PORTSMOUTH

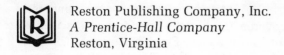
Reston Publishing Company, Inc.
*A Prentice-Hall Company*
Reston, Virginia

Richard Henderson

# Performance Appraisal: Theory to Practice

Jacob Bronowski, world famous scientist and humanist, may have uncovered the basic barrier to success in appraising worker performance. From his research on the ascent of man, Bronowski concluded that man's biological makeup dictates his view of the world. The nature of the human eye and brain and the capacity to develop symbolic language allow the eye and brain to *interpret* what surrounds mankind, rather than to perceive it as it exists absolutely.

Recognizing and accepting that what an individual sees is interpretive and not objective places a different perspective on the appraisal process. Improvement will result when those responsible for designing and administering performance use their skills and efforts to make it easier to identify performance realities. This will lead to minimizing the variations resulting from the natural individual tendency to provide a unique interpretation of reality that has deeper roots in imagination than in objective reality.

**Library of Congress Cataloging in Publication Data**

Henderson, Richard I.
  Performance appraisal.

  Includes index.
  Bibliography: p. 289
  1. Employees, Rating of.     I. Title.
HF5549.5.R3H38        658.31'25        79-26199
ISBN 0-8359-5498-6

© 1980 by Reston Publishing Company, Inc.
*A Prentice-Hall Company*
Reston, Virginia 22090

10   9   8   7   6   5   4   3   2   1

Printed in the United States of America

# Contents

Preface

It is unlikely that any managerial problem has attracted more attention or has so successfully resisted solution than arriving at an acceptable, useful, and valid method for appraising performance. Businesses frequently find that performance appraisal is a "damned if you do, damned if you don't" situation. When it is done poorly, or even done well under unsatisfactory operating conditions, it may lead to increased employee anxiety and hostility that may, in turn, lead to poor use of both human and nonhuman resources, increased costs, and declining productivity. The result may even lead to the decay and demise of the business.

Because of appraisal failures, many employees, including most union members, feel that the only solution is to eliminate it and to replace it with the one basic measuring criterion that is relatively free of subjective bias—seniority. On the other hand, if a business is to grow and prosper, it must identify those outputs, units, groups, and individuals responsible for its success. It must be able to reward and expand its areas of strength and to improve, or at least to minimize, its areas of weakness. Success in this area requires some form of performance appraisal.

Of all the parts of the reward process, probably none is more dangerous than performance appraisal. It has always been difficult to judge performance, which basically has two parts—quantity of output and quality of output. A major issue in measuring each is time. In moving up the organizational hierarchy, the period of time increases from demonstrated behavior to the ability to measure the results of that behavior.

Even in repetitive, routine, mechanistic activities, counting units produced is often an unsatisfactory measure of performance because quality is also an issue. Quality has a variety of subjective factors; quality problems can remain hidden, or they can surface at later stages in the product/service process, making it difficult to identify responsible party(ies). As modern industrial nations move from manufacturing to providing services, the quality issue becomes more important and also more difficult to resolve as it becomes harder to pinpoint.

To overcome performance appraisal dangers, many businesses do one of two things: they either do nothing, or they implement meaningless appraisal programs. Further, most appraisal systems have seldom, if ever, accomplished their mission—accurate identification of employee performance—and they are even more inadequate today. If business-provided rewards are ever to stimulate performance, improvement must begin here.

Excuses such as employees are never satisfied with the appraisal; employees are unwilling to accept average or below-average ratings; and a below-average appraisal results in a disgruntled, unhappy performer, are all unacceptable. It is imperative that those whose performance is unsatisfactory should receive additional help through counseling, coaching, and/or training. If these aids are of no avail, the incompetent employee must be removed.

Although most employees have some fears about performance measurement, they nevertheless want some form of fair, accurate, and objective appraisal. All employees want to know from their supervisors how they are performing their jobs. They not only want this information in absolute output terms, but also in terms that relate their performance to that of others doing similar work. In addition, each supervisor must be able to recognize individual differences, their relationships to worker productivity, and what is necessary to assist each person to grow and prosper.

A fundamental precondition for gaining acceptance of appraisal is the establishment of standards that are understood by the employees and that, from their point of view, are fair and just.

Performance requirements must be stated in terms that tell the appraisee:

1  What criteria will be used to measure performance;

2  How performance will be measured;

3  Who will do the appraisal;

4  When and where it will be done;

5  What inputs the employee has during the appraisal process and the type and timing of feedback to be expected;

6  What assistance can be expected to improve performance; and

7  What rewards or opportunities will be made available because of above-standard performance.

When employees have this type of information, they know what the business expects of them, what assistance is available, how to request assistance, and what they can expect when providing specific levels of performance. Answering these questions helps employees to know where they are today, where they want to be tomorrow, and what job performance can do to help them move in that direction. Most importantly, employee acceptance of the appraisal process relates directly to the trust that the employee has in the business.

Three major factors related to performance appraisal that greatly influence the development of a trusting workplace environment are: (1) collecting data that accurately describe the job, allowing and encouraging employees to make inputs into the identification of job-related behaviors that will be used for developing their performance standards; (2) designing understandable appraisal instruments in which work requirements are described in language that relates to the way that employees actually perform their assignments; (3) developing supervisor–subordinate (appraiser–appraisee) interview sessions that allow for mature interactions—those that are natural and minimize defensiveness (this does not require appraisers to change their normal behavioral patterns, but it does require them to realize the impact that their behavior has on their subordinate appraisees).

A workplace environment that generates both security and opportunity for future growth while minimizing stressful situations will certainly enhance appraisal acceptance. Establishing this type of environment goes far beyond the performance appraisal process. Every aspect of managing people and their work relates to the development of a quality work life. However, performance appraisal is an integral part of a trusting, healthy work environment.

1

# An Introduction to Performance Appraisal

Practically every employee observes and appraises the performance and assesses the potential of other members of the organization. Is it not strange though that, when an organization attempts to install a formal performance appraisal system, employees at all levels frequently do their utmost to block or foil its implementation? After implementation, both supervisors and subordinates frequently give only half-hearted or "lip service" effort toward its success. Employee embarrassment, anxiety, fear, frustration, hostility, and rejection are feelings that frequently accompany the appraisal of workplace performance. A brief review of the potential and widespread impact of performance appraisal assists in identifying why these deep-seated emotional issues exist.

The basic inputs and outputs of an organization provide a good starting point for analyzing the impact of performance appraisal. Basic inputs are monetary resources, material resources, and human resources. Basic outputs are goods and services, employee job behaviors, and performance measures.

## ORGANIZATIONAL INPUTS AND OUTPUTS

| INPUTS | | OUTPUTS |
|---|---|---|
| Monetary Resources | ORGANIZATION | Goods and Services |
| Material Resources | | Employee Job Behavior |
| Human Resources | | Performance Measures |

Even the most simple analysis of inputs quickly becomes complex when one realizes that few organizations can operate without monetary or material resources. Conversely, monetary and material resources can be wasted and soon lost if they are not properly managed or processed through effective and efficient human resources.[1]

[1] Efficient: maximizing the utilization of resources; achieving the greatest possible output with given input, or with given output, minimizing input.
Effective: achieving objectives of individuals, groups, and organizations with a minimum of unsought and undesirable consequences.

The worth of the monetary and material resources can be significantly enhanced or drastically reduced by the quality of the human resource inputs. It is easy to count monetary assets and to put a quantitative value on available or potentially available material resources, but attempting to identify the quality of the human resources is the true enigma. Knowledge, skills, certain human qualities, past performance, and prior accomplishments may be useful indicators of future performance, but situations and the relationships between job requirements and individual knowledge and skills blend in such unique ways that the resulting levels of job performance and employee worth defy the accuracy of most predictive tools.

Output analysis also quickly becomes complex when one reviews the various opportunities available for identifying the quality and quantity of output. Once again, it is the human resource factor that causes the difficulty. The human resources of the organization are what separate the successful from the unsuccessful, the winners from the losers. Producing the desired quality and quantity of goods and services within acceptable cost levels requires a work force that is ready and willing to provide availability, capabilities, and performance.

Bottom-line output performance measures, such as profit or loss, return on invested capital, sales, and market shares, are fairly easy to obtain and are useful in providing organizational measures of success. Procedures for measuring the quantity and quality of output are also relatively easy to design and implement. Their values are widely recognized and understood. One critical output measure of success that frequently defies scoring and that has minimal meaning, even when identified by some quantitative value, is the value or score that identifies and defines the level of performance of each employee.

Although it is unlikely that any single, one-time output measure provides significant information on the efficiency and effectiveness of the organization, values that identify organizational output over a period of time become extremely meaningful. No where is this more important than in the orderly and systematic identification and measurement of employee workplace behavior—job performance.

## Business, Personal, and Social Benefits

The name of the game in the 1980s for managers at all levels is PRODUCTIVITY IMPROVEMENT.

```
┌─────────────────────┐
│     PRODUCTIVITY     │
│    A measure of the  │
│        output        │
│         of an        │
│      organization    │
└─────────────────────┘
```

Managers influence productivity improvement through their skills in directing and coordinating the use of monetary, material, and human resources (inputs) so as to maximize goods and services, employee job behaviors, and performance measures (outputs). Of the three inputs, the most critical to the success of a business is the human resource. Success is possible even when monetary and material resources are in short supply if the use of human resources is maximized.

The quality of management decisions and actions is directly proportional to the availability and validity of information. The information provided through performance appraisal significantly enhances management effectiveness in making decisions that influence the directing and coordinating of human resources. Therefore, a primary objective of any business is to ensure the existence of an effective, accurate, continuous process for gathering, analyzing, and disseminating information about the performance of its members. That process is the performance appraisal system.

```
┌─────────────────────────┐
│   PERFORMANCE APPRAISAL  │
│   A measure of the output │
│          of a            │
│      jobholder that      │
│      contributes to      │
│       productivity       │
└─────────────────────────┘
```

The process of appraising performance is a sequence of interrelated events designed, administered, and operated for the intentional purpose of observing, measuring, and altering employee workplace behavior.

A major indicator of the effective use of human resources through a viable performance appraisal system is the impact of that system on productivity improvement. Productivity relates directly to the performance of all employees of the organization. After all, organizations hire employees and reward them so that they will provide the effort necessary to achieve organizational objectives and goals. Healthy improvement in profit can be related directly to increases in productivity.

> Employees are hired and paid
> to achieve results.

Employees have always expected security from the work they do. Today, employees not only want security, but they also seek satisfying, interesting work opportunities for personal growth. Well-designed performance appraisal systems decrease ambiguity concerning job requirements and uncertainty about rewards to be achieved by providing employees with information about what is expected of them and feedback on how they have performed. Organizationally provided rewards can then be distributed according to the contributions of each individual employee. Performance appraisals also grant employees more influence over the work they do and how they do it.

Continued existence of the business and the survival of individual jobs through productivity improvement lead to life style improvement that is not dependent on short-term gains made possible through inflation. Improvements made through inflation have a very negative, even disastrous, impact on long-term security and growth. Real improvements in buying power result from productivity increases made possible through the wise use of human resources. Performance appraisal systems, in turn, coordinate the efficient and effective use of human resources with available monetary and material resources.

## Performance Appraisal—A Continuing Operation

Because both on- and off-the-job situations critically influence employee workplace behavior, a one-time performance measure is of minimal importance. For performance appraisal measures to be of significant value to both the organization and the employee, appraisals must be conducted at regular bimonthly or quarterly intervals, and the resulting scores or values analyzed over the measured time frames. A series of appraisals conducted over an extended period of time can provide the type of worthwhile and valid information that managers need to make many personnel-related decisions that will hold up under intense scrutiny by all involved employees or outside agencies.

Seldom does a personnel-related decision affect only the employee at whom the action is directed. Many personnel decisions have spin-off effects on other employees who are aware of and able to observe the decision. Remember, a promotion decision affects not only the employee receiving the promotion but also all those seeking one who were not promoted and those who, although they are not currently in a promotion zone, will be looking forward to one at some future time.

## Human Resource Influences

A major reason employee performance appraisal is such a critical tool is that it is a control device that influences practically all human resource functions. The influences of performance appraisal are felt in (1) human resource planning, (2) human resource research, (3) human resource development, and (4) human resource recognition.

Human resource planning requires information about employee knowledge, skills, strengths, and weaknesses. Properly designed and conducted performance appraisal identifies required and demonstrated workplace behaviors. When this type of information is presented through performance appraisal, it assists in identifying individual training and development needs required for current job performance and for future job placement. The placement of employees in jobs where their skills and knowledge complement organizational demands is a major step toward achieving the objectives and goals of both the employees and the organization.

Human resource research information provided through performance appraisal assists in validating hiring, selection, placement, and promotion criteria. This information also assists in measuring

| Planning | Research | Development | Recognition |
|---|---|---|---|
| 1. Identify knowledges and skills | 1. Validate hiring, selection, placement, and promotion criteria | 1. Identify individual training and development needs | 1. Determine in-grade pay—merit adjustments |
| 2. Identify potential | 2. Measure effectiveness of training | 2. Establish appropriate training and development programs | 2. Determine one-time bonus payments |
| 3. Identify training requirements | 3. Appraise effectiveness of EEO/AAP programs | | 3. Determine termination, demotion, transfer, and promotion opportunities |
| 4. Identify placement opportunities | | | |

the effectiveness of training and development programs. Meeting Equal Employment Opportunity guidelines and analyzing the effectiveness of Affirmative Action Programs can be furthered through performance appraisal generated information.

Human resource development programs initially require the identification of individual training and development needs. This assists in the establishment of appropriate development plans and programs that link individual requirements to organizational demands.

Human resource recognition programs are normally a major reason, if not the primary one, for the existence of performance appraisal. Performance appraisal inputs frequently influence in-grade base pay adjustments, one-time performance bonus payments, terminations, demotions, transfers, promotions, and learning opportunities.

## An Employee's Perspective

Over the years, much has been written about separating performance appraisal outputs into specific or finite segments, e.g., establishing training and development requirements, implementing pay adjustments, and determining transfer and promotion opportunities. Many experts have recommended that the various activities influenced by performance appraisal be separated by the time and actions that occur within the specific activity. This is physically possible from an employer's point of view, but it is psychologically impossible from an employee's point of view. Performance appraisal is a continuous process; certain operations can occur at designated points in time, but it is impossible to separate the influencing activities of performance appraisal.

To understand the strengths, weaknesses, and dangers inherent within performance appraisal, it is essential to view the entire process from the emotional or psychological perspective of all involved employees and not merely as some mechanical operation requiring managers to rank or rate their subordinates relative to one or more performance variables on some official form at some specific period of time.

The following list identifies some of the psychological effects that performance appraisal has on employees—both appraisers and appraisees:

### Appraisees

1   Identifying me as an average performer will limit my promotional opportunities in the organization, and a below-

average appraisal is a stigma that will remain with me for the rest of my career in the organization.

2   Recommending additional training and development may identify me as a marginal employee.

3   Validating hiring, selection, and promotional criteria from my performance appraisal and those of others makes me feel that my qualifications are borderline.

4   Appraising my performance as superior will identify me as a "rate buster" and cause other members of my work group to be uncooperative and unfriendly.

*Appraisers*

5   The great majority of my employees feel that their performance is at least average, if not above average.

6   Appraising the performance of any employee as below average will cause that employee to dislike me; will result in reduced, not better, performance; and, although unlikely, could result in some physical harm to me or damage to my career.

7   Appraising employee performance consumes an inordinate amount of time and results in few, if any, positive organizational actions.

8   Identifying differences of performance among employees will cause intragroup jealousy, rivalries, and hostilities and dysfunctional organizational intrigue.

The reader must recognize that performance appraisal is a system. The various components of the system and the outputs of each component interact and influence, in some manner and to some degree, all previously described human resource functions.

The major components of a performance appraisal system are:

1   Identifying job responsibilities and duties and performance dimensions, standards, and goals.

2   Prioritizing and weighting performance dimensions and performance goals.

3   Determining appropriate methods for appraising performance.

4   Developing suitable appraisal instruments and scoring devices.

5   Establishing procedures that enhance fair and just appraisals of all employees.

6   Providing performance feedback to all employees.

7   Relating observed and identified performance to the rewards provided by the organization.

8   Designing monitoring and auditing processes to ensure proper operation of the system and to identify areas of weakness.

9   Granting employees opportunities for appeal whenever and wherever such action is appropriate.

10   Training involved employees in all phases of the appraisal system.

Each of these components is discussed in detail throughout the remainder of the book.

Lack of understanding and skill in the technical phases related to design, implementation, and operation are barriers to successful performance appraisal. Even though these barriers are significant compared to the psychological and emotional issues that block success in operating a formal appraisal program, they are somewhat easy to overcome. By recognizing psychological and emotional issues in the design, implementation, and operation phases, it is possible to minimize the barriers to success and the ill effects that may result from the appraisal of performance.

From an employee's perspective, possibly the most important issue in any appraisal of performance is, plainly and simply, *job security*. Practically all employees recognize that, to some degree (in a unionized setting *less* than in one that is nonunionized), their *survival*, let alone advancement, depends on the judgment, consideration, and feelings of their immediate supervisors and others holding positions of superior authority in the organization. (In reality, peers and subordinates also influence individual survival and advancement, but, generally, this does not appear to be nearly as threatening as the influence wielded by supervisors.)

Survival not only has a current time frame for most employees but also a future orientation. From the validation of hiring and selection criteria to the establishment of training and development programs and the implementation of many pay-related decisions (including transfers and promotions), employee job behavior influences both current reward opportunities and those that may be made available in the future.

Is it possible that employees do not recognize the relationship between performance appraisal and employer-provided reward opportunities? Is it even possible that employees feel that informal appraisal systems have less impact on such critical personnel issues?

I believe that employees do recognize the multifaceted uses of performance appraisal and the existence and influence of informal performance appraisal processes. They recognize that their immediate supervisors and other involved managers can subjectively assign a particular value to their performance that, in turn, affects the opportunities and rewards available and received from their employers. I also believe that employees are extremely sensitive to interrater (supervisor) differences in appraising performance. They are also aware that these differences frequently result in inequitable and unfair distribution of performance-related rewards.

If employees have these levels of awareness and recognize the implications, why do they so frequently abhor and fight the implementation of a formal appraisal system? One reason is that they do not believe that the organization has the knowledge, skill, and desire to implement a performance appraisal system that will reduce subjectivity and interrater differences and provide a more equitable distribution of performance-related rewards.

There is no doubt that personal biases and other subjective considerations heavily influence informal appraisals of performance, but does the implementation of a formal system mean the elimination of informal appraisals? The answer must be no. (Discussion throughout the remaining chapters of this book focuses on specific design, implementation, and operation characteristics that will minimize opportunities for unfair and unjust appraisals of performance.)

There are no simple answers to why employees have negative attitudes concerning formalized appraisals of performance. If there is a single, most important answer, however, it is lack of trust. Employees do not believe that organizations can conceive, design, implement, and administer a formal appraisal system that can adequately and accurately identify and measure job performance. Furthermore, they do not believe that information gathered through performance appraisal will be used in an open and objective manner to relate rewards to performance. (This is an issue that is of basic concern throughout this book because performance is just as much a perception issue as it is one of measurement. Perception rests in the eyes of the beholder and differs according to what each set of eyes visualizes and perceives.)

Another unacceptable condition emanating from poorly developed performance appraisals that can have an extremely negative impact on organizational productivity occurs from the "Guilt-Rationalization—Blame The Organization syndrome" (Figure 1-1). The process works in this manner:

1  The appraiser tells the appraisee that he or she is performing well or acceptably.

2   A guilt feeling arises because the appraisee knows that he or she is not performing to self-assessed potential.

3   Initial embarrassment concerning demonstrated behavior gives way as the employee rationalizes reasons for such behavior, i.e., (1) no one performs any better, or (2) others perform not nearly as well yet receive more and better rewards.

4   The employee internalizes the rationalization and does not change work place behavior that would lead to improved performance.

5   The individual continues to harbor deep-seated frustrations based on lack of motivation to perform to the level that he or she is capable of performing (self-actualization).

6   Continuing good and acceptable performance ratings energize this traumatic experience.

Employes believe that poorly conceived, improperly designed, and inadequately administered performance appraisal systems are far worse and more dangerous to the average employee than no formal system at all. Even under the poorest conditions, the average employee has sufficient self-confidence in his or her own ability to exist and function with practically any type of boss, but a poor performance appraisal system can only reinforce unacceptable mana-

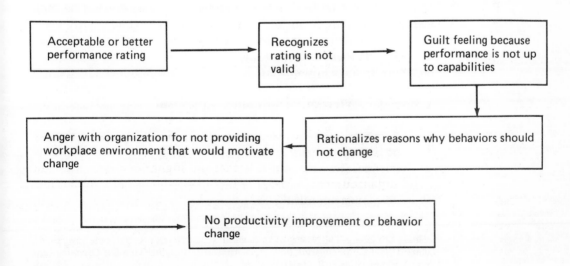

FIGURE 1-1    THE UNBREAKABLE CYCLE

gerial behavior and make workplace existence more tenuous and difficult. It is one thing for an employee to do battle with an unskilled, unfair, even unscrupulous supervisor within some type of an informal process. It is an entirely different matter for this type of supervisor to function and hide his or her behavior behind a cloak of bureaucratic immunity that can easily be provided by a formal performance appraisal system. An unacceptable formal performance appraisal system demonstrates to employees that they live in an US—THEM working environment.

## The Manager's Perspective

Not only do appraised employees object to performance appraisal, but research by Henry Mintzberg and others on the way in which managers do their work reveals many behavioral characteristics of managers that are antithetical to the successful operation of a performance appraisal system.[2] Their investigations show that a major part of the job of practically all managers is to coordinate the activities of the human resources that report to them. In supervising the monetary, material, and human resources under their command, the managers perform a wide variety of activities characterized by brevity, variety, and fragmentation. The quality of their decisions and influence depends to a significant degree on the information that they possess.

A brief analysis of how managers function reveals many daily formal and informal interactions and a reliance on information gathered from these interactions. Using information that they have gathered from a wide variety of sources, managers depend on their own intuitive judgments and rely on brief reviews and hastily made analyses in making many of their day-to-day decisions.

How do these and other managerial activities relate to and support performance appraisals?

### A Manager's View of Performance Appraisal

1   Since my job requires that I perform so many varied activities, it is very difficult, if not impossible, to appraise my performance. (Surveys indicate that the higher one moves up the organizational ladder, the less likely the use of a formal performance appraisal.)

---

[2] Henry Mintzberg, *The Nature of Managerial Work* (New York: Harper & Row, 1973); Leonard Sayles, *Managerial Behavior: Administration in Complex Organizations* (New York: McGraw-Hill, 1964).

2    The more information that I have that my subordinates do not have, the more influence I have. (This minimizes the desire to disseminate information to subordinates other than what they actually need to perform their jobs.)

3    The most trusted and useful information is that which I collect from face-to-face communications with superiors, peers, and subordinates. (The use of staff-provided data is of minimal importance.)

4    I do not have the luxury to spend considerable amounts of my time analyzing reports and reviewing records when I make decisions. (Formalized planning is truly not a basic job activity; most planning is done in conjunction with or as a part of other actions.)

5    Many of the decisions that I make require an extended period of time and an assessment of many external factors before it can be decided whether the decision is good or bad. (It is unfair and inappropriate to appraise the performance of managers.)

6    Many actions that I take involve political considerations requiring broad understanding of the situation that cannot be identified or described in a well-defined, written format. (Completing forms and reports is not really worth the time required and provides minimal insights into how decisions were made.)

7    I prefer to communicate with people who (1) can improve my position, (2) have views and attitudes similar to mine, and (3) normally are of a higher or equal status. (Providing performance feedback to subordinates within the appraisal process is threatening and frequently results in frustration and tension.)

8    Anything I do that requires that I spend extended amounts of time reviewing, analyzing, and directing my attention to past actions and, in turn, responding in a predictable manner is not typical of my action-oriented job. (Performance appraisal requires too much time pondering over past behavior and requires certain types of managerial behavior in response to specific employee behaviors.)

9    I have very little to gain by accurately appraising performance. (If I appraise an employee as a below-average performer, the employee will probably be upset and will not accept the rating as accurate.)

If Mintzberg and other researchers who have identified these managerial behaviors are correct, is it not likely that many managers feel that formal performance appraisal procedures are unnecessary? If managers have this attitude, is it not also likely that they will transmit it to their subordinates? Furthermore, is it not likely that employees will also resist performance appraisal if they see their managers not being appraised or are uncomfortable with the process?

Traveling full circle, we come back to the proposition that employees do not trust performance appraisal systems. Why should they? In many cases, management does not either.

## Is It Worth The Time, Effort, and Cost?

Since employees would rather not have their performance appraised, and since performance appraisal in many ways operates in a completely opposite manner to that in which many managers function, a question arises. Why do it? Every manager must ponder this question before deciding to implement a performance appraisal system, to improve an existing one, or even to eliminate one in which the costs exceed the benefits.

Possibly the first issue that must be faced concerns one that has already been discussed: employees do not want their performance appraised. Is this really true? Once again, management faces a paradox, and it appears that there is no right, best, or even acceptable answer. Most employees probably do want their performance appraised when the appraisal is favorable. When there is a good chance that it will be unfavorable, they resist. One approach available for analyzing this managerial dilemma is based on the concepts of equality and equity.

Equality demands that everyone be treated the same way. But is this possible or even desirable from an organizational point of view? There is no doubt that the concept of equal pay for jobs of equal value is gaining greater recognition.

Equity considerations come into play because incumbents in different jobs must accept various kinds of responsibilities with differing degrees of intensity. These responsibilities, in turn, require various levels of knowledge, skill, and motivation to be performed in an acceptable manner. Most people agree that a job at the top of the organizational hierarchy is worth anywhere from 10 to 30 times more than those at the bottom level of the hierarchy. (Even industrial unions committed to a single rate of pay for all members constantly face internal dissension among members for variation in rates of pay according to levels of skill, knowledge, and responsibility requirements of the job.)

In addition to job demands, the issue of variation in employee performance arises. Do organizations wish to pay all jobholders the same, using the worth of the job as the sole criterion for establishing differences in rates of pay? The answer in most cases is an emphatic no! Most managers recognize that each jobholder brings a different set of knowledge, skills, and desires to the workplace. This basket of qualities results in varying levels of performance, and, under normal circumstances, the range of performance varies significantly among a group of workers. In organizations that reward employees equally over an extended period of time, there is a great likelihood that employee performance will be centered very tightly around some common level and that these norms will closely relate to those employees who have low levels of performance, which is a visible and acceptable common denominator. This possibly suggests an answer to the unacceptable declines in levels of productivity in American organizations.

Productivity improvement is and will continue to be a major concern of practically all organizations. Productivity is the relationship between resources used and results achieved. Improvements in productivity occur when more or better outputs are obtained from given levels of input resources or when fewer resources are used to maintain or even to improve a certain level of output.

A primary component of any useful or meaningful productivity improvement program is its measurement system. In the input–output analysis, the quality and quantity of human resources and their efforts are critical factors influencing productivity improvement. A key human resource output measure is performance appraisal.

In productivity improvement programs, human resource inputs and outputs must frequently include changes in hiring, selection, and promotion patterns and criteria, accurate identification of work activities and standards of desired performance, and review and possible revision of staffing patterns. These types of human resource-related activities pose threats to all employees, and it is obvious that the possibility of such changes will cause employee resistance at all levels.

Recognizing the influence of human resources on productivity improvement and relating the importance of measurement systems on successful implementation of productivity improvement programs, employees cannot escape the critical nature of two basic human resource-related measurement systems—job evaluation and performance appraisal. It also becomes apparent that increases in productivity may require changes in the philosophy, policies, and operating procedures of the organization. These kinds of changes, in addition to the extent and depth of employee risks, underscore the need for the understanding, commitment, and active support of senior management and key officials in all productivity improvement programs. Developing and maintaining this type of support requires an understanding that the results obtained from many productivity improvement programs are slow in evolving. Many of the problems and opportunities related to productivity improvement also apply to performance appraisal because it is a basic tool for managing an organization.

Declining levels of productivity may be attributed to the fact that high performers have voluntarily changed employers or have internalized the equality-based system when organizations and supervisors fail to recognize differences in capabilities, desires, or actual job behaviors and reward everyone similarly. These employees have said, "The hell with it. If this is what management wants, this is what management will get." By operating in this manner, highly productive employees become frustrated and dissatisfied because they are not performing at levels compatible with the design of their own internal systems.

This leads to another issue. Many experts and managers push performance appraisal to identify and then to reward the top and bottom 5 percent of the work force accordingly. If this is the case, there are extremely simple, formal appraisal systems that document the behavior of superior and unacceptable performers. Practically all managers, upon request, can immediately identify the performers who comprise the top and bottom 5 percent of their work groups. If the organization wishes to provide highly desirable rewards to the top 5 percent and to institute job reassignment, job improvement training, demotion, or even termination actions for the bottom 5 percent, relatively simple behavior–performance documentation programs can be implemented.

It is my belief that performance appraisal focused on the top and bottom 5 percent is a cop-out. Management spends far too much of its time observing, reviewing, praising, or correcting the behavior of employees at the extreme ends of the performance spectrum. Not nearly enough time is spent on those who are responsible for most of the quality and quantity of output and the basic bottom-line figures of the business—the middle 80 to 90 percent of the work force.

Under almost any type of management, the top 5 to 10 percent will produce, with minimal supervision, at an acceptable level without any prodding from management. They *will*, however, require recognition (employer-provided compensation or noncompensation rewards) at the proper time. At the other end, the bottom 5 to 10 percent will seldom improve their performance no matter how much time management spends cajoling, teaching, or threatening. When changes in performance do occur in this group, it is more often the result of an attitudinal change, over which management probably had little influence.

Although a well designed performance appraisal program will focus its attention on the masses, it does not fail to recognize the top and bottom 5 to 10 percent. For the top 5 to 10 percent, performance appraisal becomes a vital development tool because it assists in identifying and training those who may be the best candidates for high level jobs. For the bottom 5 to 10 percent, it provides the initial documentation for implementing demotion or termination activities, which in themselves are most difficult actions to complete successfully; in some cases, it provides the information necessary to implement programs that will change attitudes and encourage skill development that lifts the employee out of the unacceptable performance category.

Another important and frequently unrecognized issue relating to the top and bottom 5 or 10 percent approach for grouping employees is that it is unlikely that employee job behavior is normally distributed to form a parametric distribution. Grouping employees by percentage groups, such as

| Superior | Good | Acceptable | | Needs Improvement | Unacceptable |
|----------|------|------------|------|-------------------|--------------|
|          |      | +          | −    |                   |              |
| 5        | 15   | 30         | 30   | 15                | 5            |

presupposes that the variable—in this case employee job performance—is normally distributed. The central tendency statistics—mean, median, and mode—are all the same in a normal distribution, and approximately 67 percent of all behavior falls within one standard deviation of the central tendency statistic. This situation is extremely unlikely.

It is far more likely that the distribution of behaviors skews (extends) far more toward the positive side than the negative side. The bottom side (poor performance) is bunched around a statistic controlled closely by minimum acceptable performance requirements, supervisory review, and peer pressure. The process of elimination also controls the distribution of behaviors since, over a period of time, poor performers and those whose skills, talents, and attitudes do not conform to organizational requirements either leave of their own accord or have their employment terminated through official means.

This type of distribution is called a nonparametric distribution, and the most suitable measure of the central tendency is the median (the middle value in the array of all values). The impact of nonparametric considerations is discussed in detail in the chapters describing performance appraisal methods and rating scales, Chapters 8 and 10. The performance appraisal system developed in this book focuses on appraisal of the total work force. There are sections that relate or are applicable to certain groups, such as management, nonmanagement, professional, technical, clerical, even the best and poorest performers.

Because of the likelihood of managerial apathy and the possibility of employee hostility, the implementation of a performance appraisal system requires the total support and commitment of senior management. From the initial design stages, senior management must be aware of the potential pitfalls, advantages, and costs incurred with performance appraisal. It must be recognized that performance appraisal is a basic output-measuring device of the organization that relates to all employees, from the Chief Executive Officer to the lowest level employee. It must be job performance oriented and should tie individual objectives and goals to those of the organization. It should be an integral part of the reward system that minimizes US—THEM attitudes and supports a WE concept. It should minimize unacceptable, subjective considerations yet recognize that any system related to human activity will always have subjective elements. Well-designed and managed performance appraisal systems set limits or parameters on subjective considerations. They provide auditing and monitoring procedures that automatically identify some levels of potentially unacceptable appraisal decisions and permit all employees to have a real opportunity to appeal an unacceptable appraisal.

Equitable treatment of employees requires observation and identification of demonstrated workplace behavior and feedback to the employee on (1) how the superior perceived the behavior, (2) recommendations on behaviors to improve and those to maintain, (3) support that the organization can and will provide to assist the employee, and (4) consequences (rewards or punishments) that the employee can expect by continuing such behaviors.

## A Framework for Developing a Workable and Useful Performance Appraisal System

To overcome the emotional, personal perception, and job-related barriers, performance appraisal must be deeply rooted in the content of the jobs themselves. Job relatedness implies two major considerations: (1) It is possible to appraise the performance of all incumbents, and (2) It is unlikely that one tool or technique will be sufficient to identify and measure the performance of all jobholders.

A systems view of performance appraisal requires an understanding and consideration of the psychological and emotional influence that each part of the system has on each employee. Additionally, a systems view demands an appreciation of different system considerations for the various levels of the organization (such as senior management, operating management, and operatives), different functional units (such as finance, marketing, production, personnel, planning, and research and development), and different occupational groups (such as office support, administrative, crafts and trades, and data processing).

A systems view starts with an analysis and identification of job content. It then develops performance dimensions and establishes performance standards useful for measuring employee workplace behavior. After these efforts have been completed, a review of the various methods, instruments, and rating scales assists in identifying the method or procedure that best fits the specific requirements, recognizing variables such as organizational level, occupational differences, psychological impact, and individual perception. The final aspects of the technical design require the tying together of performance appraisal results and rewards that the organization makes available and provides to its members. In completing the technical design of the system, all participants must be trained in how they can most effectively participate in the system and influence its outcome. Figure 1-2 describes system component relationships and the external and internal influences that affect them.

All performance appraisal systems must take into consideration government requirements and a number of other external factors. Validity and reliability issues must be faced at each step in system design and development. Each organization must redesign an approach developed by any individual or group (including the one presented in this book) to meet its own philosophy and policies, objectives and goals, and relationships to external influences.

A review of the model and the various components of a performance appraisal system brings into focus the enormity of implementing a well designed, successful performance appraisal system. At first glance, it may appear to be too large an undertaking or a mission impossible. Implementing a successful performance appraisal is a big job; it requires the talent and cooperation of many people, is time-consuming, and has a significant cost. But the same directions that apply to eating an elephant apply to carrying out a successful performance appraisal. Do it one bite at a time! The first

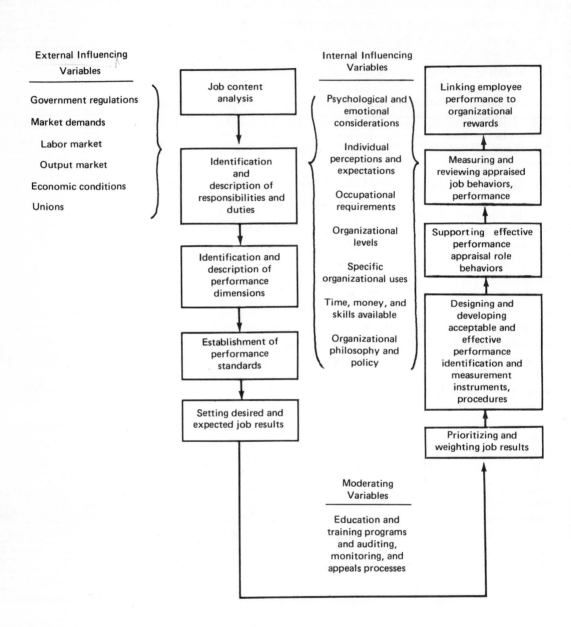

FIGURE 1-2    SEQUENTIAL PERFORMANCE APPRAISAL
SYSTEM COMPONENT RELATIONSHIPS

bite in performance appraisal is identifying and describing job content.

Although it is possible to achieve an equitable distribution of rewards without a formal appraisal of performance, the likelihood of achieving such a goal becomes significantly greater with the implementation of a formal appraisal process. The organization benefits by having employees who know what is expected of them and who recognize that they receive rewards directly related to demonstrated performance. The employees, in turn, benefit by having a much greater opportunity to influence the reward system through their job-related behaviors.

## Reaction to Legislation

In addition to those employees who truly desire recognition of their performance, there is the broad and ever-growing demand by government officials for formal, documented, measured indicators of performance. The Equal Pay Act of 1963, the Civil Rights Act of 1964, the Age Discrimination in Employment Act of 1967, and the Vocational Rehabilitation Act of 1973 all have either explicit or implied sections that require employers to document employee performance before making various human resource-related decisions. Increased government pressures may require organizations to implement formal performance appraisal systems whether they want to or not. In this event, some or all of the negatives previously identified could dominate the system, and the performance appraisal system will be a handicap rather than a positive tool for improving organizational productivity. The results will be a variety of defensive postures rather than positive performance-improvement actions. The issue that management will have to face is the tradeoff between the benefits and costs associated with a well-designed, properly managed appraisal system and one that meets minimum government requirements. Costs must include not only the time that professionals, managers, and employees spend in the design, implementation, and operation of the system but also the higher costs due to reduced (non-optimizing) productivity resulting from employee anxiety, frustration, and hostility that result from poorly designed and managed appraisal systems or when informal appraisals control the workplace destinies of the employees.

# 2

## Accomplishing the Mission of the Organization

People join together within organizations to accomplish certain purposes. Sometimes, these purposes are well defined and understood by all members; at other times, the purposes are ambiguous, causing many members to have difficulty relating their work to the desired outcomes. A commonly held belief is that the more employees understand the why, what, how, when, where, and how much of their jobs, the greater is the likelihood that their workplace-demonstrated behaviors will lead to improved organizational productivity. There is possibly no system, method, or procedure available to organizations that more effectively links available resources to the accomplishment of the organizational mission than performance appraisal.

Understanding how the mission of the organization becomes translated into productive work effort requires a knowledge and appreciation of the relationship among desired results, means for accomplishing the results, work to be done, actual results achieved, and the recognition and rewarding of employee workplace efforts. Figure 2-1 identifies the major activities involved in translating the missions of the organization into productive employee work effort. In this model, a *top-down* approach to the identification and setting of goals, a *bottom-up* development and integration of functional job activities, and a *lateral* process that links job responsibilities and duties to identified objectives and goals ties the mission of the organization to job requirements. This system uses performance appraisal as the control device to compare desired results (objectives and goals established in the top-down process) with the results achieved as employees perform job requirements. Figure 2-2 describes the role of performance appraisal as a control device in the process described in Figure 2-1. The remainder of this chapter focuses on the various activities described in these two models.

## Mission of the Organization

The mission statements identify and describe the reason for existence of the organization—what it is all about. Progressing from the dreams of one or more individuals, products and services desired by society are identified and produced through a combination of capital and technical and human resources. A framework that allows individuals with different levels of knowledge and skills and divergent desires and interests to work together for the common good include (1) philosophy statements that establish what the owner–leaders identify as acceptable and unacceptable behaviors of the or-

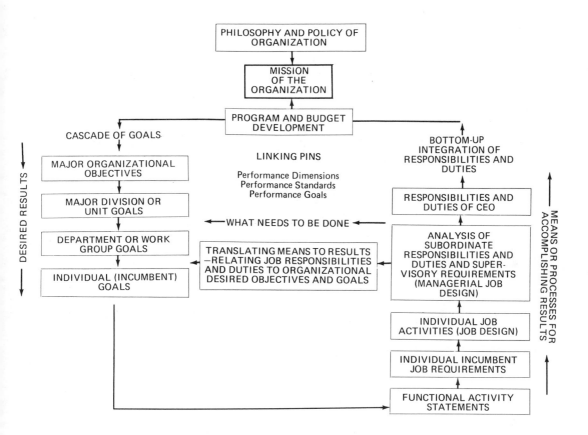

FIGURE 2-1    DETERMINING, DESCRIBING, AND MEASUR-
ING MISSION-RELATED WORK EFFORTS

ganization and its members and (2) policies that emanate from the philosophy established by the leaders of the organization that further define acceptable and unacceptable workplace behavior.

In the philosophy and policy of the organization, there is normally much room for variations in acceptable employee workplace behavior. Limitations on behavior are established by standing operating procedures, regulations, rules, and work methods. All of these behavior-related guidelines influence the types of programs that the organization implements to provide its desired outputs. The guidelines and programs in turn influence the capital outlays required to operate the organization. Various types of budgets identify the money needed and how it is to be allocated among the various

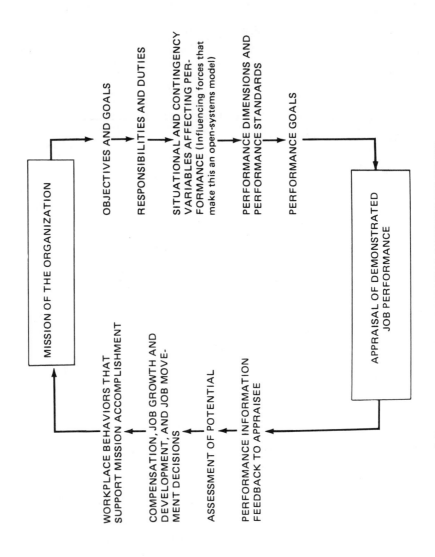

OBJECTIVES AND GOALS

RESPONSIBILITIES AND DUTIES

SITUATIONAL AND CONTINGENCY VARIABLES AFFECTING PERFORMANCE (Influencing forces that make this an open-systems model)

PERFORMANCE DIMENSIONS AND PERFORMANCE STANDARDS

PERFORMANCE GOALS

MISSION OF THE ORGANIZATION

APPRAISAL OF DEMONSTRATED JOB PERFORMANCE

WORKPLACE BEHAVIORS THAT SUPPORT MISSION ACCOMPLISHMENT

COMPENSATION, JOB GROWTH AND DEVELOPMENT, AND JOB MOVEMENT DECISIONS

ASSESSMENT OF POTENTIAL

PERFORMANCE INFORMATION FEEDBACK TO APPRAISEE

FIGURE 2-2    TYING ORGANIZATIONAL MISSION TO WORK FORCE PRODUCTIVITY

resource areas to fund the programs that make the identified and desired outputs possible. The mission statements direct the efforts of all employees toward successful completion of the intended purposes of the organization.

## Cascade of Goals

Anthony P. Raia used the term *cascade of goals* to describe a goal-setting process that starts with the formulation of long-range objectives and moves down the organizational hierarchy to where these objectives are redefined in concepts and terms appropriate to the involved level or functional area of the organization.[1] Similar to the processes described in both Figures 2-1 and 2-2, Raia's cascade of goals model is circular in that information flows from one level or stage of the model to the next, thereby permitting redirection or modification where and when necessary. (Chapter 5 describes goal-setting and management by objectives in much greater detail.) The important point here is that *initially* the identification and setting of goals is a top-down approach that allows all employees an opportunity to know what the organization desires from them at their particular level. This activity becomes the first step toward identifying, describing, and obtaining work effort that supports the overall mission of the organization.

## Functional Activity Statements

The next step in the process of translating mission statements to productive work effort is to interpret goals into employee work activities. With the division of labor, employees specialize their efforts in specific areas of responsibilities. From the newly hired, unskilled laborer to the experienced Chief Executive Officer, the organization expects specific kinds and levels of work to be performed. One approach for identifying the work to be accomplished is through a bottom-up identification and integration of responsibilities and duties. In Chapter 3, there is a detailed description of how an organization obtains job activity information and, from this information, develops and prioritizes job responsibilities.

Once goals have been subdivided into the smallest practical parts, it is possible to interpret these goals as work requirements for specific groups and to define the work group requirements as job activities. (The models developed in Figures 2-1 and 2-2 are theoret-

---

[1] Anthony P. Raia, *Management by Objectives* (Glenview, IL: Scott, Foresman and Company, 1974), p. 29.

ical and idealistic in nature and will seldom, if ever, be followed in a step-by-step sequence by an organization. In most cases, organizations that wish to use the concepts, ideas, and tools proposed and developed in this book are already in existence and have implemented many of the steps. Newly developed organizations that could use these models in totality frequently do not have the sophistication or knowledge to recognize the need for them. Most new organizations have enough trouble surviving, let alone looking at ways and means for improving management skills. These models should be of immense value for use as check lists by operating organizations to see where they are today, to identify possible trouble areas, and to develop programs that will overcome deficiencies that are blocking effective use of their available resources.)

With the bottom-up approach to the identification and description of job requirements, it becomes easier to see whether each job is carrying its own weight. Is the job necessary? Should there be any redistribution or realignment of job activities? Do the jobs of the work group support each other? Do the job requirements of the supervisor successfully integrate and coordinate the requirements of his or her subordinates? If this questioning process is continued through to the highest level of the organization, the answers should result in a description of the responsibilities and duties of the Chief Executive Officer that support and mesh with the mission of the organization.

## The Linking Pins

The circuitous route from mission statements through goals to responsibilities and duties and back to mission statements is insufficient in operating most complex organizations that hire hundreds, thousands, or tens of thousands of employees. Additional steps must be implemented to allow for more and improved integration between top-down set goals and bottom-up identified responsibilities and duties. This part of the process is frequently missing from many management planning, operating, and control systems.

Over the years, many specialists in workplace and job design have decried the need for extensive job analysis and the writing of soon-to-be obsolete job descriptions. These critics of job analysis and job descriptions say that the time that they consume and the costs involved are not worth the benefits gained. In my opinion these views are false; in fact, one of the principal goals of this book is to develop a sound foundation for justifying the expenditure of time and money on these efforts.

We will now investigate an approach available for linking responsibilities and duties to goals. This approach requires the
maximum possible participation by affected employees and the
commitment to the process by everyone in the organization. The
transition stage involves the development of *performance dimensions,* the possible identification of *critical performance dimensions,* the establishment of *performance standards,* and the setting
of *performance goals.* This stage also includes the identification of
situational and contingency variables that can either assist or block
goal achievement, and the appraisal of demonstrated workplace behavior.

Responsibilities and duties identify and describe the means or
processes for accomplishing desired results (goals). Responsibilities
and duties identify requirements void of unique individual qualities
and the environmental factors (both internal and external to the organization) that influence the way an incumbent performs. For these
reasons, procedures must be designed that recognize the impact of
these critical areas.

## Performance Dimensions

The transition to job requirements that recognize the influences of the individual jobholder and the various demands placed
on the job by an ever-changing environment starts with the identification of performance dimensions. Through the use of performance
dimensions, it is possible to recognize situational differences and to
write job requirements in terms that relate to the incumbent. Similar
to the closely related responsibilities and duties, performance dimensions describe processes that identify the specific knowledge,
skills, efforts, and desires of the jobholder. Performance dimensions
then integrate the unique qualities of the incumbent with the demands placed on the job by the situation. The fairly static responsibilities and duties are replaced by the more dynamic performance
dimensions. These job-related qualities permit the development of
job-related criteria that are useful in appraising employee job performance.

Performance dimensions can be very broad and relate to all jobs
or they can be extremely narrow and relate to only one or a very
small number of jobs. The broadest and most universal performance
dimension is simply JOB PERFORMANCE. Although this dimension
is certainly job related, it is extremely ambiguous and open to a wide
variety of interpretations. (Additional universal and general performance dimensions are identified and described in Chapter 8.) In

order for a performance dimension to be useful in the process developed in this and the following chapters, it must relate to a specific responsibility or duty and be precise enough to lead to explicit goals.

Criteria used for establishing performance dimensions can be broadly classified as human qualities and technical abilities. Human qualities may be further subdivided into categories such as personal traits and interpersonal skills. Personal traits include qualities such as dependability, resourcefulness, cooperation, and innovativeness, whereas interpersonal skills describe qualities such as the ability to promote and use feedback in group effort, to organize group activities, and to respect individual differences. Technical abilities include mechanical skills and conceptual aptitudes. Mechanical skills relate to the operation of a specific piece of equipment, the handling of various materials, and/or the processing of inputs that may range from the assembly of a manufactured product to coding, storing, or retrieving of data, etc. The ability to identify problems and the willingness to accept and understand responsibility requirements within a variety of risk-taking situations are but two examples of conceptual aptitudes.

Performance dimensions are variables useful for measuring individual workplace behaviors or for profiling incumbent performance. For these reasons, performance dimensions must (1) accurately describe major or significant behaviors required in the successful performance of the job, (2) be amenable to scaling, and (3) be able to be weighted, if necessary. Performance dimensions provide a degree of individual tailoring to each job since they set the stage for identifying the unique sets of behaviors that relate most appropriately to a specific job. Responsibilities and duties describe inputs into the work process; performance dimensions begin the movement toward identifying required outputs or outcomes by further describing processes required for carrying out a specific responsibility or duty.

When employees have the opportunity to provide the basic inputs to the development of responsibilities and duties and have a final sign-off on the description and the ordering of importance of these responsibilities and duties, there is a much greater likelihood of achieving a high degree of agreement between supervisor and subordinate as to the content of the subordinate's job. Using this as the foundation for the eventual measuring of employee performance is a rational and consistent approach for developing agreement and understanding and minimizing the fear, anxiety, and hostility that frequently accompany the appraisal of performance.

Linking performance dimensions to job responsibilities and

duties establishes a first cut at prioritizing performance dimensions, which should equate to the importance of the associated job responsibility and duty. Although this may not always be true, when work demands and situational variables require changes in performance dimension priorities, a basis for priorities has already been established. Reasons acceptable to both supervisor and subordinate can then be identified, assisting both parties to understand more clearly why and how work efforts should be redirected.

### Critical Performance Dimensions

Critical performance dimensions are those components of job performance that are systematically determined to be the pivotal behaviors required for the successful accomplishment of the job. Failure to achieve results related to these dimensions outweighs satisfactory achievement of results related to other dimensions. Here again, situational variables and changing organizational demands influence the identification of critical performance dimensions.

A quick review of the numbers involved in moving from responsibilities and duties to performance dimensions assists in identifying the need for establishing critical performance dimensions. Most jobs have from four to seven responsibilities. A complete description of a responsibility normally requires the identification of three to seven duties. For each duty, there may be one or more performance dimensions. It is impractical and unwieldy to appraise an employee relative to 15 to 30 or more performance variables. It makes far more sense to select the four to ten variables (performance dimensions) that, over an appraisal period, will identify successful job performance.

This does not mean that it is acceptable to ignore noncritical performance dimensions. What this permits is the use of a simple acceptable—unacceptable rating scale relative to these noncritical variables. Unacceptable performance in one or more of these noncritical dimensions is a flag item that requires further investigation by the supervisor and discussions with the employee.

*Number of Variables To Use.* To improve the identification and measurement of employee performance, managers and personnel specialists develop models. Appraisal forms and their various components are models of reality. Like all models, if they are too simple, they fail to improve recognition, understanding, and measurement. On the other hand, if they are too complex, those using the model will be unable to comprehend its various parts and the interactions between the parts, and they will find the model to be of little to no use. A useful model must be a valid representation of reality; and it must be neither overly simple nor overly complex.

Performance appraisal instruments must provide sufficient measurement criteria and measurement scales if they are to be useful in synthesizing the critical features of individual performance. Remember, these instruments are models of reality. In this case, reality is the actual demonstrated behavior of the involved employee.

Performance appraisal measurements depend primarily on observation. Most appraisal observations rely on transient information, which is developed in real time (the here and now), requires short but specific spans of attention, and uses short-term memory.

Short-term memory involves concept identification. In concept identification, an individual learns to identify specific dimensions through learning and to select the correct dimension when facing a specific stimuli. The appraiser is normally involved in complex situations with a short time to make observations. To be effective under such conditions, he or she must learn to classify stimuli. Most individuals can learn to respond almost perfectly to a reasonable number of previously learned and classified stimuli.

Research by George A. Miller recognized that there are severe limits to the capacity of the short-term memory.[2] He concluded that the short-term memory is used primarily for identifying lists of unconnected events. (In the world of the appraiser, these unconnected events are demonstrated behaviors of subordinates.) Short-term memory not only uses few items for measurement but also operates on a "push-down" principle for retrieving information stored in the human brain (Last-In, First-Out, is an example of the "push-down" principle).

Miller theorizes that most people can work concurrently with five to nine different items of information (e.g., criteria, dimensions, variables) when making decisions. The more different items with which an individual works concurrently and the more input information required for analysis and discrimination purposes, the greater is the likelihood of making errors. When appraising performance relative to one variable—for example, observed performance—it is possible to misidentify or inconsistently appraise certain performance features. On the other hand, too many variables overly complicate the recognition and appraisal processes, leading to ineffective or risky uses of appraisals.

---

[2] George A. Miller, "The Magical Number Seven Plus or Minus Two: Some Limits On Our Capacity For Processing Information," *The Psychological Review*, March, 1956, pp. 81–97.

Over the years, Miller and other researchers have noted that individual short-term perceptual and memory abilities normally permit discrimination of about seven variables. Most people can work with at least five variables. Using less than five may unduly restrict an individual's ability to discriminate and the result will not be as consistent as it should be. Using more than nine variables may result in an individual making discriminations that are too fine.

From his own research and that of others, Miller concludes that individuals possess finite and rather small capacities for making unidimensional judgments. An underlying reason for this characteristic is that human survival depends on adaptability which requires a little bit of information about a lot of things. The measuring of employee performance, however, requires considerable information about relatively few things. It is for this reason that essential job requirements (responsibilities and duties) and distinctive features of an employee's job performance (performance dimensions) are grouped into rather small units for identification and observation purposes.

## Performance Standards

Criteria for differentiating the level or degree of results are provided by the performance standards. To describe results, measurement terms of how much, how well, when, and in what way are used and may be further identified through (1) quantity of output, (2) quality of output, (3) timeliness of output, (4) effectiveness in use of resources, (5) positive and negative effects of effort, (6) manner of performance, and (7) method of performing assignments.

When performance standards are developed, quantitative measures may be identified through statements such as:

No more than (quantity or quality measures)

No less than (quantity or quality measures)

Within (a time measure)

By (a time measure)

No later than (a time measure)

Measures must be achievable, but they should relate to a scale of performance whereby the organization identifies an acceptable performance that it expects most employees to meet. These measures may also identify an achievable performance that requires employees to put forth extra effort, to stretch themselves; only a few employees will perform to these above-expected standards. These measures permit the identification of performance where employees are failing to meet expected standards. Some employees will, at times, fall into these categories. When standards are established and identified, care must be taken to ensure that they are stated in specific, understood terms and are attainable and valid.

## Performance Goals

The setting of performance goals follows the identification and description of performance dimensions and performance standards. This step in the transition process leads to further personalization of job requirements. Goals are specific outcomes or desired results from incumbent workplace behavior. They must be observable and measurable, preferably in quantitative terms, but qualitative measurements are satisfactory in some cases. Goals may be classifed as follows:

*Routine goals:* those that ensure a continued level of performance;

*Emergency goals:* those required to meet a specific crisis;

*Special goals:* those required to satisfy particular situations or contingency demands;

*Innovative goals:* those that promote new and vital actions; and

*Personal development goals:* those that foster individual growth.

Similar to responsibilities and duties, there is a limit to the number of goals that a person can work toward achieving at any one time. Since most formal performance appraisal programs cover a period of one year, it is unlikely that it would ever be wise to set more than ten goals during an appraisal period.

In moving from duties to performance dimensions, it is possible to identify 15 to 20 goals. When this occurs, goals should be prioritized, and only those that meet certain criteria should be used for appraisal purposes. In developing a list of goals by order of importance, the following criteria are useful:

1   Represents full range of job responsibilities;
2   Covers important aspects of job;
3   Is appropriate to work required;
4   Is meaningful to work required;
5   Is challenging to the incumbent; and
6   Is feasible and attainable.

The setting of performance goals requires the involvement of both supervisor and subordinate. The goals relate to the performance dimensions that come from the job duties. For the goals to be valuable to both the employee and the organization, they must be understood and accepted by the employees and must fit into the overall purposes of the organization. In addition to identifying results that are observable, goals should be measurable preferably in quantitative terms. This is not always possible, however, and in these cases, qualitative measurements are acceptable.

Performance goals provide the critical link back to the top-down goals identified for accomplishing the mission of the organization and represent only one of a number of checks and balances built into the performance appraisal process. Establishing performance goals attempts to ensure (1) that all goal-directed work effort relates to the achievement of the mission of the organization and (2) that the goals of each individual and each work group are compatible with and supportive of results to be achieved by other organizational groups and units.

***Non-responsibility, Duty-related Goals.***  It is quite possible that certain performance goals may not relate to job responsibilities and duties, an example of which is a growth or development goal. Among the essential responsibilities and duties of a job, there is seldom one that relates to personal growth. This type of goal may be set and used as a critical measure of job performance. Involvement in and successful completion of a wide range of training and development programs may be a critical goal. There is no problem, including these and other types of goals, that does not relate directly to responsibilities and duties. One problem that may develop is the weighting of these goals relative to those evolving from specific responsibilities and duties. Here again, final weighting may best be accomplished through supervisor–subordinate discussion and negotiation.

The concept of adding goals beyond those related to job responsibilities is similar in nature to a statement found in most job descriptions, "and other duties as assigned." Neither case is meant to be a "catch 22"—placing the incumbent in a compromising situation. Both are necessary because job requirements must be flexible enough to meet the demands of a constantly changing environment. The nagging, truthfully unanswerable issue is how to identify what is sufficient flexibility.

***Attainment Steps.***  Before actually appraising employee performance, attainment steps must be identified. This activity is by far the most personal and highly individualized portion of the entire process. Here, supervisor and subordinate discuss the various actions that the subordinate will implement in order to achieve a goal. The attainment steps provide both diagnostic and monitoring opportunities for the supervisor and subordinate. The attainment steps permit identification of:

1   Subordinate strengths and weaknesses;
2   Barriers to goal attainment;
3   Opportunities for goal attainment; and
4   Degree of progress.

During the discussion of attainment steps, supervisors identify how they will assist their subordinates to attain their established goals. Opportunities for documentation and review of both supervisor and subordinate behavior occur at this point. Although general goals may be set on an annual basis, attainment steps and specific goals may be set for a two- or three-month period with specific goals and attainment steps reset at the conclusion of a bimonthly or quarterly review session. Both goal setting and attainment steps are discussed in greater detail in Chapter 5.

## Available Options

The step-by-step process from organizational goals to job responsibilities, duties, performance dimensions, performance standards, and performance goals can be shortened. It is certainly possible to develop three to five responsibilities in very general terms, i.e., supervision, quality of work, quantity of work, affirmative action, etc., and to go from these directly to goals. It is also possible to measure results directly by reviewing how well employees have performed relative to the assigned job duties. Another option is to develop a performance dimension profile and to select the element in the profile that most closely relates to the demonstrated workplace behavior of the appraisee.

A *performance dimension profile* is a set of behaviors within a specific performance dimension that provides a scale, degree, or range of behaviors that act as standards or reference points for identifying and measuring demonstrated employee behaviors. The critical point on a performance dimension profile is the break point that describes a minimum level of competency for that dimension. Requiring a "yes" or "no" response for the break point profile statement signifies either that the behavior did or did not occur. A useful profile provides a set of behaviors ranging from unacceptable to acceptable to mastery and possibly to superior mastery. The development of scales and the identification of specific workplace behavior are discussed in detail in Chapter 8.

The following is an example of a performance dimension profile:

### Performance Dimension

Provides sufficient on-the-job training to ensure efficient use of equipment and input materials in producing a timely and quality output.

### Performance Dimension Profile

Ignores agreed-upon training procedures.

Frequently has insufficiently trained employees to fill all key jobs.

*Explains how to do the job, describes why things went wrong, but does not explain why or check to see if employees understand the reason for doing something in a prescribed manner.

Provides minimal follow-up after training an employee.

Ensures that employees know how to do their jobs but there is no inventory of available skills.

Ensures that employees know their jobs, and jobs of others in work group and can provide adequate support under most circumstances.

Uses slack time to cross train employees.

Promotes skill development and continuous training is promoted within work group.

* Breakpoint statement describing minimum level of competency.

A specific selected profile statement provides information useful for identifying training, coaching, and counseling needs and for relating demonstrated behaviors to the rewards provided by the organization. Developing performance dimension profile statements to identify and measure performance requires more of the time and effort of skilled professionals, but less time of the supervisor and subordinate than does the establishment and use of performance goals. In many jobs, however, appraising performance relative to a set of statements that profile a specific performance dimension would be more appropriate. These jobs are those:

1   that are routine in nature and require repetitive work effort;
2   that permit employees little opportunity to participate in decisions that affect them;

3   in which work rules, methods, and procedures closely define work to be done; and

4   in which authority is centralized and autonomy limits the appraisal process. (The discussion of Behavioral Anchored Rating Scales (BARS) in Chapter 8 focuses on this topic.)

A possible area of confusion occurs when differentiating between a performance dimension profile and a performance profile. As mentioned, a performance dimension profile describes a complete range of behaviors that employees may exhibit when performing their job assignments related to a specific dimension. A performance profile, on the other hand, is a set of performance dimensions that fully describes or forms the composite criterion—job performance.

The dimensions included within a performance profile should consist only of those essential to the performance of a job and should comprehensively describe it. Performance dimensions should be conceptually different, requiring different knowledge and skills to perform properly. Performance dimensions, like job responsibilities, have a tendency to deteriorate over time. Like all aspects of job requirements, they require review and reevaluation.

## Cost–Benefit Analysis

The mission-accomplishment process modeled in Figures 2-1 and 2-2 and described in this chapter does not require the use of any complex mathematical procedures, but it does consume a large amount of time, especially during the development period and in the early stages of implementation. In most cases, personnel (either internal staff specialists or external consultants) can be used to design performance appraisal programs and to teach employees the what's, why's, and how's of using these programs. These personnel should be skilled in (1) analyzing job content, (2) teaching employees how to identify and describe what they do, (3) involving employees in actively supporting the program, (4) creating a workplace atmosphere in which trust can develop, (5) teaching supervisors how the process works and why it benefits them, and (6) teaching supervisors to interact and to communicate with their subordinates as individuals and members of work groups in an efficient and effective manner.

The major costs involved in this process are communication related. Organizational communication does not have to be like the famous comment about the weather, "Everybody talks about it but nobody does anything about it." The key to sucess of a performance appraisal program is designing a program that requires employee interaction.

As mentioned in Chapter 1, one of the first and possibly most difficult hurdles to overcome in implementing a program that requires any amount of employee participation lies with middle- and the lower-levels of upper management. Their basic concerns are, first, that they lack time to do the work that is necessary and, secondly, that this process is not necessary since they can accomplish all that will come out of such a program through their own management skills and efforts.

It is my experience that what normally happens in most organizations is that managers at all levels are so busy "putting out fires" that they do not have the time to discuss with employees what their job responsibilities and duties are, the priorities that these responsibilities and duties deserve, the results that they should be achieving, the standards used to measure performance, and the rewards that are available for superior performance. The other side of the use of time issue is that many of the fires would never occur if time were spent communicating desires, expected results, support that is available, and rewards to be gained. In addition, those fires that do occur can be identified more readily and extinguished before they develop into organizational catastrophes. The true issues are where to spend time and how to spend it most productively.

A major motive for implementing any type of employee involvement program is to improve productivity. There is a widespread feeling that modern workers require more opportunities for interaction on decisions that affect their jobs than employees did 30 to 40 years ago. The performance appraisal process developed in this book involves employees in their jobs from initial identification and weighting of responsibilities and duties to the setting of goals and establishment of standards used for appraising their goal–achievement success to the right to appeal any decision they feel to be inaccurate or unfair. The basic premise underlying the responsibility–goal–appraisal process is that employees want to know what is expected of them, how their performance will be measured, and what they can expect from specific levels of performance.

As mentioned earlier, it is possible to omit steps in the process. Omitting steps reduces the initial cost and permits more flexibility, but it may lead to misunderstandings, misinterpretations, and the possible eventual scuttling of the entire program. Performance appraisal programs and requirements must be specific enough to ensure understanding by all involved individuals. They must promote fair and considerate decisions and, whether from an organizational point-of-view or from government demands, be valid and reliable. Stable and consistent performance appraisal programs can only develop when there is widespread understanding and acceptance. When basic steps in a plan are omitted because of cost considerations or because managers at certain levels feel insecure or uncertain when confronting their subordinates regarding "What exactly is my job?" and "What exactly do you want me to do?", it may be worthwhile to consider doing nothing. There may be a very good chance that money expended in developing and implementing the program will be absolutely wasted. Even more importantly, a poorly designed and implemented performance appraisal program can do more harm than good; a poor performance appraisal program does not achieve *zero* results, it achieves *negatives*. It arouses frustration, increases insecurity and hostility, and could easily result in reduced employee performance—the exact opposite of the intent of most performance appraisal programs.

A question that frequently arises is why do middle- and upper-level managers fight the implementation of performance appraisal programs. Although some reasons have already been identified, an essential point to recognize is that managers at these levels normally require as much flexibility in working with their subordinates as possible. These managers are constantly facing changing work situations. Any time they have to state precisely what they expect from their subordinates, they are in trouble. They know from experience that the one sure thing about their job is that what is demanded now may change in 30 minutes or tomorrow. Possibly, the one approach open in the modern organization is to develop a working environment in which all employees recognize the dynamics of the work situation and are willing and able to make the necessary adjustment to achieve goals that may change or have changing priorities. Practically everyone in some manner would like to have a job that exudes *certainty* and consistency, especially when it comes to the appraisal and the rewarding of performance. In the great majority of cases, this is an unattainable goal.

The appraisal system recommended in this book uses precise, step-by-step procedures. Attempts are made to define and to describe each step carefully. This in no way infers that there is no room for flexibility. Rather, the entire process recognizes the impact that forces both internal and external to the organization will have on job requirements (the higher the level of the job, the greater the impact). The responsibility—duty—performance dimension—performance standard—performance goal process identifies areas in which mutual involvement and agreement on basic job requirements are possible and critical.

Agreement in these areas permits improved identification and increased understanding and awareness by supervisor and subordinate of job-related obstacles that face the incumbent. Interactions in these areas permit supervisors to inform subordinates of the opportunities that they have and what the future may hold for them.

It is practically impossible for a supervisor and subordinate to obtain any kind of meaningful results in a once-a-year discussion of performance issues. Supervisors and subordinates must work together on ordering priorities, setting goals, and establishing standards of performance. Creating a working environment in which disagreements and misunderstandings are identified and worked out through continuous two-way communication is the intent of this performance appraisal process. This type of supervisor–subordinate relationship must not be left to chance. It must be part of a well designed, properly implemented, management system.

Although performance is the ultimate criterion, it is important to recognize that performance, in itself, is a theoretical construct. Normally, various empirical dimensions must be used to measure performance. It may be extremely difficult, if not impossible, to measure total performance because of various environmental limitations. An appraisal system that includes a set of responsibilities and duties that comprehensively cover job requirements and performance dimensions, as well as performance goals that represent the significant or most important part of work assignments will provide the information and criteria necessary to appraise performance.

3

From Job Content
to Individualized
Job Requirements

Over the past thirty years, many respected scholars and successful managers have expressed the need for and the benefits available from a participative approach to management. A major reason for implementing participative management is to increase the opportunity for dignity and respect for all employees. The question that then arises is, "What can employers do in order to increase the dignity of work and to provide respect for those employees whose efforts make possible the successful accomplishment of organizational objectives and goals?"

A review of programs and projects implemented for improving employee quality of work life stresses the importance of employee demands to have a significant voice in and influence over decisions that affect their jobs. Before employees will commit the quantity and quality of energy necessary for successful operations, they want to know (1) what the organization wants from them, (2) where they now stand, (3) where they are heading, and (4) what they can expect. Answers to these important questions require disclosure of information that frequently is not made available to many employees throughout the organization.

## A Legal Analogy

The four issues identified in the previous paragraph provide the framework of a due process concept to job ownership. A basic step in job ownership is an employment contract. Of course, an employment contract can be terminated by either side at any time for any reason whatsoever unless the contract or higher laws provide otherwise.

The National Labor Relations Act provides the right to employees to bargain collectively with their employers. The Fair-Labor Standards Act and its amendments establish minimum pay, overtime pay for hours worked in excess of 40, and equal pay for equal work. The Age Discrimination in Employment Act of 1967 and a 1978 amendment protect persons between the ages of 40 to 70 from discrimination on the basis of age in any terms or conditions of employment. Title VII of the Civil Rights Act of 1964 and its amendments require employers to act in a nondiscriminatory manner when making personnel-related decisions. The Employee Retirement Income Security Act (ERISA) protects employees against unwise administration and capricious use of retirement plans. The Occupational Safety and Health Act (OSHA) is designed to promote the safety and health of employees at the work site. The Rehabilita-

44

tion Act of 1973 requires most government contractors and subcontractors to make reasonable accommodations to persons having physical or mental handicaps. The Vietnam Era Veterans Readjustment Act of 1974 requires government contractors and subcontractors to employ and promote qualified disabled veterans and Vietnam Era veterans.

These and other acts are establishing a body of due process in human resource jurisprudence which provides protection to employees in all kinds of work situations. However, unless specifically stated through legislation, employers are not required to provide individual rights to employees on the job. Good management practices necessitate additional considerations.

Although employees do not have full *legal* ownership to their jobs, it is in management's favor to recognize that a contract is being established when it provides a wide array of rewards in exchange for employee-provided availabilities, capabilities, and performance. To ensure that both parties understand the stipulations of the contract, instruments must be developed that identify certain obligations.

Possibly the most important documents that management can prepare and use are those that identify job content and job requirements and those that identify and analyze job performance. The job description, in essence, becomes a deed and title to the job, and the performance appraisal system and its accompanying instruments provide the due process that identifies and communicates the desired and actual results. To ensure continuing possession of their jobs, employees must accept responsibility for satisfactory performance of these workplace obligations. In turn, employees should be secure in the knowledge that they will have continued job ownership.

## Providing Job Information

Reducing job-related uncertainties should be a major goal for all employers. It should be noted that the very process of providing employees with more job-related information may, in some cases, temporarily result in greater uncertainties than previously existed. Managers must recognize that the release and transfer of job and organizational information in itself is no guarantee for improving employee job-related satisfaction. However, without quality job-related information, employees have a difficult, if not impossible, assignment in making quality decisions regarding their work and the effort that they expend in performing their jobs.

Making job-related information available and granting employees the opportunity for increased influence over job-related decisions must be accomplished in a systematic and orderly manner. Once senior management makes the decision that there should be greater disclosure of job-related information to employees, the questions that arise are what to include in the disclosure and where to start. A very general outline includes information on these topics:

1　Job responsibilities and duties.

2　Job performance dimensions and standards.

3　Performance goals and attainment steps.

4　Employer performance expectations.

5　Job performance as perceived by management.

6　Job rates of pay.

7　Performance-related reward opportunities.

By promoting this type of job-related information, organizations have the opportunity to minimize distortions and fallacies carried through rumor and gossip channels. A first step in an orderly and systematic approach for presenting job-related information to employees is through a process of job content analysis that *requires* employee participation.

"Requires" may appear to be an inappropriate word when discussing employee participation, but acceptance of obligation on the part of employees for improving workplace decision processes is not always readily attainable or provided on a voluntary basis. Long-standing distrust of employer investigations into what employees do on their jobs blocks employee willingness to participate in providing job-related information. Influencing employees to participate requires well conceived and orderly systems that lead back to the one-bite-at-a-time approach.

From the concept of participative management, worthy ideas, such as job enrichment, quality of work life, and productivity improvement, have arisen. The sad part of these glorious ideas is that, to date, much of the work regarding them has consisted of oral and written platitudes and a minimum amount of activity leading to the improvement of the work life of employees and the increased productivity of the organization.

One possible answer to the large volumes of praise and the minimal amount of operational success is the failure to recognize the facts that employees "own" their jobs and that the proprietary contract between employer and employee includes payments to be made in both directions. To maintain job ownership, employees must be (1) available to perform job assignments and activities, (2) capable of performing these assignments and activities by demonstrating that they have the necessary knowledge and skills, and (3) willing to perform at levels sufficient to meet or surpass acceptable job standards. On the other side of the bargain, employers implicitly state that they will provide (1) work opportunities, (2) training and development necessary for employees to meet changing job demands, and (3) rewards for provided availability, capability, and performance.

A primary action taken by an organization that recognizes employee job ownership occurs when the employer requests employees to identify what they do in performing their jobs. Employees must recognize that a basic ownership responsibility and right is the opportunity to describe what they do on their jobs. Also, they should have final approval over any documents that describe their jobs and the standards that will measure their performance. This does not mean that employees must have the skills necessary to write a job description and to set performance standards. It also does not mean that they must be the sole individuals with the authority to establish job responsibilities and duties and to appraise work performance. It does mean that they have a significant and meaningful voice and input into all parts of any system or process that influences job requirements and measures work performance.

## Employee Involvement in Job Content Analysis

In most workplace activities, little worthwhile occurs without spending much time, effort, and expertise on the design and implementation of the activities. Nowhere is this more apparent than in the activities related to job analysis. At first glance, it may appear that analyzing, identifying, and describing job content is a fairly simple process. One approach includes two steps:

**Step 1**  Ask an employee what he or she does on the job.

**Step 2**  Write what the employee says on some formal document.

A different, but also fairly straightforward approach is to observe a person perform job activities and then to describe what happened. A third approach is either to interview the responsible supervisor and have him or her describe the job or to request the supervisor to furnish a written description of job activities. A fourth approach is to use some standardized list of job activity statements and have employees select from the list those statements that best describe what they do on the job.

These approaches appear to be adequate and straightforward.

If, however, they are to provide the quality and quantity of information that organizations need for performance appraisal, they are not as simple as they appear. It is unlikely that any one of the above-listed approaches will provide information of sufficient quality and quantity to implement a successful performance appraisal program. Because of the already-identified barriers to a successful performance appraisal, it is critical that its foundation be set in concrete and that the appraisal of an employee's workplace behavior relate directly to accurate and valid job content information.

To obtain information that completely, accurately, and validly identifies and describes job content, the first step is to identify in words and terms understandable to everyone involved in the process what is meant by activities, responsibilities, and duties. Active involvement and support of incumbents and knowledgeable supervisors make it possible to identify, classify, and prioritize job-related activities. These same individuals must also assist in describing the education, experiences, and skills necessary to perform work assignments. With the collecion of this information, care and consideration must go into properly describing an activity and the format used for displaying job content information.

Individual preference certainly plays an important role in this first step in developing a performance appraisal system, but the following described procedure is relatively simple and leads into and supports each succeeding step of the appraisal system.

In performing job content analysis, certain words and terms that have varied meanings must be defined. By defining these words and terms, everyone involved will be working from the same base.

> *Task:* An assigned piece of work that is normally clearly identifiable, usually finished within a prescribed period of time, and relatively easy to measure.
>
> *Activity:* A group of tasks that form part of an employee's job.
>
> *Duty:* One or more activities performed in carrying out a responsibility.
>
> *Responsibility:* A group of duties that identify and describe a major purpose or primary existence of a job.

Figures 3-1 and 3-2 are examples of job responsibilities and duties. A detailed description of how to obtain this type of information and how to display it follows these two figures.

These two listings of responsibilities and duties identify certain issues that arise from an analysis of jobs at all levels in an

1   Commits unit to new courses of action.

   **a**   Allocates resources to individuals and projects that will have the greatest impact on the achievement of organizational goals.

   **b**   Directs activities of unit to adapt to changing environmental conditions.

   **c**   Recognizes disturbance issues and redirects efforts to minimize resulting ill effects.

   **d**   Negotiates issues that may or will have a negative impact on organizational performance.

2   Monitors, collects, and transmits information for work unit.

   **a**   Scans environment, interrogates liaison contacts, and receives unsolicited information.

   **b**   Disseminates privileged information with subordinates.

   **c**   Passes information between subordinates who do not have readily accessible communication channels.

   **d**   Sends information to people outside the organization for subordinates.

3   Maintains interpersonal relationships with individuals both external and internal to the organization.

   **a**   Directs efforts of immediate subordinate/own staff personnel.

   **b**   Encourages all employees to coordinate efforts in order to meet group, unit, and organizational goals.

   **c**   Acts as a liaison with individuals outside the vertical chain of command.

   **d**   Performs assignments of a ceremonial nature.

FIGURE 3-1    RESPONSIBILITIES AND DUTIES OF THE JOB OF AN EXECUTIVE* (*PARAPHRASED FROM HENRY MINTZBERG, "THE MANAGER'S JOB: FOLKLORE AND FACT," *Harvard Business Review*, JULY–AUGUST 1975, pp. 49–61.)

1   Plans and schedules work assignments.

   **a**   Establishes and reviews group and individual goals.

   **b**   Sets workplace methods and procedures.

   **c**   Schedules daily work assignments.

   **d**   Coordinates work activities with related work group.

   **e**   Ensures that subordinates have necessary equipment and material.

   **f**   Establishes and maintains records and reporting systems.

2   Monitors performance to ensure acceptable levels and quality of output.

   **a**   Observes employee performance at work site.

   **b**   Compares individual performance to group norms.

    **c**   Compares actual performance with present performance standards.

    **d**   Conducts specified number of quality inspections.

    **e**   Investigates accident and damage claims.

    **f**   Resolves grievances and informal problems.

**3**  Develops employees and maximizes performance potential.

    **a**   Reviews records to identify low performers.

    **b**   Instructs employees on preferred procedures.

    **c**   Schedules formal training programs.

    **d**   Detects through observation unsafe work practices.

    **e**   Inspects equipment for safe working conditions.

    **f**   Appraises employee performance.

    **g**   Provides training to correct knowledge- and skill-related deficiencies.

**4**  Schedules employees to ensure work coverage within guidelines pre-scribed by government legislation, corporate policy, and union contract.

    **a**   Assigns hourly tours to provide appropriate job coverage.

    **b**   Develops weekly work schedule to ensure 8 hours per day and 40 hours per week work load.

    **c**   Establishes holiday and vacation schedules.

    **d**   Rotates work to allow for equal distribution of various types of work assignments.

FIGURE 3-2    RESPONSIBILITIES AND DUTIES OF THE JOB OF A FIRST-LEVEL MANAGER

organization. These issues arise from analysis and identification of all aspects of the job from work activities to performance goals.

1   The higher the level the job is, the more complex are the job requirements and associated incumbent behaviors.

2   The more complex the requirements and behaviors are, the more difficult it is to describe them in clear, unambiguous terms.

3   The more complex the behaviors are, the more difficult it is to identify relevant behaviors that are observable and measurable in quantitative terms, although qualitative measurements are certainly acceptable.

4   The higher the level the job is, the greater the likelihood that identified job behaviors represent only a sample of necessary or required behaviors.

5    As jobs increase in importance, the cognitive and affective domains become more important, and the psychomotor domains become less important.

    *Cognitive Domain:* intellectual pursuits characterized by thinking, reasoning, and understanding skills.

    *Affective Domain:* feelings and emotional pursuits characterized by interests, attitudes, openness to change, and appreciation of differences.

    *Psychomotor Domain:* physical pursuits characterized by motor skills involving synchronized and coordinated movement of hands, arms, legs, torso, head, and eyes.

Figure 3-3 describes the relationship of these three domains with jobs at increasingly higher levels in an organization.

There are a number of additional points to be discussed from these examples.

1    *Format.* In an outline form, responsibilities and duties may be easily identified, thus minimizing the chance that they will be lost in some paragraph or will be hidden behind another

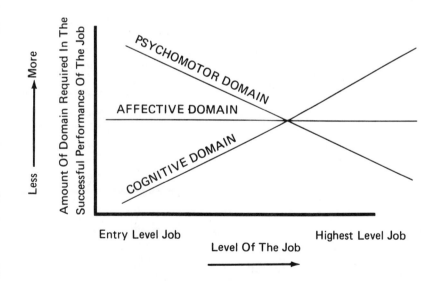

FIGURE 3-3      RELATIONSHIP BETWEEN COGNITIVE, AFFECTIVE, AND PSYCHOMOTOR DOMAINS AND JOB LEVELS

statement. Such a format permits responsibilities and duties to be clearly separated and prioritized.

2   *Separating Responsibilities and Duties.* It is not necessary to ask an employee to provide responsibility and duty statements. What is necessary is to request employees to describe the work activities required in the performance of their jobs. The intent of requesting activity information is to minimize confusion that occurs when employees are asked to list responsibilities and duties. For example, many employees are unable to differentiate between responsibilities and duties. Employees should simply rank their activities in order of importance. Figure 3–4 is a useful document for collecting job activity information. It is also useful for collecting other types of job content information that assists job analysts to identify, describe, and prioritize responsibilities and duties.

From the information generated by a Job Activity Questionnaire, an analyst can identify and write responsibility and duty statements. The following guidelines will assist the analyst to select appropriate responsibilities and duties from the list of activities.

Practically all jobs can be fully and completely described by from three to seven responsibility statements. These responsibilities cover the major knowledge and skill requirements of the jobholder and the major functional areas in which the jobholder has work assignments. The knowledge, skills, and functional activities may relate to general areas, such as operational, technical, financial, and interpersonal. For example, in Figure 3-1 operational performance areas include those described in responsibility 2: "Monitors, collects, and transmits information . . ."; technical and financial performance areas in responsibility 1: "Commits unit to new courses of action"; and interpersonal in responsibility 3: "Maintains interpersonal relationships with. . . ." Other major and universal performance categories are:

1   Frequency and type of supervision received.

2   Frequency and type of supervision given.

3   Interaction or involvement in teaching, counseling, coaching, training of others.

4   Ability and requirements for analyzing and evaluating action-oriented information.

5   Requirements for following instructions or orders.

6   Amount and quality of direction, instructions, and suggestions transmitted.

7    Degree of accountability for human and nonhuman resources in planning, operations, and/or control of the job.

8    Physical demands.

9    Emotional demands.

10    Special demands.

Responsibilities and duties establish not only the what and how of the job but also why the job exists. The important point to remember in defining the responsibilities and duties is that the key issue is why the activity is being performed.

In most cases, employees identify from 10 to 30 activities that they perform. The major effort facing the analyst writing responsibility and duty statements is selecting the most suitable and appropriate responsibility statements and collecting the activities that best fit and further describe a specific responsibility.

When a responsibility is being identified and then described, it may be necessary at times to combine two or more activities into one responsibility. After identifying the responsibilities, the analyst reviews the activity list and places under a specific responsibility those activities that best describe or relate to it. Again, three to seven activities or duties are normally sufficient to describe a responsibility completely.

After developing a first draft of the responsibilities, the analyst should review the information that the incumbent provided on order of importance, time spent, and difficulty. This review should provide the analyst with enough information to establish an order of importance for the responsibilities. The same procedure is used to establish a ranking of duties for each responsibility.

When writing the final draft of responsibility and duty statements, the analyst should list the responsibilities in order of importance. It is preferable to use the same procedure when listing the duties for each responsibility. This approach allows for a needed uniformity among job responsibility and duty statements. Anyone receiving such a list would know that the first responsibility listed is the most important, the second listed is the second most important, and so on. Likewise, the ordering of duties within a responsibility would carry the same meaning to a reviewer.

The following guide is helpful in developing an orderly arrangement of words or phrases for responsibility and duty statements:

1    Start each statement with an action word—*verb.*

2    Explain the requirements of the job by amplifying the verb

1. Job Title:_____ 2. Code: _____ 3. Date:_____

4. Name: _____ 5. Department: _____

6. Name of Supervisor: _____ 7. Supervisor's Job Title: _____

7. Time In This Job: _____ years _____ months.

You are the person best qualified to provide information about your job. You know the exact work activities that you perform. From the information you will provide, it will be possible to develop a description of the responsibilities and duties of your job. The completeness and accurancy of the job description will depend to a great extent on your interest and attention in completing this questionnaire.

8. *List of Activities:*

List the various activities that you do on your job. An activity is a set of interrelated tasks that produce an observable output. Number each activity consecutively. Follow the description of the activity, state whether it is (1) a *regularly* recurring activity or (2) an *irregularly* occurring activity. If it is a regularly occurring activity, state whether it occurs (1) daily, (2) weekly, (3) semimonthly, (4) monthly, (5) quarterly, (6) semiannually, or (7) annually.

This is the most important section of the questionnaire. You will be referring to it throughout the remainder of this questionnaire. Please take the time to list the activities that comprehensively cover all parts of your job.

9. *Importance of Activities*:

Review all of the activities that you identified in item 8, List of Activities. Identify in item 9.1, Most Important Activities, the activities that you consider to be most important in their descending order of importance. In item 9.2, Least Important Activities, list the activities that you consider to be least important. The first activity listed will be the least important of all activities that you perform. (The alternative method of ranking is helpful in performing this ranking. First review the list of activities and identify the one that *you* consider most important, circle the number, and enter the number in item 9.1. The circled number will indicate that it has already been used and requires no further analysis. Next, review the list and circle the number of the activity that you consider to be least important and enter the number in item 9.2. Continue this process, circling the numbers and entering them in the appropriate list, until you have identified all the activities listed in item 8.)

9.1 *Most Important Activities:*

9.2 *Least Important Activities:*


10. *Difficult Activities:*
    From the List of Activities in item 8, list (by number only) the activity or activities that *you* think are difficult to perform (require the most skill, experience, effort, etc.). Beside each activity number listed for this section, briefly explain why you consider this activity to be difficult.


11. *Time Required to Perform Activities:*
    Return to your list of activities in item 8 and review them, this time thinking about the amount of time that you spend performing each.

    11.1 List by number only and in order of importance those activities that consume the largest amount of your working time.


    11.2 List by number only and in order of importance those activities that require very little of your working time.


12. *Inappropriate Activities Being Performed:*
    Are there any activities that you now perform that you feel you should *not* be doing? List these activities below by number only, and provide a brief explanation of why you feel you should not be doing them (for example, the activity is already being performed by another employee).


13. *Appropriate Activities Not Being Performed:*
    Are there any activities that you do *not* now perform that you feel you should be doing? If so, please describe these activities along with a brief explanation of why you feel you should be doing them.

FIGURE 3-4    (con't)                                                                                    **55**

through a phrase that tells *what* is done—describes a specific outcome, a product of certain effort. These outcomes should be observable.[1]

For example, from the executive job description statements (Figure 3-1):

Maintains (verb)

Interpersonal relationships (what is done)
    With individuals both external and internal to the organization (who)
Encourages (verb)

All employees to coordinate efforts (what is done)
    In meeting group, unit, and organizational goals (why)

If sufficient and understandable instructions are provided to assist employees to give quality job information and the analyst is given the materials and instructions useful for writing responsibility and duty statements, the quality of the statements will improve and the time and effort required to write them will decline. With proper instructions and assistance, supervisors or certain individuals within a work unit can be given the assignment to write job responsibility and duty statements and can be expected to do a good job on the assignment.

An additional aid for writing responsibility and duty statements is a list of action words. Such a list appears in the Glossary of Richard Henderson's *Compensation Management*, 2nd ed. (Reston, Va.: Reston Publishing Co, 1979). Lists of typical functional areas associated with the jobs under study are also extremely helpful in identifying responsibilities and duties and in developing responsibility and duty statements.

In a large organization having many jobs in particular occupational groups, standardized and quantified job analysis questionnaires provide analysts with help in identifying responsibilities and duties. These types of questionnaires assist in supporting information gained from employee-completed job content questionnaires and possibly help in identifying missing information. Since these questionnaires provide information about a wide range of jobs, they also enable organizations to compare jobs in various settings. Job analysis instruments, such as the Position Analysis Questionnaire

---

[1] This procedure is applicable and appropriate for writing standards of expected or desired behavior throughout the job evaluation–performance appraisal process.

(PAQ) and the Job Analysis Questionnaire (JAQ), use preestablished, standardized sets of job profile statements to identify similarities and differences in jobs.

Additional bits of job information that are vital to understanding the job are lists of knowledge and skills required in the performance of listed job activities.

### Definition of Terms

*Knowledge:* Prerequisites for thinking and action required to perform assignments necessary to produce acceptable output.

*Skill:* Demonstrated level of proficiency of an ability.

*Ability:* A natural talent or acquired proficiency required in the performance of work assignments.

An additional question for the Job Activity Questionnaire (Figure 3-4) could be:

"14.  *Knowledge and Skills Required:*

a    List the basic knowledge and skills required to perform activities listed in item 1 (for example, knowledge of federal regulations regarding monopolistic activities; skill in speaking before large groups at public functions; skill in making decisions with a minimal amount of information).

b    List any tools, equipment, vehicles, and machines that you use in performing your work assignments.

c    List any licenses or certificates required before you can legally perform your work assignments."

## Performance Measures Not Attainable Through Job Analysis

Job analysis is not the only method used to measure workplace performance. For example, Chapter 8 contains a discussion of the industrial engineering application of work methods analysis. Industrial engineering methods, techniques, and procedures provide information on quantity of output and are particularly useful in worker-controlled manufacturing operations. Some clerical jobs are also amenable to this approach for determining acceptable or standard levels of output. Other measures that identify quality of performance that do not arise from job analysis are quality factors, such as error rates, and scrap or waste resulting from work efforts.

Other measures of performance that identify or measure employee job-related behaviors are tardiness, absenteeism, and possibly rates of injuries. These measures vary significantly in importance from one kind of job to another. Before measures such as scrap, absenteeism, tardiness, or injuries are used, it must be demonstrated that these are valid and relevant indicators of workplace performance.

## Job Performance—A Multidimensional Variable

The obvious reason for implementing performance appraisal is to analyze and identify employee job performance. Job performance must be the ultimate criterion. The problem that faces appraisal system designers, administrators, appraisers, and appraisees is whether it is possible to use the basic criterion to measure employee workplace behaviors. In the great majority of cases, the answer is no!

There are a number of reasons for the emphatic negative response. One that stands out is the fact that the job performance criterion consists of many performance variables (criteria). Each of these variables probably requires different sets of incumbent knowledge and skills in order to be accomplished successfully.

Recognizing that there are different knowledge and skill requirements for different performance criteria leads to the obvious conclusion that employees on the same job will not perform each criterion identically. Moreover, their overall job performance will vary according to the manner in which they perform each performance criterion. Additionally, it is likely that the numerous variables that make up the global variable—job performance—vary in importance; therefore, the differences must be recognized through some weighting process. Quite likely, the importance of some, if not most, of the performance criteria will vary over time. In addition, some performance criteria will cease to exist and new ones will appear. There is little doubt that situational changes will occur that will require both changes in the performance criteria and in their intensity.

Analyzing the global or universal criterion and identifying the various performance criteria that constitute it are critical in developing any performance appraisal system. The classification of performance criteria must also recognize the existence of individual differences in the perception of similarities. Essential to the success of a performance appraisal is agreement among all those involved in the design and administration of the process that the performance criteria are appropriate and important.

The performance criteria proposed and used in this section are those that emerge from the job itself. This approach to classifying performance criteria is an interactive process that rests on the philosophy that (1) appraised employee job behavior must relate to job requirements; (2) incumbents, workplace supervisors, and specialists responsible for analyzing and describing job content must have inputs to the identification, description, and weighting of performance criteria; and (3) the best way to identify, define, and classify job content information is through job analysis.

Successful appraisal of employee performance based on job content-related criteria requires the identification of work activities into an orderly and natural arrangement. Defining, describing, and ordering appraisal factors into a natural arrangement is not a simple or inexpensive operation. Establishing and operating an appraisal that by its very design is subjective in nature but that at the same time minimizes individual biases which may distort final results is a major assignment.

A critical design and implementation goal in any performance appraisal system is to limit nonperformance-related biases of the rater/appraiser. Complete elimination of subjectivity in performance appraisal is an impossible assignment. The very foundation of performance appraisal is set on expert judgment. The expert, in most cases, is the immediate supervisor of the individual being appraised. The supervisor/appraiser must set a value on or estimate the worth of the performance of the subordinate. Those involved in the design, implementation, and administration of performance appraisal systems must recognize that human judgment is fallible and that there is an indiscernible link between the conscious and unconscious processes of the human brain. This link will almost always result in subjective considerations regarding performances that "replays" of employee performance during the appraisal period would not substantiate or justify.

Possibly the best approach available to minimizing the opportunities for distortions that rest within human value systems and appraiser perceptions, knowledge, and skills is to provide adequate and useful guidelines for appraising performance. When guidelines are inadequate or unavailable, appraisers frequently allow considerations such as central tendency, overly lenient or excessively strict interpretations, halo and horn judgments, and initial impressions and the latest events to contaminate their appraisals of subordinate performance. (A detailed discussion of these contamination factors appears in Chapter 6.) The key to a quality performance appraisal system is limiting appraiser biases that distort the description of an employee's performance. A major opportunity available to attain such a lofty goal is to maintain a continuous focus on the work that an incumbent does in performing the job.

To minimize the opportunities for distortion in any performance appraisal system, it is critical to focus on behavior that relates directly to job performance. The more job-related and specific the performance criteria are, the greater is the likelihood that the employee will receive a valid and fair appraisal. Guiding or directing appraiser attention through the use of job performance criteria is the reason for the focus and emphasis on job analysis. In the job analysis process described earlier, stress was placed on what may at first appear to be an academic but "nonreal world" issue: the specific and precise differences in the definitions of the terms job activities, job duties, and job responsibilities. Not only were definitions provided, but procedures were presented to assist job analysts to identify, describe, and prioritize responsibilities and duties. Attention was also placed on permitting and, in some cases, requiring employees to provide job activity information and to review responsibility and duty statements for adequacy, comprehensiveness, and accuracy.

There are a number of important reasons for the amount of attention and effort being placed on the identification, description, and prioritizing of responsibilities and duties. First, this approach lays the foundation for developing a valid and acceptable ordering of jobs by worth or value to the organization (job evaluation). Secondly (and the focus of this book), it provides a basic building block for establishing a performance appraisal system that is job related. Such an approach also provides organizations with the opportunity to develop a system that is flexible enough to meet and relate to changing employee, organization, and job demands. On the other side of the coin, employees have the opportunity to express themselves concerning their job requirements and to gain recognition and organizational rewards for job innovation that expands job worth and individual productivity.

## The Transition Process

Moving from depersonalized job responsibilities and duties to the highly personalized behaviors of an employee performing a job is the next step in the process. After an individual has been placed on the job, the organization must make every effort possible to ensure that he or she demonstrates the three C's necessary for acceptable workplace behavior.

1   Capabilities to perform as required;
2   Comprehension of job requirements; and
3   Competency in performance.

Providing a basis for addressing the capability, comprehension, and competency issues involves the further classification or restatement of responsibilities and duties. Starting with responsibilities and duties establishes a job content foundation for everything that follows. Minimizing the opportunity for varied individual interpretations of performance and gaining greater supervisor and subordinate understanding, acceptance, and agreement on what constitutes a certain level of performance also require further classification and more precise and individualized descriptions of job requirements. These additional steps include the development of performance dimensions, the establishment of performance standards, the setting of performance goals, and the identification of goal attainment steps.

The responsibilities and duties listed in Figure 3–1 provide the basis for developing performance dimensions for the job of an executive. It is possible to use the responsibility statement as the basis for the performance dimension; however, more specific and possibly more useful performance dimensions evolve from the duties. For example, from duty 1(c), "Recognizes disturbance issues and redirects efforts to minimize resulting ill effects," the following performance dimensions evolve:

1  Recognizes possible unionization activities and identifies individuals and units responsible for minimizing their efforts.

2  Reorganizes weak divisions to increase their productivity.

3  Eliminates nonprofitable divisions in most expeditious and least costly manner.

Again, the major reason for specificity is to provide the maximum amount of objectivity possible for the appraisal of performance. Established and accepted performance dimensions must relate directly to the job itself. Finally, performance dimensions and actual job performance must be recognized similarly by the different individuals who have appraisal responsibilities. An example of the entire transition process of moving from responsibilities to duties, to performance dimensions, to performance standards, and finally to performance goals is developed in Chapter 4 and modeled in Figure 4-3. Figure 3-5 provides definitions and describes the sequential relationship of the principal components of a performance appraisal system.

Establishing an appraisal system that uses individualized job requirements is more costly in terms of development time, effort expended, and skill required than some already-designed, standardized methods that use universal performance dimensions that are neither job specific nor incumbent related. Costs, strengths,

| Job Responsibilities | Job Duties | Performance Dimensions | Performance Standards | Performance Goals | Attainment Steps | Circumstances | Actual Results |
|---|---|---|---|---|---|---|---|
| Principal processes that describe what is to be done and, possibly, how it is to be done. Verbal descriptions representing demands for work activity. | Underlying processes that further describe the principal job processes—responsibilities. Verbal descriptions that more completely describe work activities consistent with related job responsibilities. | Statements that adjust associated responsibility and duties to environmental demands and unique qualities of the incumbent. Statements that lead to the development of observable measurements that can be defined in either quantitative or qualitative terms. | Clear and precise identification of what can be or is expected in the performance of a job. | An expected end result from incumbent's work place behavior. | Specific behavior performed for the purpose of accomplishing a performance goal. | Personal or environmental factors that either facilitate or inhibit the achievement of a performance goal. | Identifiable and measurable output of incumbent's job-related behavior. |

WHAT IS TO BE DONE ——————→ HOW IT IS TO BE DONE ——————→ WHAT ACTUALLY WAS DONE

AN ACHIEVEMENT-ORIENTED PROCESS, NOT A PRESCRIPTION.

FIGURE 3-5    DEFINITIONS OF PRINCIPAL PERFORMANCE APPRAISAL COMPONENTS

weaknesses, substitutability, and reinforcement are discussed in Chapters 8 and 9.

Costs related to the use of a particular performance appraisal technique or method do not provide sufficient information to justify performance appraisal decisions. Rather, costs must be analyzed from a systems view. A systems view of performance appraisal costs includes front-end costs incurred in the design and establishment of performance criteria, costs incurred in the administration of the system, and, possibly the most important and difficult to calculate, personnel costs involved in implementing a performance appraisal program. These include costs that occur from increased employee (appraisers and appraisees) frustration and hostility and, possibly, decreasing levels of productivity.

Throughout the remainder of the book, an in-depth discussion concerning the limitations related to any one method of performance appraisal occurs. In many cases, a particular method is sufficient and satisfactory for a specific organization, for a particular group of employees, or for a particular use. In other cases, an organization may require a combination of approaches and methods to achieve desired performance appraisal goals. Positive and negative attributes (including involved costs) are discussed concerning various performance appraisal methods, rating scales to be used, those that have appraiser responsibilities, approaches for reviewing appraisals, timing of appraisals, procedures for conducting appraisals, feedback of appraisal information to appraisee, and intended use of appraisal results.

As with practically all management tools that relate to directing and measuring human resources, there is no one right, best, or optimal method for appraising employee performance; however, optimization would not be worth the costs involved even if achievement of an optimal or one best way were possible. Instead, managers seek and implement procedures and methods that are satisfactory and produce results that are sufficient to meet the demands both of today and tomorrow. In many cases, the use of a combination of procedures and methods will minimize costs while maximizing the attainment of desired results. An appraisal system with a foundation based directly on specific job content has a much greater likelihood of being credible and acceptable to appraisers and appraisees. The gaining of credibility and acceptability is a major barrier that all organizations must overcome if they are to achieve the desired results from their appraisal programs.

# 4

## A Weighting
## and Scoring Process

It is now time to get down to brass tacks—establishing weights and scores for measuring employee performance. Throughout the remainder of the book, various scales, scoring devices, and measurement methods that are useful for assigning a specific score or value to an employee's performance are introduced. In this chapter, attention focuses specifically on weighting responsibilities and duties, developing performance dimensions, establishing standards, setting desired results, and measuring and scoring achieved results, i.e., employee performance.

In the early days of the twentieth century, industrial engineers developed various methods for establishing acceptable daily outputs for many types of jobs in industrial settings. The procedures used for setting work standards went into detailed analysis, such as identifying the fundamental motions required in the performance of a job. A basic job analysis identified actions such as "grasp object weighing three pounds in left hand" and "transport object five inches." In this manner, each observable and measurable element of work was identified. Through actual observations, motion pictures of the job being performed, or a synthetic design of fundamental work motions, it is possible to identify very precise and accurate times required to perform job tasks and, from these times, to establish hourly or daily output measures for workers performing specific assignments.

This approach for setting performance standards is still applicable today to jobs that are routine, repetitive, and require considerable amounts of physical effort, skill, and dexterity to perform. The issue facing managers today that is different from those facing many managers at the start of the century is the changing nature of jobs.

Today, more people have service-related jobs than there are those who have jobs in industrial settings. The output of most service-related jobs requires some degree of systematic and logical understanding of the work to be performed. Also, in moving up the organizational hierarchy, jobs require less physical activity and more intellectual abilities. (In Chapter 3, there was a discussion of increasing job complexities and the relationship of complexities to the cognitive, affective, and psychomotor domains.) In the movement from work requiring physical effort to work requiring intellectual abilities, the industrial engineering approach for measuring work activities becomes less valuable. Many workers in industrial settings now direct and monitor the operation of complex technological systems that perform the physical work.

In the cases of many service-related workers and of those performing many technical, professional, administrative, and managerial assignments, the quality and quantity of work cannot be observed and measured by analyzing the physical movements of the worker. Worker performance depends on intricate interactions (black box activities)[1] inside the brain of each employee. It is, however, possible to measure the results of worker performance although this also is by no means a perfect solution to the measurement problem. (Even the industrial engineering studies using detailed method and motion analysis make allowance for time required for personal activities. Those responsible for setting time standards must also establish a leveling factor that relates actual time required by a worker to perform a specific task to the time that an average employee would take to do the same task. In addition, these studies also have difficulty in relating quality of work to quantity of work.)

A practical and useful approach for measuring the performance of workers who must use a greater proportion of intellectual effort than physical effort is through goal setting. Goal setting is a very natural process. Practically every human being sets some kind of life-style goals and then works toward achieving them. To the young child, being a teenager and having teenage opportunities is a very real and meaningful goal; to the teenager, acquiring a driver's license and owning a car become an important goal; to young adults, acquiring a spouse and having a residence of their very own become goals worth achieving. Job-related goals can also be set, and the degree of achievement of these goals becomes a useful measure of job performance.

## Weighting Responsibilities and Duties

In Chapter 3, there was an extended discussion about prioritizing responsibilities and duties. The process required the incumbent to list job activities by order of importance, to identify the amount of time spent on each activity, to list activities that are most difficult to perform, and so on. From this information, the job analyst (a staff specialist or a designated individual within the unit) develops, prioritizes, and lists responsibility and duty statements.

In reference to the responsibilities and duties of an executive as

---

[1] The term black box refers to the human brain. Because of the complex structure, design, and operational characteristics of the human brain, man is still unable to understand how it actually functions. It is currently impossible to recognize, much less to analyze, how inputs to the brain relate to behavioral outputs. Because of this lack of knowledge, man cannot predict the actions resulting from internal function. Although this severely limits man's ability to predict human behavior, it is still possible to identify certain fairly universal behaviors that result from certain external stimuli or consequences of those behaviors.

identified and described in Figure 3-1, let us assume that the analyst performed the assignment in a creditable manner and that the responsibilities and duties are in order of importance. The designer of the performance appraisal system then interviews or requests information from individuals familiar with the job to weight each responsibility (the Delphi Technique[2] may be useful in this stage of the process). Instructions to individuals providing weighting information may take this form:

The following three responsibilities for the job of an executive were assigned the following hierarchical orders (listing by importance):

1   Commits unit to new course of action. <u>100</u>%

2   Monitors, collects, and transmits information for work unit. _____%

3   Maintains interpersonal relationships with individuals both external and internal to the organization. _____%

Please follow the instructions listed below:

1   Responsibility 1 (the highest-ranked responsibility) has been given a worth of 100 percent. Compare responsibility 2 with responsibility 1. Then, assign a worth to responsibility 2 that indicates how closely you believe responsibility 2 compares with responsibility 1. (If, for example, you felt "Monitors, collects, . . ." is about 90 percent as important as "Commits units, etc.," write the value 90 in the blank space following the listing of responsibility 2.)

2   Return to the list and compare responsibility 3 with responsibility 1 and place your comparison value in the blank following responsibility 3.

3   This same procedure is used when rating all listed items. The important point here is always to compare the items (responsibilities in this case) with the first item. The first item always receives a value of 100 percent.

---

[2] The Delphi Technique uses a committee of experts to evaluate particular types of information. Each member independently answers specific questions relative to the provided information. The answers are collected, analyzed, summarized, and returned to the committee for comparison. All responses are kept anonymous. The process minimizes pressure of the expert among experts and stimulates individual innovativeness. However, the time lag and the lack of personal contact in the process may minimize the opportunity for stimulation resulting from group-related brainstorming.

In this case, if the three responsibilities received the following values:

| Responsibility | Relative Value |
|:---:|:---:|
| 1 | 100 |
| 2 | 90 |
| 3 | 70 |
| | 260 |

a numerical weight for each responsibility could then be obtained by dividing the relative value for each responsibility into the total value of items:

$$R_1 = \frac{100}{260} = 38.5$$

$$R_2 = \frac{90}{260} = 34.6$$

$$R_3 = \frac{70}{260} = 26.9$$

$$100.0$$

The next step is the setting of values for identified duties:

Determining the weight of each duty follows the same procedure described for each responsibility. The same mathematical process is used for determining the value of each duty with the individual familiar with the job providing related worth data for each duty and with an additional step of multiplying the relative values for the duty by the value assigned to the specific responsibility.

For example, the duties listed for responsibility 1 are assigned the following relative values:

| Duties | Relative Values |
|:---|:---:|
| 1. Allocates resources to ... | 100 |
| 2. Directs activities of ... | 95 |
| 3. Recognizes disturbance issues ... | 84 |
| 4. Negotiates issues that ... | 78 |
| | 357 |

| | Relative Worth | | Weight Assigned Responsibility 1 | | Weight Assigned |
|:---|:---:|:---:|:---:|:---:|:---:|
| $D_1 = \frac{100}{357} =$ | 28.0 | X | 38.5 | = | 10.8 |
| $D_2 = \frac{95}{357} =$ | 26.6 | X | 38.5 | = | 10.2 |

$$D_3 = \frac{84}{357} = \quad 23.5 \qquad X \qquad 38.5 \qquad = \qquad 9.1$$

$$D_4 = \frac{78}{357} = \quad 21.9 \qquad X \qquad 38.5 \qquad = \qquad 8.4$$

$$\text{100.0} \hspace{6.5cm} \text{38.5}$$

## Weighting Performance Dimensions

Following the weighting and scoring of responsibilities and duties, a systematic and orderly approach to the setting of goals can begin. The first step in the development of a goal-setting appraisal process is the identification, definition, and weighting of performance dimensions. Following this step comes the establishment of performance standards and the setting of performance goals. Figure 4-1 describes the steps leading to a responsibility–goal appraisal process.

It is possible for one or more performance dimensions to relate to a specific duty. The performance dimension is the bridge between the impersonal responsibility and duty statement and the highly personal attainment goals of the jobholder. Performance dimensions provide a degree of flexibility to the stable job duties. Changing job situations and demands may not require a change in a job duty, but they are recognized in the performance dimensions. The transition from duty to performance dimension(s) provides a more specific description of what is expected of an incumbent in successfully performing assigned job duties.

In reference to the job of the executive (Figure 3-1), the path from duties to performance dimensions takes the following form. The duty 1(a),—"Allocates resources to individuals and projects that will have the greatest impact on the performance of organizational goals," has two performance dimensions:

(i)   Reviews major programs that support mainstream of business operation and authorizes capital fund expenditures for these projects.

(ii)  Reviews existing operations and capital requirements, identifying expenditures for continuing growth of the business while improving long-term debt obligations.

If there is only one performance dimension, it normally has the same weight as that assigned to its associated duty. When more than one performance dimension is used to describe a duty in behavioral

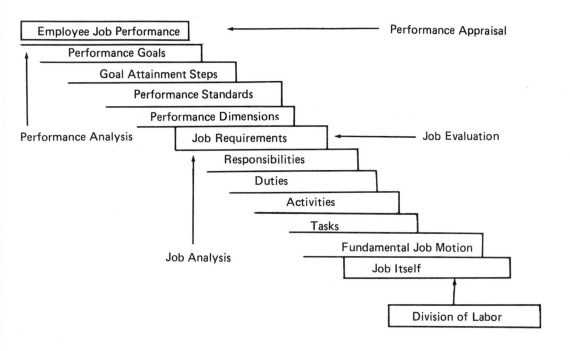

FIGURE 4-1        STEPS LEADING TO A RESPONSIBILITY—GOAL
                 APPRAISAL PROCESS

terms, the weighting and scoring of the performance dimension follows the same procedure as that used for weighting and scoring
duties. In this case, performance dimension 2 is considered most
important. The weighting and scoring process takes this form:

| Performance Dimensions | Comparison Value | Assigned Weight | Associated Duty Weight | Performance Dimension Weight |
|---|---|---|---|---|
| 2 | 100 | $\dfrac{100}{175} =$  57 | X  10.8  = | 6.2 |
| 1 | $\dfrac{75}{175}$ | $\dfrac{75}{175} = \dfrac{43}{100}$ | X  10.8  = | 4.6 |

There may be times when situations or other business demands vary the weight of the performance dimension relative to its corresponding duty. When this occurs, the predetermined weight of the duty at least provides a base or standard for the changes to be made.

## Determining Performance Standards

The description of the results to be expected—the performance standard—follows the identification and weighting of performance dimensions. A standard indicates whether or not each performance dimension is being accomplished in an acceptable manner. The standard should be specific, realistic, and feasible. If at all possible, standards should include tangible measures, such as how many, how well, time of completion or time consumed, and costs. These measures should be described in clear, concise terms.

As with other parts of the process, employees should have an opportunity to make inputs into this stage. Although they may have minor inputs as to what is a measure of satisfactory performance, they must understand the standards. The standards should be consistent and facilitate the setting of performance goals. There must also be flexibility in the setting or changing of standards in order to meet changes brought about by variations in resource allocations or conditions.

For example, the performance standards that relate to previously described performance dimensions 1 and 2 of duty 1 are:

| *Performance Dimensions* | *Performance Standards* |
|---|---|
| (i) Reviews major programs that . . . | 1. Increase operating revenues by approximately 12% from manufacturing operations; use long-term, low-cost industrial revenue bonds for capital expenditure projects. |
| (ii) Reviews existing operations and . . . | 2. Reduce short-term bank debt to $15 million; reduce ownership in units that do not indicate a return on equity of at least 10%. Hold cost increases to less than 6% for the year. |

## Setting Performance Goals

Although performance goals can be set by the supervisor or a person other than the appraiser or appraisee, setting goals is another ideal procedure for involving the appraisee in the appraisal system. A discussion of employee involvement in the development of the appraisal process should consider the totality and not merely an isolated view of each individual's participation opportunity. Figure 4-2 identifies opportunities provided for employee involvement in the responsibility–goal appraisal process.

The process developed here permits/requires employee intervention at key stages. Each succeeding employee input builds upon preceding inputs. Beyond the philosophy that nobody knows a job better than the incumbent and that the incumbent's inputs are essential for developing a complete and accurate description of job activities is the concept that it is in the "doing" that learning increases. The more opportunities that are available for employee involvement, the better the employees understand the importance of performance appraisal, how they influence it, and the impact that it has on their work lives.

In reference once again to the job of the executive, it is possible to set one or more performance goals relative to each of the performance dimensions. Possible goals for performance dimension 1(a)(i), "Reviews major programs that support mainstream of business operation and authorizes capital fund expenditures for these projects," could be

- Within program year, expand operations that provide acceptable margins of profit and have the greatest potential for increased shares of the market.
- Avoid major financing this year; raise needed capital by selling certain assets.

Normally, the associated responsibility–duty–performance dimension process determines the weight or value of the goal, and follows the same procedure as that used for determining the weight for each stage in the process. When more than one performance goal is set for a specific performance dimension, the sum of the value of the goals must equal the weight assigned to the related performance dimension; when only one goal describes and personalizes a performance dimension, it has the same weight as the performance dimension. The process of varying the weight of a goal is identical to that described for varying the weight of a performance dimension. A word of caution: the total weight must equal 100 and if one dimension or goal is weighted upward relative to its corresponding duty, other dimensions or goals must be decreased in order to maintain the total weight of 100.

Because of specific requirements, it is possible that the relative weights assigned to the goals will differ from the relative weights

Employee identifies job activities and describes their importance.

Employee reviews responsibility and duty statements for accuracy, adequacy, and completeness.

Employee describes critical incidents that relate to various types of job behaviors.

Employee assists in establishing performance dimensions and setting performance goals.

Employee lists performance goals.

Employee and supervisor review goals and establish goals to be attained and their priority.

Employee and supervisor identify attainment steps required to attain goals.

Employee describes results or accomplishments related to identified goals or targets.

Employee and supervisor review job-related performance and appraise goal achievement.

Employee and supervisor approve performance rating set by supervisor.

Employee and supervisor set goal(s) and attainment steps for next appraisal period.

Employee appeals to higher levels unacceptable performance ratings or even job requirements or performance goals.

FIGURE 4–2    EMPLOYEE INVOLVEMENT OPPORTUNITIES IN THE DEVELOPMENT OF THE RESPONSIBILITY GOAL APPRAISAL PROCESS

74

assigned to their respective responsibilities or duties. In this case, the procedure described for weighting responsibilities is used for weighting goals. The major issue that must be faced when the weights of goals differ from their responsibilities is the difficulty in relating a specific score that one incumbent receives for goal achievement to a score that another incumbent receives for performing a similar or identical job. A major problem in any kind of goal-setting performance appraisal program is the establishment of equivalencies among the goal achievement of different employees.

## Analyzing Performance

Following the setting of goals or targets comes the "moment of truth." The employee lists his or her actual results or accomplishments relative to each individual goal. An example of results relative to the goals set by the executive are:

1   Approved funding for the expansion of two polyethylene plants. (Improved technology will reduce production costs and substantially increase profits in a market in which we currently have a large share.)

2   Sold European automotive parts division, generating $250 million in revenue and eliminating $47 million in required capital expenditures.

Following this process comes the identification of conditions that helped or hindered the achievement of the identified results. Circumstance information is not always required, but it assists the appraiser to understand and recognize the conditions or situations that favored or blocked the achievement of goals. Information here may temper, either up or down, the final grading of a specific result.

## Rating Performance

The time of reckoning arrives when the appraiser rates the employee's performance. This process may have a 4-, 5-, 6-, or 7-interval scale. The actual number of intervals on the scale is a matter of personal choice. Those favoring an even number of intervals feel that this type of scale requires the appraiser to move away from a central tendency (average) score and to rate an individual as being above or below average. An odd number of intervals permits the identification of an average value.

A typical five-interval scale may take this form:

1 Inadequate. Performance far below standard or below the level achieved by other employees doing the same work; fails to meet minimum requirements.

2 Below standard. Performance below what can be reasonably expected of an employee normally working in this area; improvement necessary to meet desired level of performance.

3 Standard. Solid performance; that typically expected of a competent employee.

4 Above standard. Exceeds normal performance; above that expected of a fully competent person.

5 Outstanding. Conspicuous performance; rare or uncommon to witness such results.

A six-interval scale could take the same form as the five-interval scale except that the standard interval would be replaced by two intervals, interval four (above standard) would become five, and interval five (outstanding) would become six. the new intervals three and four would be:

3 Adequate. Performance almost meets that typically expected of a competent employee; usually, but not consistently, satisfactory; some improvement desirable.

4 Competent. Performance consistently satisfactory; meets expected standards and, at times, exceeds stated performance requirements.

If a five-interval scale is used for rating performance and a procedure as previously described is used for the weighting of performance dimensions, the maximum score that any employee could receive is 500 (points) and the minimum score is 100 (points). This approach assumes that the total score (weight) assigned to all performance dimensions is 100 and that 5 is the highest attainable performance score ($100 \times 5 = 500$).

Figure 4-3 collects and summarizes all of the appraisal-related information generated on the example job of the executive. In this case, the weighting and scoring process included (1) the weighting of responsibilities (the particular responsibility received a weight of 38.5), (2) the weighting of duties (the duty received a weight of 10.8), (3) the weighting of two performance dimensions (4.6 and 6.2), (4) the identification of performance goals (each goal personalizes a specific performance dimension and receives the weight assigned to

| Responsibilities | Weight | Duties | Weight | Performance Dimensions | Weight | Performance Standards | Performance Goals | Weight | Results | Circumstances | Performance Rating | Performance Score |
|---|---|---|---|---|---|---|---|---|---|---|---|---|
| Commits unit to new courses of action. | 38.5 | (a) Allocates resources to individuals and projects that will have the greatest impact on the achievement of organizational goals. | 10.8 | 1(a)(i)Reviews major programs that support mainstream of business operations and authorizes capital fund expenditures for these projects. | 4.6 | Increase operating revenues by approximately 12% from manufacturing operations; use long-term, low-cost industrial revenue bonds for capital expenditure projects. | Within program year, expand operations that provide acceptable margins of profit and have the greatest potential for increased shares of the market. | 4.6 | Approved funding for the expansion of two polyethylene plants (improved technology will reduce production costs and substantially increase profits in a market in which we currently have a large share. | Currently, surplus of polyethylene in world markets but future uses and changes in marketing opportunities indicate favorable future for our capacity. | 3 | 4.6×3=13.8 |
| | | | | 1(a)(ii) Reviews existing operations and capital requirements, identifying expenditures for continuing growth of the business while improving long-term debt obligations. | 6.2 | Reduce short-term bank debt to $15 million; reduce ownership in units that do not indicate a return on equity of at least 10%; hold cost increases to less than 6% for the year. | Avoid major financing this year; raise needed capital through the selling of certain assets. | 6.2 | Sold European automotive parts division, generating $250 million in revenues and eliminating $47 million in required capital expenditures. | Increasing rise in European labor costs cast a shadow over the value of this investment but negotiation with "XYZ" Manufacturing identified positive benefits for both buyer and seller. | 4 | 6.2×4=24.8 |

Rating Scale
1 – Inadequate
2 – Below Standard
3 – Standard
4 – Above Standard
5 – Outstanding

FIGURE 4-3    PERFORMANCE APPRAISAL WORK SHEET

the respective dimension—4.6 and 6.2), (5) the rating of goal achievement performance (goal 1 was rated at a 3, and goal 2 was rated at a 4), and (6) the determination of a performance score (multiplying goal weight times performance ratings for a total of 38.6).

Although the information developed for this example came entirely from research-based information (responsibilities and duties) generated by Henry Mintzberg and some imaginary information (performance dimensions, standards, performance goals, results, and circumstances) that I generated, this example models reality closely enough to present some additional thoughts and areas requiring further consideration.

One of the reasons for using an example that relates to the job of an extremely high-level executive is to present in the early stages of this book the concept that the performance of all jobs can be appraised within a formal structure. Of course, the higher the job is in the organizational hiearchy and the broader the job requirements are, the more complex they are and the more difficult they are to describe. Another important issue with higher-level jobs is the increasing length of time required to identify successful performance. This, however, does not negate the requirement to provide rewards on a current basis to all employees, from a newly hired assistant maintenance worker to the Chief Executive Officer. In every job, there is some degree of latency regarding the ability to identify quality performance. The major issue regarding latency is that it becomes increasingly more pronounced and important as one climbs the organizational ladder. This does not excuse the appraiser (in the example of the job of the executive, the appraiser may be the Chairman of the Board or a select group from the Board of Directors) from making decisions regarding the quality of current performance and opening opportunities for either rewarding or penalizing the individual relative to actual performance.

## Variations in Responsibilities—Goals—Results Approaches

There are probably unlimited variations to the appraisal process presented in this chapter, but the basic elements—identification and description of responsibilities and duties, determination of performance dimensions and standards, setting of performance goals, and measurement of goal performance—should be included in the process. The variations arise in weighting responsibilities and duties, identifying performance dimensions, establishing performance standards, setting performance goals, selecting a rating scale to be used, and actually rating performance.

## Changes in Responsibilities and Duties

Although the responsibilities are probably the most static component of the appraisal process, it is quite likely that, over an extended period of time, responsibilities will change in importance. Changes in both external and internal forces not only vary the relative importance of responsibilities, but new ones may appear while others may disappear. Changes in responsibilities may be a flag item or an indicator that the job itself has changed to such a degree that its worth should be reevaluated and that specifications for recruiting, hiring, and selecting candidates for the job should be modified. Changes in job training and employee development programs may also be indicated.

Prior to changes in responsibilities, duties will probably go through some type of transition, and the overall configuration of duty assignments relative to a specific responsibility may herald job changes that require further recognition. Changes in responsibilities and duties may require that they be reweighted.

There may also be a need to permit flexibility in the weighting of responsibilities and duties among jobs that have identical or similar evaluations. It is conceivable that the importance of responsibilities and duties will vary among jobs because of changing job demands even though the responsibilities and duties themselves remain unaltered. Incorporating this needed and desirable type of flexibility allows for a manipulation of the appraisal process. One potential opportunity for manipulation is for the individual(s) who have the right to vary the weight of responsibilities and duties to change them to favor or disfavor a certain jobholder rather than because of changes in job demands. (Again, the ugly head of unfairly biased subjectivity arises—a possibility in any system. As already mentioned, these issues are identified, throughout the book and some opportunities for minimizing their influence are listed. It is important to recognize, however, that bias and antibias opportunities are as numerous as the outputs from the human brain.)

The manner in which changes in weights of responsibilities and duties affect incumbents occurs in the following manner. A supervisor or person having the responsibility for changing job responsibility and duty weights to meet changing workplace demands favors an individual that he or she would like to see appraised in a most favorable manner. Recognizing both individual strengths and weaknesses and job requirements, the supervisor weights more highly those responsibilities and duties that would provide an unfair advantage to a specific jobholder. This same process can also be reversed, placing a jobholder in an unfavorable light.

This issue will surface at every step at which the opportunity for flexibility permits staff or managerial personnel to change weights unilaterally. This situation may occur anytime managers have flexibility for interpreting and administering policy regulations, etc. There is no total answer to this most difficult and inherently dangerous condition, but the control matrix offers aid for identifying behaviors that have the potential for destroying any appraisal system. This is but one approach available for monitoring managerial behavior. It is designed to minimize unacceptable interpretations and administration.

*The Control Matrix.*    Again and again, I have identified the need for and the dangers inherent within individual subjective considerations throughout the entire appraisal process. A major approach already discussed for minimizing unfair or illogical subjective considerations is to use inputs from many individuals who are well versed on the subject under review. By permitting many knowledgeable people to rank or set a value on specific job responsibilities and duties, it becomes possible to assign objective weights to them. Through the use of various mathematical procedures, subjective measures can be translated into objective weights. In many cases, it is not possible to obtain immediately the opinions of various experts on a particular topic (e.g., they may not be familiar with situational requirements, time demands, and unique qualities of the job itself), and the best, possibly only course available is an after-the-fact approach.

The use of a control matrix is basically after-the-fact. When it is employed, those who may wish to practice conscious manipulation of the appraisal process may have second thoughts and even those who may be performing injustices unconsciously will minimize these actions by directing more effort and greater care into each part of the appraisal program. Appraisers exercise more care when they realize that their appraisal behaviors are being identified and recognized and that they will be held accountable for and must substantiate and justify deviations from a norm.

In the specific case of responsibility and duty weighting, responsibility and duty control matrixes are developed for each job. Figure 4-4 is an example of a Job Responsibility Control Matrix. The matrix consists of a list of each individual weight assignment. The matrix permits visual and rapid analysis of assigned weights and easy identification of weights that vary from the accepted or standard value. A weight different from the norm does not mean that something is wrong; it just indicates that further investigation may be required. This type of analysis is extremely compatible with computerized data processing. Software packages are readily available for collecting, storing, and displaying such data. This type of analysis can also

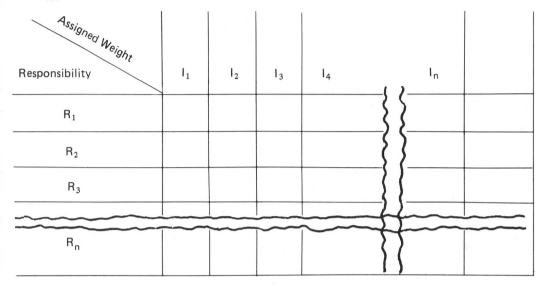

1.  This simple matrix may be used to display a wide variety of appraisal-related information
2.  Actual listing and complete identification and description of responsibilities may be found on the job description
3.  Listing of individuals responsible for weighting may be found in a separate printout

FIGURE  4-4     JOB RESPONSIBILITY CONTROL MATRIX

identify deviations—for example, individuals whose scores deviate more often than what may be considered an acceptable frequency.

This monitoring and control device does not relate well to the opposite case in which changes in weights should have been made but never were incorporated into the appraisal process. Possibly the best answer to this problem is incumbent involvement through each step. By implementing various programs that increase employee understanding of how the process works and by expanding their awareness of how they may influence it, there is a greater likelihood that they will accept the responsibility for identifying necessary changes.

## Changes in Performance Dimensions and Standards

Dimensions and standards normally relate directly to responsibilities and duties; thus, changes in responsibilities and duties directly influence performance dimensions and standards. Once dimensions and standards are set, possibly the best control device is the use of the "exception principle." Supervisors must report any changes that they make in performance dimensions and performance standards. Their changes or requests for changes should include substantiating reasons that justify the changes to be made.

### Setting Performance Goals and Measuring Performance

The greatest opportunity for individual manipulation of the system lies in this step of the appraisal process. Here, both the appraiser and appraisee can vary goals and, thus, through the measurement of achievement, allow an individual to appear from appraisal scores to have performed far better or far worse than deserved. Jobholders can set or influence the setting of goals so that they require a minimal amount of the appraisee's abilities and efforts, are easily achievable, and ensure a relatively high performance rating. From an opposite approach, appraisers/supervisors can set relatively high or unrealistic goals for their subordinates, place them in an untenable situation, and practically ensure that they receive a low performance rating.

Possibly the best solution to this problem is extremely close review of goals and goal achievement by the supervisors of the appraisers or by those having review responsibilities—on additional components of the monitoring process. A goal achievement score matrix is also useful here. A control matrix of this type monitors the goal achievement score given to each employee by each supervisor. This matrix is valuable in identifying supervisors who tend to be overly lenient or excessively strict in their ratings. It also identifies central tendency, horn, and halo effects (these appraiser distortions are discussed in detail in Chapter 6).

A basic weakness of the appraisal process discussed in this chapter appears when analyzing the results of performance appraisal of large numbers of individuals who (1) serve in various locations, (2) have different supervisors, (3) perform different jobs, and (4) have the same jobs but with responsibilities and duties that vary in importance. These variables may cause such differences in the performance score that an individual with a score significantly lower than another individual may have actually outperformed the employee receiving the higher score. The organization, however, provides reward–compensation opportunities (e.g., desirable transfer, promotions, in-grade pay increases, and merit bonuses) relative to performance scores.

The approach presented here may be all that is necessary for appraising performance in a small or centralized organization or in one where the managers who appraise and measure performance do so consistently and uniformly. When these conditions do not apply, it may be necessary to supplement this approach with other appraisal techniques, procedures, and methods. Other chapters in this book discuss additional techniques, procedures, and methods that reinforce the appraisal process developed in this chapter or cover in greater detail certain critical elements of the process.

5

Goal Setting

A major area of concern expressed throughout this book relates to employee understanding and acceptance. Many of the identified and described appraisal methods and procedures focus on employee involvement and participation with the major intent of expanding employee awareness, understanding, and acceptance.

A few years ago, a number of managers were meeting with and asking questions of one of the individuals responsible for the design and administration of a very successful productivity improvement program. A portion of the discussion that related to reasons for the success of the project took this form:

**Q:** What would you identify as possibly the most important reason for your success?

**A:** The establishment of a TRUSTING environment.

**Q:** How did you establish such an environment?

**A:** Quite simply—over the years, we just did not screw our employees.

Establishing a trusting environment is and will continue to be a paramount issue facing every organization interested in and wishing to improve productivity. What can an organization do to establish such a workplace atmosphere? There are almost limitless variations about where to start and what to do. In this connection, very real opportunities are available to every organization in the identification of work requirements, the establishment of performance standards, the analysis and appraisal of job-related behaviors, and the recognition of such behaviors by offering or withholding certain employer-provided rewards. These opportunities identify the major components of a performance appraisal system.

All of the emotional issues that are constantly surfacing to block implementation of a successful performance appraisal program pose a question that must be answered. Is it possible to appraise performance and, at the same time, to develop and maintain a trusting environment? Although this question has already been answered in a different context, the answer is yes. In my opinion, job security—a paramount issue with practically all employees and the keystone of a trusting environment—is impossible if employees do not know what is expected of them, how they are doing, and the relationship between employer-provided reward opportunities and employee-demonstrated workplace behavior. This is the guts of performance appraisal.

The critical issues here are employee awareness, employee understanding, and employee acceptance. One of the best, possibly the only approach available to management for achieving employee awareness, understanding, and acceptance of goals is to involve employees as much as possible in the planning, operation, and control of workplace activities.

Although much of the learning process is still a mystery to specialists researching this area, there is widespread agreement, and centuries of empirical knowledge, that one learns by doing. Learning job requirements extends beyond manipulating a keyboard, placing items in certain files, operating a piece of equipment, and so on. Successful performance in many jobs in modern organizations requires that employees understand how the inputs they receive are developed, what happens to their outputs, the reason for the existence of their jobs, and the location of their efforts in the overall scheme of organizational objectives.

The more opportunities that are available for workplace planning and control, the greater is the likelihood that the employee will understand what is to be done, how it is to be done, and the kind and amount of rewards to be expected. There is little argument that each individual has different demands about the opportunities available for influencing his or her job. Quite likely, a few people only want their employers to tell them what is expected of them, what they will receive in return, and then to be let alone. Others want to have their job requirements identified to the most minute detail and then they want to perform with the least possible amount of change. In between are the great majority of employees; for this group, management must determine the appropriate methods for involving employees in programs and procedures that directly influence their on-the-job behavior.

## Participation in Goal Setting

Over the past thirty years, researchers and practitioners involved in productivity improvement programs have spent much time and effort in generating evidence to support the hypothesis that the more opportunities are made available to employees in the identification and determination of goals and in the review and appraisal of goal attainment, the greater is the likelihood that employee workplace behavior will be goal directed. Research into goal-setting activities has also focused on issues such as whether or not goal-directed workplace behavior (1) leads to the attainment of organizational objectives, (2) enables the organization to be more productive, and (3) assists employees receive more satisfaction from the work they do.

Although there is much evidence available to support the hypothesis that goal setting can improve organizational productivity, the data also support the thesis that ambiguity must be minimized concerning what is desired, what was done, and the consequences of specific behavior. Goal-setting programs are of little value for improving organizational productivity if they (1) require or permit supervisors to set the goals of their subordinates unilaterally, (2) relate goals solely to job activities, (3) permit little to no interaction by the individuals responsible for achieving the goals, (4) function with irregular, too few, or too many appraisal reviews, (5) relate principally to a short-run perspective, or (6) pay minimal attention to the means used for achieving goals. In fact, goal-setting programs that operate in this manner probably do more harm than good. If management implements a program with these features yet extols its interest in and desire for programs that stress the importance of its human resources, employees will only look upon management's actions and words as a charade. Further, they will feel that management does not support their words with suitable actions and, above all (or least of all), they cannot be *trusted*.

Except for those employees covered by collective bargaining agreements and minority groups protected by federal and state legislation, employee job security rests firmly in the hands of management. Like it or not, most employees must place their future in the hands of their managers. (In reality, employers place the security of their businesses in the hands of the employees, but this is not a perception commonly held by many employees.) Granting employees an opportunity to make decisions that may influence the way in which they perform work activities is one way for employers to state that they trust the judgment of their employees.

Participation in goal setting must permit employees to influence outcomes that will affect and, in turn, favor them. To achieve such results, employers must fully understand job content and job requirements. They must also recognize jobholder perceptions of what the job is and what is acceptable or desired performance. Developing congruence between job requirements as identified by management and as perceived by incumbents is a critical component of participative goal setting.

Participation in goal setting begins with the employee and supervisor agreeing on the purpose of the job and the job requirements. Once there is this type of mutual understanding and agreement, the supervisor and subordinate can independently prepare goals, confer, and reach agreement on the importance of goals and the attention and effort necessary to attain them.

Goals must integrate organizational requirements with individual demands. Employees should receive information (feedback) frequently enough to assess progress made toward goal attainment. When situations arise that require modification of goals, both the employee and supervisor should have adequate opportunity to review changing conditions and the impact of these conditions on the goal(s).

A healthy, participative goal-setting relationship is one in which the supervisor provides coaching support and the employee accepts and uses such assistance to solve problems and to overcome barriers to goal attainment. Recognition of both the short- and long-run influences of goal attainment leads to the identification of and concern for the means used to achieve goals.

Finally, participative goal setting includes regularly scheduled reviews of goal-directed behavior. The actual intervals between goal setting and formal goal reviews vary somewhat according to the type of job, level of job, and the employee's time of service on the job. In any case, it is quite unlikely that only an annual goal-performance review is adequate. Goals may be set for periods up to one year in length. However, if performance reviews are not held on a two- or three-month basis, the impact of the goal on the behavior of both the employee and supervisor decreases significantly. The bimonthly or quarterly review may be a relatively brief session for the person who knows the job and has a minimal amount of environmental forces influencing goal attainment, but it is crucial to the employee who is working in new areas or on new goals.

## Goal Difficulty

Researchers and practitioners writing about participation in goal setting frequently discuss issues related to the setting of both difficult and easily attainable goals. They note examples of employees setting goals that are, for all practical purposes, impossible to achieve. This condition will almost certainly lead to goal achievement failure, which destroys desire and promotes an unwillingness in the involved employee to continue active participation in the process.

The opposite condition of employees setting goals that are relatively easy to accomplish and provide little or no challenge can exist just as easily. The result is that the organization receives minimal benefit from the employee's goal achievement effort. In reality, the employee plays the "how much can I get away with, how little can I do" game with management.

The issue here is that *difficulty* is individually oriented. For another individual (supervisor/appraiser) to determine the degree of ease or difficulty of a specific goal requires black box (human brain) inspection. This is workplace witchcraft. The idea developed in this section is to keep appraisers outside the black box and to focus appraisal attention on demonstrated behavior.

Instead of concentrating concern on goal *difficulty*, attention should focus on the following issues:

1   Goals should cover the complete range of job requirements with sufficient intensity placed on each goal to cover adequately the corresponding responsibility–duty–performance dimension sequence.

2   Goal attainment should be a challenge, not a mission impossible, for each individual. The extra effort required "stretches" the employee, facilitates growth and development, and provides the challenge that so many people expect and demand from their jobs.

Minimizing the importance of goal difficulty also tends to lessen jobholder emphasis on difficulty and the importance of a specific goal. The responsibilities, duties, and performance dimensions have already laid the groundwork for identifying the importance of specific work efforts. A major reason for the entire process is to minimize the need for the employee/appraisee to be unrealistic concerning work effort in order to provide job security (to ensure complete and successful accomplishment of all assignments).

## Attainment Steps

A valuable addition to participative goal setting is the identification of attainment steps. This feature goes beyond the model developed in Figure 4-1 and provides yet another opportunity for linking appraiser and appraisee in a job-related, performance–oriented atmosphere. The major purpose of the attainment step feature is to reduce another part of the appraisal process to bite-size pieces (making it easier to eat the elephant).

Attainment steps are specific activities that the employee (and, at times, the supervisor) will perform in order to achieve a certain goal. Over the years, a review of unsuccessful and unsatisfactory goal-setting programs attributed failures to issues such as (1) too many goals, (2) lack of specificity and structure, (3) failure of management to provide sufficient support, and (4) extended intervals of time between goal setting and goal reviews.

Inherent within participative goal setting is the concept that the subordinate owns the goals. In order for the subordinate to recognize and accept ownership, he or she must make meaningful inputs into the process and know the relationship between actions taken and results achieved. The employee should also recognize both the short-term and long-term impact of any action and the benefits or costs of the action over an extended period of time.

When a goal-setting program is initially implemented, it may be impractical for certain jobholders to set meaningful goals, and managers in various settings may find it useful to work the subordinate into the process gradually. The "text" approach states that the appraiser and appraisee should independently prepare a set of goals and then discuss their lists and agree to an ordering of the goals. There may be times, due to individual characteristics of the appraiser and appraisee, job demands, and situational requirements, when the results of the goal-setting session are significantly or even 100 percent influenced by the thoughts of the supervisor. There may be nothing wrong with this approach.

This process, however, must not grant the subordinate the opportunity to abdicate goal-ownership rights. Through the use of attainment steps, the subordinate can be brought into the goal-setting process in a very meaningful way. The counterpart of the identification and description of attainment steps in the entire performance appraisal process occurs when jobholders identify and describe the activities that they perform in doing their jobs. The counterpart of the review of attainment steps occurs when employees review and approve the list and ordering of responsibilities and duties.

Similar to the concept that the employee doing the job is the individual who can best identify what is done is the belief that the individual responsible for attaining a goal is the person who can best describe what he or she will do in order to achieve it. Job activity descriptions stress the impersonal nature of the job. A list of job activities identifies what any jobholder must (or should) do in order to perform the job and to meet certain preset standards or desired results. Goal attainment steps, on the other hand, are highly personal in nature, permitting, if not requiring, the appraisee to analyze each goal in a problem-solving mode and to recognize personal benefits, costs, strengths, weaknesses, and desires. From this personal analysis, the appraisee can recognize real-world opportunities and goal attainment barriers and integrate these issues with personal assessment in as innovative a manner as possible to achieve the goals.

The identification and description of goal attainment steps permits the accomplishment of a number of basic parts of participative goal setting. For example, in Figure 4-3 for the goal, "Avoid major financing this year; raise needed capital through the selling of certain assets," the attainment steps for this high-level executive may take this form.

1  Review with responsible division heads the use and value of all capital expenditures over $10 million dollars by February 1.

2  Arrange meetings with the President of XYZ Manufacturing and the Secretary of Industry in the federal government to arrange the sale of ownership of European automotive parts division before March 1.

3  Discuss sale of European automotive parts division with President of European National Bank in order to gain their approval of prospective sale and involvement in the financing of the sale.

4  Meet with environmental agency administrator and discuss relaxation or extension of time period for implementing new pollution control requirements.

These attainment steps relate to the work of a top executive and may appear to be fairly nebulous and not specific enough because of the nature of the job. In reviewing a lower level job, however, it is possible to provide more specific and precise examples of attainment steps. A review of attainment steps identified by a sales representative for the automotive parts division may take this form:

*Goal*

Achieve an average of four calls per sales day in which average daily sales exceed $2,000 for the next three months.

*Attainment Steps*

1  Awake each sales day by 6:00 a.m. instead of 7:00 a.m. so that I am in the office of my first customer by 8:00 a.m.

2  Spend the time necessary each weekend to plan all calls for the coming week. Make an extra effort to identify the best time to call on each account in order to improve my chances of seeing the person who can make a purchase decision. Plan my itinerary to minimize the time spent traveling so that I can

spend the greatest amount of time possible in the offices of my customers.

3   Review past sales and recent payment and credit histories of customers before making a sales call.

4   Each night, reevaluate calls scheduled for the next day, adding or changing calls and routes on the basis of progress made that day.

These attainment steps permit the appraisee and appraiser to discuss and monitor goal achievement in very concrete terms. In many cases, even when a goal is quantified, the goal remains difficult to conceptualize and to put into operational terms. To begin with, attainment steps permit the appraisee and appraiser to discuss what they think is necessary in order to achieve the goal. This discussion may uncover perceptual differences on the part of both individuals as to what the goal is. It sets up a nonthreatening environment in which the subordinate can say, "What do you think I should do?" and "What support can I expect from you and the organization relative to this matter?" The supervisor can state, "What would you like me to do?" and "I really think that you are biting off more than you can chew with that step." In discussing the steps, they set priorities and develop strategies that will assist in implementing or performing a certain action. The discussions permit the employee to state why he or she thinks that the action is appropriate. In return, the supervisor can provide information gleaned from personal observations and experiences that may be helpful to the subordinate.

When the time comes to review goal achievement, attention focuses primarily on the attainment steps and not on the goal itself. With the review of each step, there is a stream of conversation—talking and listening. Whether the goal is being achieved or not, both the appraiser and appraisee want to know why. If they can identify steps that are blocking success or are making it possible, they both will have a better idea of which behaviors to repeat, which to change, and which to eliminate. The review process may also identify missing steps that should be incorporated into the list of desired actions.

## Attainment Step Checklist

1   Is the current situation properly and accurately described?
2   Have desired goals been properly and accurately described?
3   Have major goal-blocking factors been identified?

4   Have major goal attainment factors been identified?

5   Over which blocking and achievement factors does the employee exert control?

6   What must the employee do to achieve a desired goal?

All too often, supervisor and subordinate buy off on goals verbally, but their goal-oriented behaviors indicate that it was strictly a verbal commitment and not one involving the expenditure of intellectual and physical energy.

Setting and reviewing attainment steps provides the vehicle for involved appraiser–appraisee interaction. Here lies an excellent opportunity for implementing a bottom-up approach to the management of human resources. As the subordinate identifies and defines the steps required to achieve a goal and then reviews goal attainment success relative to a specific goal, he or she recognizes ownership of the steps. Thus, the development of a logical and workable procedure for attaining a goal permits the employee to buy the goal.

## Goal Attainment Plan of Action

1   Identify personal actions and their sequence of occurrence.

2   Assign responsibilities for these personal actions.

3   State the time of occurrence for each action and the resources required to perform it.

4   Establish "costs" for each action.

5   Determine whether supervisor and subordinate can accept these costs.

If the attainment steps are not viewed as manipulative devices designed by management to trap or coerce the employee into behaving in a certain manner, the likelihood of goal ownership by the employee increases significantly. A purpose of the attainment step–goal achievement process is to stimulate initiative and innovativeness. Self-direction and self-control are the keys to a successful goal attainment program, but they are only possible when the employee has access to relevant and current performance-related information and recognizes how to use this information for improving performance. Through the use of attainment steps, performance-related information becomes a central part of the process. In this manner, the chance that a goal will become an unattainable burden becomes smaller. There is a constant search for new and better ways to achieve a goal. Reviewing success relative to the attainment step may also lead to the setting of new goals or the modification of those already set.

The establishment of attainment steps as part of a goal-setting program came about when managers found that goals set and reviewed on an annual basis seldom led to an improved, motivating work environment. They found it difficult for managers and their subordinates to relate over a period of twelve months to a specific goal or set of goals, no matter how well goals were described. The stress and strain that occur constantly at the workplace tend to destroy the effectiveness of goals in directing workplace behavior. The implementation of attainment steps with reviews every two to three months places life into rather static, goal-setting programs. Behavior that follows paths identified by the attainment steps and that leads to goal achievement enhances progress visibility and reinforces goal-directed behavior.

Organizations and their managers have found that the attainment step process removes a considerable amount of the US–THEM atmosphere from the appraisal of performance. This helps to alleviate a previously alluded to and very real problem—the dread supervisors and subordinates feel at the very thought of another appraisal session. Both parties see only negatives such as confrontation, hostility, and back stabbing. Developing a program in which the supervisor and subordinate can sit down together and talk in a meaningful and acceptable manner is one of the finest types of support that organizations can provide for all their employees. (Remember, in all cases, appraisers also become appraisees, supervisors become subordinates.)

In many cases, a barrier to improved employee performance is not "getting a supervisor off my back"—overly close supervision—but almost the opposite—persuading supervisors to talk to their subordinates, which gives the supervisor a chance to know what the subordinate is actually doing and how well he or she is performing. A large number of employees would like the chance to ask these types of questions of their "boss" (but in a nonthreatening atmosphere):

"What is happening?"
"What can I do about this problem that I am having?"
"What do you think my chances are of doing . . . ?"

Most employees feel that the best contact they have with their organization is through their immediate supervisor (who is also normally their appraiser). With the possible exception of information regarding corporate financial conditions and new opportunities through research, acquisitions, or product changes, it is the immediate supervisor who can best provide "little" and "big" pictures of conditions that affect each employee. The attainment step process is a part of the formal management program that has the capability of developing a very positive, trusting, security-oriented atmosphere. It accomplishes this by providing channels of communication where employees can receive information and make inputs that can positively influence their on-the-job and off-the-job lifestyles.

The major weakness of the attainment step process is the time that it requires of all employees. The stumbling block that supervisors will present is that they just do not have time to do all this talking with employees. This is a very real and valid concern. The first answer to removing this barrier is to think about what happens if you do not do it. How much time do you spend correcting problems that would never have occurred if employees had done the job right in the first place? How much time do you spend training and directing new or replacement employees because a capable employee quit or is laying off for the day? How much more would you get from each employee if they really knew what you wanted, understood your motives, trusted and respected you, and truly wanted to do their best for you?

Is it not possible that if you had a "turned-on" work group you would not be spending your time putting out fires? Is it not also possible that if you established a program in your work unit where there is free and open communication that is both job-requirement and employee-performance oriented you could have a "turned-on" group of employees? Furthermore, is it not possible that a steady flow of honest and accurate job-related information would minimize the need to present job-related bad news?

No employee appreciates or wants unacceptable surprises, and most people have a distaste for carrying "bad" news. Unacceptable appraisal of performance is hardly ever enjoyable, but a steady identification of unacceptable behavior at least removes the mystery and sets the scene for the final showdown. Employees are not concerned about receiving an unacceptable appraisal rating when it is deserved but about receiving one that they feel is undeserved or comes with no prior warning.

Most employees worth their salt know when their performance is below par. They may not like the idea that their unacceptable performance is being recognized, but these employees also do not respect supervisors who fail to recognize such levels of performance and consider them unworthy of holding supervisory positions.

The use of attainment steps may be one of the best training

opportunities available to supervisors for enhancing employee development and growth. Employees have a first-hand view of the relationship between their job-related behavior and the results that they achieve, whether good or bad. By being able to monitor what they do relative to what they have set out to accomplish, they can make changes accordingly. This is learning at its finest.

Attainment step-oriented appraisals of performance may require a reanalysis of how supervisors spend their time. Reallocating work time for activities involved in the appraisal of employee performance may just be the best way for supervisors to perform their jobs. In reality, the issue is not "I do not have the time to appraise subordinate performance" but rather "I must find the time and make the opportunities to appraise employee performance."

The entire appraisal process presented in this chapter and in Chapters 2 and 3 relates to individual differences and variations caused by situational requirements. The process, however, is independent of the level of job in the organization, the type of job, and the variation in job design. Often variables such as job level, occupational differences, type of work, or organizational demands require variations or changes in the performance appraisal process. When these occur, a wide variety of additional procedures and appraisal methods are available for supplementing or even substituting for the responsibility–goal appraisal process developed in these chapters.

## Group Goal Setting

Much recent work toward improving organizational performance has focused on the work group. Such emphasis minimizes the importance of individual appraisal. Goal setting is as effective for appraising group performance as it is for appraising individual performance. The major problem is that the appraiser requires even greater teacher–leader–counselor skills than when he or she practices individual goal setting. The same basic procedure used for establishing and weighting individual goals applies to group goals.

## Management by Objectives

Over the past twenty-five years, a concept that identifies an approach to managing organizations has been developed under the title of management by objectives (MBO). MBO may be considered a generic title that includes a wide variety of programs developed by various individuals and organizations and operating under different functional titles. These programs have as a common central theme the concept that identified and understood objectives lead to improved performance in organizations. Underlying MBO is the view that establishing a motivating workplace environment in which human resource inputs are successfully integrated with the capital and material resource inputs requires linking individual, work unit, and organizational goals.

MBO is a system for managing organizations that ties together long-range strategic plans with short-range operating plans. It embraces all functions of management from planning, to doing, to controlling organizational activities. MBO includes organizational responsibilities for identifying and defining workable and measurable goals and for providing employees with opportunities for participating in determining the direction, amount, and timing of their work efforts in achieving both organization and individual goals.

A description of the MBO process by Anthony P. Raia, one of the pioneers and leaders in the development of MBO, takes the form shown in Figure 5-1. The major difference between this model and the one initially developed by Raia is the use of the words objectives and goals. In line with the materials and procedures presented in this book, objectives are defined as being long-range in nature and often difficult to quantify whereas goals are short-range in nature and easier to measure. In this sense, goals are subobjectives. (Raia's definitions are just the opposite. Goals and objectives may also be used synonymously—it is a matter of personal choice. The only important issue is that those involved in objective- and goal-oriented programs know the full meanings of the words objectives and goals if they differ in any way.)

This approach starts with a clear, concise statement of the central purpose of the business by the Board of Directors. This statement provides the guidelines for the formulation of long-range objectives and the strategic plans to be used to accomplish them. From these long-range objectives, more specific short-range goals are identified and defined. This redefinition of objectives to goals and subgoals continues throughout the business hierarchy, where individual job requirements are restated in terms of responsibilities and duties.

Organizations must set goals that transcend employees and their work groups. Only in this way is it possible to minimize suboptimizing work patterns. (Suboptimizing refers to behavior leading to the achievement of goals that support or favor an individual or specific unit but that damage or block the achievement of organizational objectives and goals.) By identifying and redefining objectives into a hierarchy of goals that unites the whole work force, a business sets one of the first conditions that is necessary in order to produce an environment in which both management and employees recognize the value and necessity of their contributions. In its most democratic

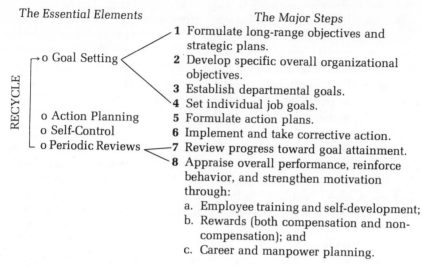

| The Essential Elements | The Major Steps |
|---|---|

RECYCLE

- o Goal Setting
- o Action Planning
- o Self-Control
- o Periodic Reviews

**1** Formulate long-range objectives and strategic plans.
**2** Develop specific overall organizational objectives.
**3** Establish departmental goals.
**4** Set individual job goals.
**5** Formulate action plans.
**6** Implement and take corrective action.
**7** Review progress toward goal attainment.
**8** Appraise overall performance, reinforce behavior, and strengthen motivation through:
  a. Employee training and self-development;
  b. Rewards (both compensation and non-compensation); and
  c. Career and manpower planning.

FIGURE 5-1    THE MBO PROCESS

form, the goal-setting process involves the subordinate in the identification of required performance behaviors. In this way, the process helps to reduce employee fears that are inherent in any system that measures individual behavior. Loyalty and allegiance to broadly based business objectives go a long way toward minimizing unsatisfactory behavior at work—behavior that can lead to suboptimizing work patterns.

It is evident that this process is far more than merely a method of appraising performance. It is a system that is available to managers for operating organizations that recognize and stress the importance of human resource inputs and that provide a procedure that promotes employee involvement and interaction at all levels. The setting of objectives and goals becomes an iterative process that starts with the formulation of very general desires and philosophy of owners and senior managers and repeats itself at every level in the organization. With the narrowing and increasing specialization of work requirements, job goals become more specific and more applicable to quantification.

By relating employee goals to job responsibilities, it is possible to minimize discrepancies between information available for performing work assignments and information required for adequate job performance. Improving understanding between the supervisor and subordinate about what constitutes adequate and acceptable job performance *must* have some bearing on the working climate of the organization.

MBO is a process that integrates self-control, which includes individual appraisal of one's own performance, with formalized organizational appraisal of performance. The process includes activities that identify what is expected of a worker and that permit employees to state what they plan to do in return. To enable employees to meet goals, supervisors state the support that they and the organization can provide, and employees identify what they feel they require from management (the organization) in order to achieve their performance goals.

Organizations have few members who do not wish to make their lives more meaningful through their work efforts. The activities that employees perform on their jobs and the environment in which they work affect both the on-the-job and off-the-job quality of their lives. A sense of wholeness between work life activities and nonwork life activities expands for many employees when the work that they do provides a feeling of competence, of self-worth.

For many workers, improving their understanding of the relationship between what they do and the goals and objectives of their work units and organization enhances a feeling of importance—adds a sense of significance to the work that they do. In addition, most people enjoy keeping score of changes in activities or things that they can observe or in which they have an interest. A very basic place for scorekeeping is with on-the-job inputs and outputs; scorekeeping identifies the "what I have done" inputs with the "what I am getting" outputs. In essence, this becomes the basis for establishing work equity measures.

MBO provides a mechanism for relating the input of workplace behavior to both short-run and long-run results. It focuses on the means for accomplishing a result as much as on the result itself. It is especially valuable for identifying possible suboptimizing behaviors. Suboptimization is a danger that exists in any activity involving human labor. It is a natural trait for people to compete to accomplish the most or to provide the best for themselves and their close associates (family, friends, team members). Although a competitive spirit is critical to successful operation, cooperation is also necessary. An essential area of cooperation is the unification and similarity in direction of all goal attainment behavior.

The basic ingredients of a workable and useful MBO system are the same as the requirements for a sound performance appraisal system. The system must be:

1   Logically sound;
2   Internally consistent; and
3   Empirically relevant.

The responsibility–goal appraisal process developed in this book could be a basic part of an MBO system. The underlying *logic* of the responsibility–goal appraisal process states that within the content of a job lie the factors for measuring the quality of an incumbent's on-the-job performance.

The procedure for determining performance dimensions and performance standards is *identical* and *consistent* for all jobs, yet the various procedures provide flexibility for changing job demands, whether these changes occur because of internal or external influencing forces. Through on-the-job observations and experiences (*empirical* activities), it is possible to identify and describe clearly and completely job activities and their meaning and value to the organization and to the involved employees.

# Documenting Workplace Behaviors

From the first chapters, this book has stressed the importance of focusing on observable, identifiable, and measurable workplace behaviors. Initially, the thrust related to the identification of job content requirements, and these efforts resulted in the development of job responsibilities and duties. To individualize these job requirements, the next step was the development of performance dimensions, goals, and goal attainment steps.

Until now, the principal vehicle discussed for collecting job-related information has been the job analysis questionnaire. Although it is effective, this technique has certain limitations. These limitations center on its inability to identify specific employee job behaviors and to provide sufficient information for what may be considered inappropriate, appropriate, and superior job behaviors.

This chapter describes procedures and techniques available for documenting actual workplace behaviors and behaviors that employees perceive to be either acceptable or unacceptable. The discussion includes not only the "how" but the "when," "what," and "why" of such documentation procedures.

Possibly the best place to start a discussion is to review the obvious and, at times, not so obvious reasons for documentation. Throughout this book, there has been concern over the issue of subjectivity when performance is appraised. From my point of view, subjectivity is an inherent part of the entire process. It is impossible to eliminate unfair or biased ratings because there is some kind and degree of favorable or unfavorable predisposition toward other people wired into every individual. It is possible, however, to minimize these biases, and one of the principal approaches available is for supervisors to document employee behaviors as they occur and to relate back to the documentation in the formal employee appraisal activities.

## Typical Rater Errors

Although they were briefly identified earlier in the book, here are definitions of some of the typical types of subjective errors that appraisers make that contaminate their appraisal of performance:

*Halo Effect.* Rating appraisee excellent in one quality, influencing the appraiser to give the appraisee a similar rating or to rate the appraisee higher on other qualities than actually deserved.

*Horn Effect.* Rating appraisee unsatisfactory in one quality, influencing the appraiser to give the appraisee a similar rating or to rate the appraisee lower in other qualities than actually deserved.

*Central Tendency.* Providing a rating of average or around the midpoint for all qualities. This is the most common and serious kind of error. Since most employees do perform around an average, it permits an easy escape from making a valid appraisal decision.

*Strict Rating.* Rating appraisee lower than the normal or average appraiser; being overly harsh in rating appraisee performance qualities.

*Lenient Rating.* Rating appraisee higher than the normal or average appraiser; being overly loose in rating appraisee performance qualities.

*Latest Behavior.* Rating appraisee by most recent behavior; failing to recognize most commonly demonstrated behaviors during the entire appraisal period.

*Initial Impression.* Rating appraisee on first impressions; failing to recognize most commonly demonstrated behaviors during the entire appraisal period.

*Spillover Effect.* Allowing past performance appraisal rating to unjustly influence current ratings. Past performance ratings, good or bad, result in similar rating for current period although demonstrated behavior does not deserve the rating, good or bad.

Two approaches available for overcoming rating errors are (1) to require appraisers giving poor ratings to outline procedures for improving appraisee performance and/or initiate termination proceedings, and (2) to require appraisers giving high ratings to verify such ratings and to make recommendations for promotion. The adverse impact of these two courses of action is that it pressures appraisers into giving satisfactory–average ratings.

There is probably an unlimited number of reasons why appraisers make these types of errors. The first clue to understanding why these types of errors are made is to recognize that appraisers are human. They are subject to the same problems and forces that influence all human behaviors.

Even the best trained and most observant individuals have limitations when recalling and processing observed behavior. The supervisor in the normal daily chain of events observes a wide variety of behaviors of various employees under a broad range of conditions. The observed behaviors in some manner modify those previously observed, and recollections of past behaviors will, in fact, vary perception of actual behaviors.

To overcome human weaknesses in processing, storing, and recalling observed behavior, there must be continuous documentation of behavior as soon as possible after its occurrence. These human weaknesses also underscore the necessity for training supervisors in observing behavior and then providing feedback on what was observed. The ability to obtain accurate information and then to provide it in a nonthreatening, growth-producing manner is not an easily obtainable quality. The success of the entire performance appraisal process eventually relates to the supervisor's ability to accurately recall and disseminate job behavior information.

Some of the major behavior-influencing forces that affect practically everyone are:

1   Desire to be accepted;
2   Concern with job security;
3   Concern with self-protection;
4   Affiliation with those holding similar views or having similar qualities; and
5   Limitations due to lack of prior education, previous experience, or developed skills.

***Desire to Be Accepted.***   All human beings have both instinctive and learned behavior determinants regarding social processes. The need for social affiliation may be stronger and easier to observe in some individuals than in others. But each person requires some type of social interaction, and underlying any successful interaction is a feeling of concern, comradeship, respect, and so on. When one employee rates the performance of another, there is a distinct possibility that this rating could damage the acceptance of one by another.

***Concern With Job Security.***   All supervisors worth their salt know that their success depends on the cooperation, effort, and contributions provided by subordinates. If in the appraisal process they inappropriately (not necessarily inaccurately) rate certain employees, the performance of the entire work group (not just the inappropriately rated employee) may suffer. Most supervisors realize that the performance of their work unit and job security usually go hand in hand.

***Concern With Self-Protection.***   Anyone who has ever worked with people realizes that the range of behaviors that people can demonstrate relative to some incident or issue defies the imagination. Performance appraisal can be very crucial to an individual. An individual's response to an unsatisfactory performance appraisal can range from absolute indifference to becoming so distraught that the appraisee murders the appraiser. Very few appraisers like to be in such a position, and, although the chance for such a drastic action is very unlikely, concern for personal retaliation often influences appraisal ratings.

*Affiliation with Those Holding Similar Views or Having Similar Qualities.* It is always easier to relate to people who have similar perspectives. The factors that influence perspective may relate to race, sex, national origin, religion, educational background, work experience, physical characteristics (height, weight, length of hair, etc.), place of birth, or location of residence. Factors that influence perception are innumerable, but it is easier to communicate and be with people who have similar views. It is also easy to see that those who do possess such qualities will probably receive higher appraisal ratings than those who do not. These differences often do not arise because of specific, conscious action but may result in a subconscious minimization of unacceptable activities by an individual holding similar views and a subconscious negative overreaction to those holding different views.

*Limitations Due to Lack of Prior Education, Previous Experience, or Developed Skills.* Although it is important to recognize the other four influencing forces, most businesses have fairly large limitations on what can be done to minimize these unsatisfactory influences. Education, experience, and skill limitations, however, are fertile grounds for improvement.

Education opportunities abound within every aspect of the performance appraisal process. Appraiser educational programs can include instruction on:

1   Purpose and use of the appraisal process;
2   Business objectives and goals;
3   Standards used for measuring performance;
4   Design of the appraisal instruments (the appraiser must understand each factor—dimension—and the scales used for measuring its demonstrated degree);
5   Measurement indexes used to identify the demonstrated degree of a performance quality;
6   Meaning of appraisal to employees;
7   Procedures available for *preparing* for performance appraisal;

**8** Ways to implement appraisal interviews and to provide employees feedback on performance. (Of every aspect of performance appraisal, this is probably the one area that offers the greatest opportunity for improvement. The costs involved in improving an appraiser's skill in implementing face-to-face conversations with subordinates on performance issues are outweighed by the benefits derived.)

**9** Practices of observing, describing, and rating behavior as it actually occurs;

**10** Range of subjective influence on performance appraisal and types of rating errors made by appraisers and possible ways of minimizing them; and

**11** Recognition of equity and equality and the impact of appraisal on these two vital areas of concern to all employees.

Educational assistance can also include preappraisal forms to be completed by the appraiser. They require the appraiser to collect and review relevant data and information that in essence necessitate doing the self-instruction "homework" necessary to be ready for the appraisal.

Appraisal experience opportunities can be enhanced in many ways. Through role playing, educational programs, and the use of instant-replay video tape recordings, appraisers can develop their observation and rating skills. By having experienced appraisers go through the entire process with them, appraisers can increase their familiarity and understanding of the process. They can learn physical movements and even facial expressions that facilitate success. They can also learn to eliminate actions that may lead to failure.

Skill improvement starts with identifying the skills necessary for accomplishing an appraisal. The next step is to identify those currently possessed skills that are sufficient to meet appraisal demands and those that must be developed. After recognition of skill strengths and weaknesses, appraisers can make their choices regarding the interest and effort that they wish to expend for these needed improvements.

## Supporting Appraisals

The impact that the previously mentioned variables have on employee appraisal makes it apparent that methods, procedures, and practices that tie appraisal to actual workplace behaviors are very important. It is essential that the identification of workplace behaviors be as accurate as possible. Passage of time clouds human memory, events become blurred, and other emotions blunt awareness of what actually happened. One of the best ways to keep past performance as fresh and accurate as possible is to document behavior as it occurs. Documentation must be job related. Information related to traits and other individual characteristics is valuable and useful only when the traits or characteristics relate directly to work-required behavior or have an influence on future career opportunities.

Direct observations are better than those that emanate from second- or third-hand sources. This does not mean that it is improper to use hearsay information; it just means that it is not as good as what you observe yourself. (But, remember, even first-hand observation may be clouded by perceptual barriers, and what you thought you saw may not have been what actually happened.) There are times when it is impossible or impractical to obtain first-hand observations. These conditions may result when an employee is temporarily assigned to another supervisor or to a work unit operating in some remote location or is working independently and the client/consumer of the services or workplace results provides the behavioral information. This situation also occurs when an employee is assigned to a special task force or work group requiring actions that are not under the control of the immediate supervisors.

Figure 6-1 is a preprinted behavior identification form that could be supplied to all supervisors. This form assists the supervisor to identify relevant, specific information required for documenting employee performance. A supervisor who completes such a form as soon as possible after the occurrence of a specific activity will build a file that is helpful for guiding and supporting appraisal decisions. A review of the form identifies some of the critical elements that must be included in any performance documentation form:

*Employee's Name.* No question as to who behaved in the identified manner.

*Job Title.* Permits easy review of work-required responsibilities and duties. Useful also if employee was temporarily assigned to another job and this relates to work performed when on the assignment.

*Date, Time, Location of Occurrence.* When and where behavior occurred.

*Date, Time, Completion of Form.* Accuracy of recall rapidly declines as time increases between occurrence and description.

*Observed Behavior.* Description of what occurred, circumstances affecting behavior, and results of behavior. (Each individual

Employee's
Name _____

Employee's
Job
Title _____

Date of
Occurrence _____

Time of
Occurrence _____

A.
P.

Location of
Occurrence _____

Identify Observed Behavior (If reporting hearsay information, identify source and location of actual observer.)

Date Form
Completed _____

Time Form
Completed _____

A.
P.

Signature and
Title of Person
Completing Form _____

_____

Items to be considered in identifying behavior (may be used as a checklist)

What specifically occurred?
Is there sufficient detail to support future judgment?
Have you described results of behavior?
What circumstances influenced behavior?
     Was there an emergency situation?
     Did unusual or adverse conditions exist?
Behavior Being Documented:
     Insubordination                          Theft
     Attendance                               Malicious Damage
     Quantity of Work                         Interpersonal Relations
     Quality of Work                          Acceptance of Job Enlarging
                                                   Responsibilities

Second-Party Observations:

     Remote Location          Temporarily Assigned to Others
     Works Independently

FIGURE 6-1    PERFORMANCE    DOCUMENTATION    FORM
(IDENTIFICATION OF EMPLOYEE ON-THE-JOB
BEHAVIORS)

description of a workplace behavior may not appear to be sufficiently important to take the time required for documentation; however, over an extended period of time, a systematic identification of behaviors provides powerful support for actions that a supervisor must take in performing his or her responsibilities.)

Many supervisors find it difficult to complete a formal document such as described in Figure 6-1 shortly after the occurrence of a behavior that should be identified. It may be necessary for a supervisor to keep a notebook available for listing and briefly describing behaviors that should be described in greater detail at some more appropriate date. With the declining cost and increasing availability of all types of recording instruments and systems, these devices provide splendid support in this area. The purpose of the notebook or taped observation is to preserve as accurate a description of the behavior as possible. In this way, it is more likely that the behavior will be described in writing and that the description will relate closely to what actually happened. (The Critical Incident Technique (CIT) discussed in detail in Chapter 8 is a similar approach that is useful for documenting employee workplace behavior.) A major reason for documentation is to minimize unfair and unjust appraisal of employee workplace behavior. Practically everyone is subject to biased thoughts and feelings. Written descriptions assist appraisers to maintain a true perspective of what the employee is doing while performing work requirements. The documentation must use "hard" information. Hard refers to information that can be documented, relates to something that happened, can be measured in quantitative terms or in actual results that describe qualitative measures, and can be identified by date, time, and location of occurrence. By providing some kind or degree of measurement to demonstrated behavior, it becomes much easier to assess the effectiveness of employee performance. Supervisors must be aware that documented employee behavior must be available and open to that employee's review. This information is critical both to the operation of successful organizations and to the future security and progress of the employee. Documentation is not an opportunity for unsupported innuendoes or rumors; it is an opportunity for stating facts.

The form described earlier for writing responsibility and duty statements, performance dimensions, and goals applies equally to the description of employee workplace behavior. The most appropriate or descriptive action verb should be selected, then modified by describing as specifically as possible what occurred, the results of the behavior, or the factors that influenced the behavior. The more often supervisors use this writing style, the easier it will become, and the more skilled they will be in written communications. The entire writing process should result in the supervisor thinking in terms of action verb plus modifiers or descriptors. This assists in keeping supervisor attention focused on what the employee is doing, not on some nonrelated trait or characteristic that can only distort actual behavior.

## Preparing for an Appraisal Review

Prior to an appraisal session, a supervisor reviews the demonstrated behavior file of each employee. At this time, it may be useful to summarize the behaviors relative to specific performance dimensions or goals. Figure 6-2 is useful for summarizing and analyzing behavior with regard to performance dimensions and goals. Consolidating a series of behaviors occurring during the appraisal period provides a more accurate picture of what actually happened than does any one single event or dependence on memory.

Summarizing behavior relative to a performance dimension or goal makes it easier and permits a more accurate appraisal of employee behavior relative to that quality. It may only be necessary to summarize behaviors relating to performance dimensions or goals that have been previously identified by appraiser and appraisee as critical components of job-related performance. This documentation should enhance the opportunity for having a constructive, positive appraisal experience by both appraiser and appraisee. Decisions made regarding these performance dimensions or goals may directly affect compensation, training, and promotion opportunities.

Performance Dimension/Goal Summarized _____

Dates of Performance Documentation Form _____

Briefly describe how workplace behaviors support identified dimensions/goals both positively and negatively:

FIGURE 6-2      PERFORMANCE DIMENSION—GOAL ATTAIN—
               MENT SUMMARY SHEET

# Performance Interviewing and Counseling

From the moment of the first contact between the supervisor and subordinate, feelings, values, and various other emotional and intellectual considerations develop that enhance or block future productive relationships. In fact, most supervisors sooner or later realize (and rightly so) that there are interpersonal issues and situational demands over which they have little or no control that influence their relationships with their subordinates. This in no way minimizes the requirement for a supervisor to be a skilled diagnostician in understanding and explaining why employees behave in a certain manner.

The skills required of a supervisor are many and varied, but the most difficult to master are those used in interpersonal relationships. Supervisors must talk, listen, analyze, and negotiate with others. They have at their disposal a most valuable and useful tool—the performance appraisal review. This tool requires careful study and application. Using it can be dangerous because of the possibility of error and miscalculation in attempting to make adjustments between *what is* and *what is perceived*. Supervisors may feel certain that they have the facts and know *what is* and that the views of their subordinates are merely perceptions. A common base for understanding requires concern for both perception and reality. Both are vital issues.

To be effective as a supervisor requires being effective as an appraiser of performance. To be effective as an appraiser of employee performance, the supervisor must be able to assess and understand:

1  job requirements,
2  short- and long-term job-related goals,
3  employee capabilities and energy levels,
4  employee goals and demands, and
5  on- and off-the-job conflicts that affect workplace behavior.

Initiating and carrying out a successful appraisal session requires both interviewing and counseling skills. Interviewing skills normally focus on the ability to gather and assess information relating to job performance whereas counseling skills aim at facilitating the achievement of change and the redirection of job behavior so that it is beneficial to both the individual and the organization.

Effective appraisal involves face-to-face interaction between appraiser and appraisee. Conducting these personal interview and counseling sessions effectively requires an understanding of intra- and interpersonal dynamics. At an appraisal session, anything may happen at any moment. The session may be extremely dull with the appraisee's response being merely an occasional nod of the head or an appropriate yes or no. On the other hand, the appraisee may take a major exception to the supervisor's analysis of behavior, with the result being a bitter and hostile confrontation. Because it is difficult to predict the way in which an appraisal session will go, the first requirement for conducting an appraisal is to do the necessary homework: to prepare carefully for the session.

## Preparing for a Performance Appraisal Review

The performance appraisal review is too important and serious to be left to chance. Appraisers should not enter an appraisal review session unprepared. They should know what they want to learn during the review session, and should not expect to follow some well defined order of events. As mentioned repeatedly in earlier chapters, employees basically mistrust anything that relates to a review or measurement of their performance; therefore, by expecting the least and the unexpected, the results will not be disappointing.

Subordinates frequently are reluctant to discuss their work-place behavior. This does not mean that appraisers cannot obtain a complete picture of what has happened. The appraisers must acquire on a piecemeal basis what may appear to be information about a number of unrelated activities and join these data together like pieces of a jigsaw puzzle. They must realize that detailed or specific information on isolated issues is of far less value than information that pertains to the overall job behavior of the appraisee.

As also mentioned in earlier chapters, most supervisors have minimal amounts of time available for involvement in the performance appraisal process. Possibly the most time-consuming activities relate to preparing for and conducting the performance review. In preparing for the review, the appraiser must gather all the information that has any bearing on the discussions. The appraisal information must be carefully analyzed, and the various events that transpired during the appraisal period must be identified. By instituting a systematic, orderly, and in-depth preparation for an interview, the appraiser becomes more prepared for the unexpected. The better the preparation is, the greater is the opportunity for flexibility. By knowing what information is wanted and what is already available, the appraiser can accept fragmented pieces of information, place them in a particular compartment, and collect additional information that will provide an overall picture of the employee's behavior.

One approach that may be extremely useful in developing a constructive review session is for the appraiser to review performance–related information and to develop an agenda for the meeting. This agenda should identify the major points to be discussed during the interview. The appraiser can hand the agenda to the appraisee who, in turn, can review it and make additions or deletions regarding topics to be discussed. This provides an additional dimension for facilitating employee awareness of what to expect and how to prepare for the coming meeting more effectively.

The appraiser must allow sufficient time to conduct the review. It is not fair to either the appraiser or appraisee to terminate an uncompleted review because of another commitment. Because of both the importance and sensitivity of the performance review, it does not make sense to cancel a review or even to make an appraisee wait because of other job requirements. Any of these things can happen, but good planning can keep cancellations or delays to a minimum.

### The Appraisal Session

To be an effective reviewer of performance requires both interviewing and counseling skills. To be successful in interviewing and counseling, the appraiser must have knowledge and skills both in asking the right question at the appropriate time and in being a constructive listener. This section will focus on types of questions to ask, when to ask them, when to listen, and how to stimulate appraisee responses.

In the performance review session, information must be shared. If the information flow is predominantly in one direction, neither the appraiser nor appraisee will benefit from this time-consuming but vital human resource activity.

Appraisees must feel that their concerns are critical to the process—that they influence the outcome of the review and that the session is in their best interests. The review must be job performance related. It must pertain to job requirements, how job activities are performed, changes that could be made, and future opportunities for the appraisee.

Three major methods are available for use in face-to-face encounter sessions in which there will be both a gathering and dissemination of information, an appraisal of past workplace behaviors, and recommendations for the direction of future behavior.

These methods are the directive, nondirective, and combination reviews. Before each approach is analyzed, a review of what the appraiser should gain from an appraisal session will be of assistance in identifying which approach is best for the given situation.

### Behavior-Influencing Information Acquired in a Performance Review.

1. Distinguish between cause of behavior and effect of behavior. For example, a cause is that a child is at home sick or that the spouse ran off with a salesperson; an effect is a series of unexplained absences and tardiness.

2. Identify factors leading to certain behaviors, such as peer pressures resulting in reduced quantity of output.

3. Separate internal and external pressures. Examples of the respective pressures are, "Spouse thinks that I should be making more money" and "My pay is low compared with that of my coworkers."

4. Assess employee strengths and weaknesses. Examples are employee cooperates well with co-workers and employee demonstrates little interest in guiding group efforts.

5. Indicate employee's potential for success and failure. Examples of the respective traits are employee appears to have unlimited energy and willingness to perform assignments, and employee has minimal skills in speaking before a group.

6. Identify the capability of the employee to tolerate or resolve stress-related issues. For example, novel or unusual situation frequently results in complete disruption of expected employee output.

7. Identify opportunities for supporting employee and directing behavior so that it benefits both the employee and the organization. For example, employee is seeking marketing job; schedule employee so that it is possible for him or her to complete graduate-school program and also to attend in-house marketing-oriented training course.

    The performance review session should provide knowledge that assists in (1) better understanding employee feelings, attitudes, and situations; (2) determining courses of action that are most beneficial to the employee; and (3) relating rewards to demonstrated workplace behavior. A discussion of the three approaches to interviewing–counseling follows.

### Directive Approach

The directive approach follows a specific format in which answers to specified questions are sought. The appraiser may either develop the questions, or they may be in a standardized form, in which case he or she must ask the questions exactly as they are worded and in the exact order of their appearance. Questions must not be added or deleted. The check list assists in recalling and recording information. The range of questions can be very wide, and the check list can cover the topics relevant to a specific issue. For example:

"Do you like your job?" Yes _____ No _____

"Can you identify one thing that you find enjoyable in doing your job?"

### Nondirective Approach

This approach follows no rigid format but requires more question-asking and listening skills on the appraiser's part. The appraiser must depend on his or her own skills because the interview and counseling session is extremely flexible. This approach frequently makes use of very broad, general questions, such as:

"What do your co-workers do that assists you in performing your assignments?"

The appraiser can focus questions on specific areas when in-depth information is needed. The major advantage of the nondirective approach is that it draws the appraisee into the process. It permits the employee to come to grips with real issues and to discuss feelings or problems that are disturbing or adversely affecting his or her performance.

### Combination Approach

Both the directive and nondirective approaches have weaknesses. The directive approach does not grant the flexibility necessary for analyzing workplace problems and developing solutions to unacceptable workplace behaviors. The nondirective approach is too time consuming; it allows too many opportunities to miss points that should be covered and places demands on an appraiser who may have neither the knowledge nor the skills to meet them. So, the appraiser can, in most cases, combine the two, using the strengths of each to his or her best advantage.

Identifying topical areas and developing a list of relevant general questions focuses the review session on the subject at hand—employee past, current, and future performance. Here, the appraiser has considerable freedom to formulate additional questions and to reword or reorder suggested questions. The combination approach provides sufficient structure and order to cover the subject but enough flexibility to allow the appraiser to follow the natural flow of events as they arise during the review session.

## The Physical Setting

The need for "doing homework" (gathering, analyzing, and summarizing information that identifies and characterizes demonstrated workplace behaviors) before the review session has already been mentioned. Preceding the actual meeting, the appraiser should obtain a physical setting that will enhance interviewing and counseling success. If at all possible, a neutral meeting place should be sought. The basic requirement is a private room in which the appraiser and appraisee can discuss the issues at hand in total confidentiality, preferably with NO outside interruptions.

If it is desirable that the appraisee discuss personal feelings and points of view, he or she must feel secure that the appraiser alone is hearing what is said or, at least, that confidentiality of information is well defined. There should be no distractions, such as the ringing of the telephone, interruptions by a secretary, or a jovial "What's new?" from a passing colleague. If available, coffee and ashtrays should be provided; if the appraisee is a smoker, this is one time that smoking should be permitted.

## Introduction

A brief but thoughtful introduction to the review session may make the difference between a successful and an unsuccessful performance review. The appraisee frequently enters the session apprehensively. First and foremost in his or her mind is "What am I going to be chewed out for today?"; then, "How are 'they' going to get me?"

The appraiser should put the appraisee at ease as quickly as possible. The room should have a comfortable chair. If possible, a desk or other physical barrier between the appraiser and appraisee should be avoided. A moment or two for some light discussion, such as "You're looking well today" and "Congratulations on the new baby" will break the ice. There should be a brief discussion about what is to be accomplished during the session. The appraiser should invite the appraisee to share in the responsibility for successful completion of the review and explain how the appraisee's views can influence the results of the meeting. A simple statement like, "I realize that there are always two sides to every story, and I certainly would like to know your side when you think it is appropriate," will underscore a desire for the appraisee's participation.

### Body

During this stage of the review session, a flow of questions, responses, unsolicited statements, and probably many nonverbal communications will facilitate accomplishing the reason for the meeting. In addition to identifying information to be provided and requested, the opportunity for success can be improved by employing empathy, penetrating questions, objectivity, problem analysis, constructive listening, and keen observation.

*Empathy.*   This quality is essential in conducting a performance review, but there is truly no place for *sympathy*. If the time is right and the interviewee feels that he or she can pull it off, out comes the "sob story," the tale of woe. This is not the time to hide performance failure behind a situation that requires compassion. This does not mean that it is possible to eliminate the sad story. When it arises, the appraiser should listen courteously, and, as soon as possible, redirect attention to the subject at hand—workplace behavior and what can be done in spite of certain unsatisfactory events. On the other hand, *empathy*—understanding why a person behaves in a certain manner, seeing something through the eyes of the other person— gives the appraiser a better understanding of why and how certain things transpire to cause unacceptable workplace behavior.

*Penetrating Questions.*   The successful combination approach to interviewing and counseling requires that the appraiser ask the right questions at the proper time. The right questions provide structure for the review session. Questions that may increase the accuracy, scope, and relevance of information fall into three major categories: responsibilities and duties, job stress, and job opportunities.

The following questions focus, in one way or another, on job performance, performance requirements, and possible barriers to acceptable performance. Remember, the appraiser should ask only one question at a time; phrase the question in simple, understandable words; keep the question as brief as possible—a general rule is that any question over two sentences is too long; be as specific as possible; keep the question in as positive a vein as possible; and when possible, avoid questions that permit a yes or no response. Throughout the review, the appraiser should be sure to follow up on any leads provided by the appraisee. A "why" question may be useful in further investigating a specific point.

Some questions that may be of value are:

### Job Responsibility and Duty Related

Which of your job responsibilities and duties do you feel that you are unable to perform satisfactorily?

What responsibilities and duties are you currently performing that are not included in your job description?

What responsibilities and duties are you *not* currently performing that you feel that you should be performing?

Which of your responsibilities and duties do you feel should be performed by someone else?

These questions provide a nonthreatening, job-focused opening to the review discussion. Both the appraiser and appraisee should bring to the session a copy of the appraisee's current job description. (Each employee should have a formal job description to bring to the review session; there should be one in the employee's personnel file that the appraiser can use for this part of the review.) From the above questions, job responsibilities and duties can be updated, and, above all, the appraiser and appraisee can be on the "same wave length" and can reach common understanding of what the job is and is not.

### Job Stress Related

What do you like about your job?

What do you find most enjoyable in what you do?

What job activities do you find most difficult to perform?

What in your job is working against you?

What do you find most demanding about your job?

What do you dislike about your job?

What do you consider good about your job?

Who provides you with the most support in doing your job?

Where do you obtain job-related support?

What problems do you have in working cooperatively with other members of your work group?

What troubles have you encountered in obtaining the cooperation of others in working toward group goals?

Do your peers, subordinates, or supervisors cause you any undue, unnecessary stress?

Is your job causing you any emotional or health-related problems?

Recognizing that performance review is, in itself, a stress-laden situation for many people, the appraiser must realize that it is not easy, and at times not possible, to learn what he or she needs to know. An important point to remember during the review session is that *what one hears is not necessarily what one needs to know.* Whether acquired through learning or instinct, survival is fundamental, and what we say often has a way of coming back to haunt us or hurt us. Appraisers should remember that "foot in mouth disease" has a very special meaning to appraisees. Consciously or subconsciously, appraisees think, "I will tell them what they want to hear" or "what I *think* they want to hear"; "I will not say anything that could put me in a bad light"; "I must be careful about what I say about my work companions—after all, they belong to my church or my social organization. They go fishing or hunting with me. I will be working with them for the rest of my life. A slip of my tongue could place them in jeopardy, and their friendship is certainly more important to me than this organization and its performance"; "Even if I do speak my mind about what is wrong, the bosses will not do anything about it anyway—except possibly get me in trouble with my associates." These are just a few examples of the many thoughts that may go through an appraisee's mind that block or prohibit the transfer of valid, meaningful, and timely information.

People seem to have an innate protective device that prohibits them from explicitly and precisely stating real and valid issues. Providing information about job-induced stress frequently has negative connotations, and many employees are not too anxious to discuss such issues. Throughout the performance review session, appraisees will at times respond to questions with answers that they feel are socially acceptable or even with what they *think* the appraiser wants to hear, but not what the appraiser wants or needs to know. The appraiser may find it necessary to return to a point several times before it is understood by both parties.

A particular stress-related situation occurs when the appraiser must provide a performance rating during the interview session. A classic study conducted in the early 1960s at the General Electric Co. indicated that supervisors had a very difficult time providing negative feedback to employees during a performance review session. From these findings, General Electric researchers concluded that it is best to split the role of performance appraisal, conducting performance rating and reward identification in one session and providing feedback useful for motivational and development purposes in another session.

Other studies indicate that by inflating the ratings, appraisers overcome the stress of providing information regarding appraisal ratings that are lower than the appraisee expects. (Again, General Electric studies in the early 1960s indicated that the great majority, over 90 percent, of employees interviewed felt that they performed in an average or above-average manner.[1]) Designing an appraisal system that permits or forces appraisers to give untrue ratings is a disservice to the appraisee and to the organization.

## Job-Related Opportunities

What additional job-related support from me would you like to have?

What types of training would you like to receive?

What additional resources or support can the organization provide?

Do you desire or are you seeking a promotion? To what job? Where? When?

Are you prepared/ready for a promotion?

What promotion assistance do you need?

What do you want from your job?

The questions that the appraiser asks determine, to a large extent, the responses that he or she will receive. Some of the previously listed questions can be answered with a simple yes or no. To elicit a more in-depth response, the appraiser may ask for more elaboration:

**Q:** Is your job causing you any emotional or health-related problems?

**A:** Yes.

**Q:** Would you please tell me what is causing these problems?

[1]Herbert H. Meyer, Emanuel Kay, and John R. P. French, Jr. "Split Roles in Performance Appraisal," *Harvard Business Review*, January–February 1965, p. 126.

The open-ended question (one that does not require a specific response but permits the respondee to develop his or her own answer) will usually provide better and more useful information. Open-ended questions require answers that are more time-consuming than questions that may be answered with a yes or no or with answer "b" rather than "a" or "c."

There may be times during a review session when there is a need for information of a very sensitive nature. When this situation arises and the appraiser feels that a direct open-ended question is inappropriate, he or she may phrase the question relative to some hypothetical situation; this is called the projective method of questioning. In this case, instead of requiring the appraisee to describe how he or she personally feels about an issue, the appraiser develops a hypothetical situation and the employee responds according to his or her true feelings. For example, "If you were responsible for meeting this delivery date on Product XYZ and two of your key subordinates were having interpersonal problems and were not supporting each other, what would you do?" In this case, the type of responsibility or product would not be within the job domain of the appraisee.

Projective questions are difficult to phrase, and the answers are often even more difficult to interpret. Although this type of question can be a very worthwhile addition to the appraiser's interviewing and counseling techniques, he or she must have considerable knowledge and skill in order to use it properly.

*Objectivity.*   A difficult but important perspective that the appraiser must maintain is one of objectivity. He or she must be as fair and impartial as possible. Facts must provide the basis for performance-related decisions. Personal feelings and prejudices must not cause the distortion of facts or their unjust use.

Maintaining a nonjudgmental attitude is not always easy. It is all too possible to be overpowered by the smooth and glib talker, the well groomed, physically attractive appraisee. However, when tempted to make a less than acceptable judgment based primarily on the speech or appearance of the appraisee, the appraiser should remember that the employee may be a "diamond in the rough" who is only giving a partial picture of the contributions that he or she has made during the appraisal period. (Of course, this employee could also be just a piece of cut glass.)

When an appraisee demonstrates a bias and there is an indication that the information being received may not reflect an accurate or honest assessment of the situation, further questioning in this area may be in order. It may not be appropriate to continue the discussion on the subject at that time, but the appraiser may want to file a mental note and return to the subject when the time is right. In relating to consistency of information, the appraiser should constantly be alert not to ask questions that cause appraisees to give the responses that they think the appraiser is seeking.

*Problem Analysis.*   A major purpose of the appraisal review is to assist in the identification and definition of problems that affect the performance of the appraisee. Successful problem solving relates directly to the quality and quantity of available information about the problem. Everything discussed in this chapter involves gathering, extracting, analyzing, and summarizing performance-related information. It is possible to probe only so far, and then nothing more is forthcoming.

The appraisee must realize that he or she is part of the problem as well as part of the solution. The review session should build rapport and trust. When appraisees understand and appreciate that there is an opportunity for improving an unsatisfactory solution, there is much greater chance that they will feel encouraged to elaborate on the problem area and frequently to develop their own solutions.

*Constructive Listening.*   When one person is talking, it is difficult to hear what the other person is saying. The amount of time that the appraiser should spend talking is a matter of current debate. There are those who believe that a rule of thumb for interviewing and counseling should be that the appraiser should talk for no more than one-third of the total interview. Others take the opposite view and state that the supervisor should spend about two-thirds of the time talking.

Those who propose the two-thirds–one-third *appraisee* speaking ratio contend that the major purpose of the review session is to grant the appraisee the time to discuss his or her job and job-related problems. It is impossible to hear what the appraisee has to say when the appraiser does most of the talking.

The supporters of the two-thirds–one-third *appraiser* speaking ratio take the approach that the major benefit that the appraisee gains from the interview is to know what the appraiser expects and how he or she views the appraisee's past performance. The appraisee also expects to learn from the appraiser future actions and job-related opportunities that may be available. The appraiser is expected to be the major source of official job-related information.

As in most cases of this type, the best approach to how much time should be spent talking and how much time should be spent listening is "It all depends on the situation." There is no one right way. There may be times when the appraiser spends two-thirds of the performance review session talking, and other times when two-thirds of the session is spent listening. Both may be correct. The most important thing to learn here is that careful preparation for the session will assist the appraiser to recognize what is appropriate and best serves situational demands.

The following is a list of guidelines to constructive listening:

1   When an employee has something on his or her mind, the listener should allow that person to talk it out. The listener should not respond with sharp answers or identify the unreasonableness of the statement.

2   The listener should minimize, even set aside, the use of any clever retorts to an employee's problem.

3   The listener should restrain the natural impulse to be curious and to avoid asking questions that show a bias. The employee may later regret answering such questions.

4   If feelings or emotions become the center of discussion, they should not be abruptly dismissed. Discouraging the expression of emotional issues can inhibit an employee's ability to work with and relate to critical problem areas.

5   Violent and deep-seated negative expressions require understanding rather than judgment. If possible, the employee should be permitted to develop his or her own solution to the problem.

6   Although it may be difficult to be silent, the listener should speak as seldom as possible. A series of "eloquent and encouraging grunts" may be all the sound that is needed. A few seconds of silence may frequently be appropriate. The expectant pause is one of the ways by which to indicate a sympathetic willingness to hear more—along with acceptance of the fact that the employee does not have to say anything.

7   New ideas should not be introduced nor should the direction of a conversation be changed. It is perfectly acceptable to repeat what the speaker has already said. A slight rephrasing of the topic may assist the speaker to realize what he or she has been saying.

8   The listener should not moralize. The role of the listener is not to make the speaker over in his or her image. The listener

should not only avoid saying, "You're wrong," but also re-frain from saying, "The other person is wrong."

9    Acceptance does not require agreement. It is not necessary to say, "I think you are absolutely right." Possibly the only thing to say that is worse is, "I think you are absolutely wrong."

10   A trap to be avoided is giving advice on personal matters. An old saying states, "A wise man does not need advice; a damn fool will not take it." Constructive listening leads the speaker into deciding which is the best approach.

To be an effective appraiser it is important to be both a willing and a skilled listener. It is not easy to get a subordinate with a problem to open up and to describe areas of conflict. Bitter experiences have taught many people that the best defense is to say nothing. The ability to encourage subordinates to talk requires (a) an active interest in them as unique individuals and in their problems, (2) a feeling on the part of the subordinate that the appraiser really wants to be of assistance, and (3) an understanding of the situation so that the appraiser can ask the right questions at the right time.

*Keen Observation.*    Appraisees constantly give both verbal and nonverbal clues regarding their understanding and acceptance of a specific topic. The appraiser must watch for these clues in order to determine when further clarification is required or when an issue is understood. The lighting of a cigarette, raising of an eyebrow, checking the time, or uttering a barely perceptible, "I'm not sure," may provide the appraiser with the clue to what his or her next step should be.

The appraiser's actions affect the quality of the review. Are his or her eyes focusing on the appraisee, on a sheet of paper, or out the window? The appraiser's questions, responses, and body movements also send a special message that may intimidate or inhibit the appraisee, which, in turn, may affect his or her response.

The appraiser must be in charge of the interview. Through keen observation, he or she will be able to recognize what must be done in order to direct the session toward the desired goals.

## Summary

The review session is now coming to a close. The major goals have been accomplished. The appraiser and appraisee have had "their day in court." However, it is still necessary to summarize what happened, what has been agreed to, what recommendations are to be made, the accuracy of the identified behaviors, and what will take place from now until the next performance review session.

If at all possible, the appraiser should record all pertinent information immediately following the session. The following questions may be useful as a check list for identifying what should be recorded upon completion of the performance review:

1   Were job requirements reviewed?

2   Does the employee understand job requirements?

3   Were areas of job conflict discussed?

4   Were job goals reviewed?

5   Were goal attainment steps analyzed?

6   Were performance standards discussed?

7   Was there a discussion of what the employee would like to accomplish from the job?

8   What was the appraisee's reaction to the review?

Personal reactions and impressions of the review session should be noted. This type of information may prove to be invaluable in preparing for future reviews or for analyzing what happened during this review at some future date.

Personal feelings should influence neither the appraiser's future performance reviews nor those conducted on the same individual by other supervisors. On the other hand, it may be extremely useful for future reviewers to know how the appraiser felt during the review and about behaviors that both parties exhibited (ease, pleasantness, hostility, anger, frustration). Recognizing the possibility of exhibiting an adverse performance review behavior that may block achievement of a successful review may force the appraiser to avoid undesirable behaviors. As much as humanly possible, the appraiser should keep the tone of the review on a positive, constructive base. Understanding one's potential weaknesses from a general consideration or as related to a specific appraisee can only help the appraiser to improve the interpersonal dynamics exhibited during a performance review.

A performance review should relate to job requirements and demonstrated workplace behavior. However, all involved parties are subject to their individual perceptions. Subjectivity and unfair biases can occur in any review. The best defense against an unfair review is to be aware of inadequate or inconsistent emotions. Such awareness can minimize the possibility of their occurrence or of unfair slanting of an employee's performance review.

# Review of Goals and Goal Attainment Steps

Chapter 5 focused specifically on the setting of goals and the identification of goal attainment steps. When goal setting is a major part of the performance appraisal process, it becomes a key part of the performance review session.

In fact, goal setting and the development of attainment steps minimize both appraisee defensiveness and autocratic manipulation of the review by the appraiser. When performed properly, goal setting and goal attainment focus as much on *how* the work was done as on the why or what of the demonstrated behavior.

The process starts when a supervisor and subordinate sit down and jointly discuss and develop goals for some future period. These goals become standards by which to measure the subordinate's future performance. In a review session that follows, the supervisor and subordinate assess actual goal accomplishment. This process provides the supervisor with an excellent opportunity to discuss the subordinate's work behavior and to provide appropriate feedback on demonstrated performance.

In this goal-setting technique, the supervisor acts as a teacher–leader–counselor. When properly performed, this technique emphasizes the supervisor's role as counselor and minimizes the role of judge. To be a successful counselor in these sessions, the supervisor must be a good listener and observer. The process is basically one of self-appraisal; performed in any other way, it is of minimal value.

A performance review session developed and conducted in this manner minimizes the need for criticism. A major barrier to the success of any performance review session is the amount of criticism directed at a subordinate's demonstrated workplace behavior. All employees have self-images that they will protect at almost any cost. The more criticism they receive, the more defensive they become. The more defensive they are, the less willing the employees are to accept ratings of poor performance. Psychological denial of inadequate performance limits the opportunity for implementing constructive changes.

When an appraisee knows that a major part of the review session will center on the goals and goal attainment steps identified and described at the last review, there is a considerable reduction in the amount of uncertainty that frequently accompanies a performance review. The entire process is one in which feedback minimizes psychological costs related to stress and risk taking involved in the review of workplace performance.

When an appraisee has performed below acceptable levels,

there is a good chance that this level of performance has been recognized by the individual when he or she compared work effort results with preset goals. Discussion related to negatives are seldom, if ever, enjoyed by either appraisers or appraisees. In a goal review session, the opportunity for injecting surprises into the situation decreases while the opportunity for constructive criticism increases.

By using goals as the standard for identifying levels or quality of performance, both appraiser and appraisee know the criteria for acceptable performance. By having goal attainment steps, it is easier to identify areas of weakness. Opportunities for arbitrary confrontations decrease. It is easier to focus on important facts or pertinent issues. The redirecting of behavior toward the accomplishment of meaningful and acceptable goals is the major contact point between the appraiser and appraisee.

Briefly, the goal-setting, goal attainment step process works in this manner:

1   The supervisor and subordinate discuss the objectives of the business and work group in simple, straightforward language and relate the work activities of the subordinate to these objectives.

2   The subordinate sets one to three goals for the coming period (which should seldom extend beyond the next two or three months). The subordinate has usually worked on developing these goals before the meeting. The special influence of such goals in the appraisal process is that, unlike global dimensions of performance, i.e., quantity of work, they are very specific and provide a facet of demonstrated job behavior in which feedback becomes meaningful and provides the appraisee with an opportunity for learning that can lead to growth and development.

3   The subordinate and supervisor mutually agree on each goal, analyze all of them, and identify as many attainment steps as possible that will lead to reaching the goals successfully. (Attainment steps are the heart of the goal-setting process. They are work–behavior activities that are identified as fundamental to the successful attainment of a particular goal. For operational success, there is a limit to the number of goals set, but no limit to the number of attainment steps identified in the problem-solving process—the more the better.)

4   The subordinate and supervisor discuss the likelihood of successfully performing each attainment step and the priority that one step has over another.

5   The supervisor tries to provide any information that the sub-ordinate needs or wants to know.

6   At all times, the supervisor must convey through demon-strated behavior that the goals are those of the subordinate. The supervisor is a resource person ready and willing to assist the subordinate in every way possible, but the subordinate owns the goals and has primary responsibility for achieving them.

7   Each goal should be specific, stimulating, achievable, and relevant.

8   Each goal and its attainment steps should be set in writing.

In the appraisal follow-up session, the subordinate and super-visor analyze the subordinate's successes and failures. This session focuses primarily on the attainment steps rather than on the goals. If the subordinate failed to reach a goal, each attainment step is re-viewed in an attempt to find the barriers to success. The subordinate and the supervisor may decide that they have not identified the critical attainment steps, or they may decide that the goal was unat-tainable considering the existing situation. On the other hand, it is important to recognize those steps that led to success. This informa-tion may benefit others pursuing similar goals.

The purpose of the goal-setting session is to improve organiza-tional performance through the growth of the individual. It is a cooperative venture in which the subordinate has the opportunity to exercise self-control, to assess progress, to self-appraise work be-havior, and to initiate corrective action.

## Ten Helpful Performance Review Hints

*Plan the Review.* Think ahead. Do homework. Identify what is to be done and determine a procedure or process for gaining and providing the desired information.

*Pinpoint Key Information.* Identify information that must be pro-vided or acquired.

*Minimize Wasted Time.* Courtesy and friendliness are essential but time is a precious commodity. Use it wisely.

*Pause.* Yes, time is valuable. But a pause here and there may not only be refreshing but critical, allowing both parties to regroup their thoughts and to move ahead.

*Listen and Observe.* Focus on the appraisee. Do not be concerned with the next question or a brilliant remark.

*Orient and Clarify.* Keep the review on the subject. To clarify, repeat a statement or ask a question.

*Keep an Open Mind.* Do not decide an issue until all the information is at hand. Be careful not to be overly influenced by unfavorable information.

*Summarize.* At appropriate times, summarize what has transpired. Increase the likelihood that everyone is on the same wave length.

*Follow up.* Fulfill all obligations made during the review. Do not make promises that cannot be kept.

*Avoid Bloodbaths.* Be careful with the information gathered in a review. Do not betray a confidence. Your reputation for integrity is at stake. This is where confidence and trust begin.

8

# Performance Appraisal Techniques and Methods

A principal reason for centering on the responsibility, duty-goal approach, as featured in Chapters 2 through 5, is because it provides meaningful job standards and accurate and valid identification of quantity and quality of contributions. I believe that this approach permits increased employee participation and enhances the likelihood of worker acceptance. Most businesses recognize that, if they are to increase productivity and lower costs, employees must accept as fair those standards of performance that affect the rewards that they receive for the work they do.

I have mentioned throughout this book that there is no cookbook or one special method for appraising worker performance. Although it is my belief that the responsibility, duty–goal achievement approach can have widespread usefulness if appropriately modified, it may be inadequate for a particular organization or business. Most businesses find that it is impossible to imitate or duplicate a performance appraisal program of another business and achieve success.

When designing and implementing an appraisal system, each business must take into account the many variables that are unique to its own situation. For example:

1   Type of goods or services produced.
2   Methods of producing or delivering outputs.
3   Ability to specify quality and quantity of output.
4   Physical locations of work sites.
5   Employee needs, perceptions, and demands; personal history and background.
6   Business requirements, history, and background.
7   Legal requirements.
8   Level(s) or unit(s) in organizational hierarchy to be appraised.

Each of these factors requires consideration in the design phase of a performance appraisal system and must be monitored constantly to ensure continued viability and validity. Performance appraisal must recognize contributions, promote achievement and risk taking, and lead to appropriate rewards. Therefore, it requires the rare combination of technological workability, organizational reliability, and employee trust. Performance appraisal must promote the willingness of employees to work together as a team and not to divide their loyalties by promoting an "US–THEM" atmosphere.

Since employees basically mistrust any method or procedure

used for appraising performance, the individuals involved in designing or approving a particular appraisal method must carefully review the performance standards that relate to it.

Work- or job-related standards used for appraising employee performance must meet two basic criteria:

1 Standards must be consistent; that is, a standard must recognize similar employee inputs by providing similar employer outputs. (Similar work effort and contributions by employees performing similar assignments should result in comparable performance appraisal ratings.)

2 Standards must be fair. Those whose performance is measured against a standard should accept the standard as being just and reasonable.

Within many businesses, the immediate supervisors, personnel specialists, and industrial engineers establish the performance standards. Some businesses are also now involving the employees themselves in this activity. The immediate supervisor is held accountable for the outputs of his or her subordinate and thus should have a voice in the setting of standards for that employee. The final standards are usually a shared responsibility that may involve the employee, immediate supervisor, personnel department, and industrial engineers.

After the usefulness or suitability of the other appraisal methods described in this chapter have been analyzed, it may be wise to consider the skills required for designing and implementing the method, the availability of the skills, and the quality and acceptability of the standards inherent within a particular method.

Techniques in addition to the responsibility, duty–goal achievement approach available for appraising employee performance vary from detailed workplace industrial engineering time and methods measurement studies to those that focus on human traits that appear to influence job performance significantly. These various appraisal techniques and methods can be classified under general categories, such as

1 Work Methods Analysis
2 Narrative Descriptive Review Technique
3 Ranking Technique
4 Check List Technique
5 Rating Scale Technique
6 Goal-Setting Technique

## Work Methods Analysis

In the latter part of the nineteenth century and the early years of the twentieth century, industrial engineers developed methods, techniques, and procedures for generating job-related data and information and for establishing criteria that are both valid and useful for identifying job competency and performance effectiveness.

Industrial engineers study jobs to find ways to standardize, simplify, and specialize work procedures and to establish performance standards. Among the various methods found useful here are time and motion studies, micromotion analysis, and work measurement. Each method not only provides engineers with a better understanding of the job and ways in which to make it easier for a worker but also increases the overall productivity of the worker and the work group. These methods require a careful, detailed analysis of work requirements and usually have the major goals of finding a best way to do the job, determining what should constitute a fair day's work, and setting performance standards that provide fair pay for work performed.

Each of these methods was developed primarily for industrial applications and relates to jobs having observable and measurable manual labor inputs. Because of the costliness of these methods, they are normally used for routine and repetitive type jobs. They all provide work standards that come from an analysis of job content. They are not, however, free of subjectivity, and all require skill in the method being used. Both a strength and weakness of work measurement is that each job standard requires an individual analysis, which is time consuming and thus costly.

### Time and Motion Study

In this oldest and most simple of the three methods, an analyst makes a time study by closely watching a worker and using a stopwatch to time performance. Most studies include a detailed analysis of each work element. These studies relate each element to the normal time required for the entire work cycle.

Time and motion study provides data on the time required of a "normal" worker to perform a specific operation. A "normal" worker refers to a qualified, experienced employee performing at an average pace while working under the conditions that usually prevail at the work station.

Time-study analysts must have an understanding of the job and be able to develop a harmonious relationship with the employees being studied. They must also possess skill in rating workers (establishing the degree to which the employee being studied performs better or worse than a "normal" worker.)

## Micromotion Analysis

A more sophisticated approach than time and motion study is micromotion analysis, which requires photographing a worker performing a job. The camera operates at a constant speed, usually 1,000 frames per minute. By studying the film, the analyst can determine work patterns for each part of the body. By studying each movement and counting the number of frames necessary to document a complete cycle of work, a work-methods analyst is able to determine acceptable methods and set standards. Using this approach, Frank and Lillian Gilbreth established basic elements or fundamental human manual motions that proved most valuable for analyzing physical work relationships.

## Work Measurement

Following the work of the Gilbreths, time-study engineers devised methods for combining standard time value with each basic work element. By assigning time values to these fundamental motions, engineers are able to work in a laboratory, to synthesize the motions necessary to perform an assignment, and to set a time standard for the work under study. Some of the better known synthetic time systems are Methods-Time Measurement (MTM), Work Measurement, Basic Motion Time-Study (BMT), and Dimensional Motion Times (DMT).

## Narrative Descriptive Review Technique

The constant search for new and better ways to appraise performance has led to the development of a number of performance appraisal methods within the narrative descriptive review technique. These include the essay, critical incident, and field review methods. Each of these methods requires the appraiser to provide a written description of the employee's performance.

## The Essay Method

In the essay method, the appraiser must describe the employee within a number of broad categories, such as (1) the appraiser's overall impression of the employee's performance, (2) the promotability of the employee, (3) the jobs that the employee is now able or qualified to perform, (4) the strengths and weaknesses of the employee, and (5) the training and development assistance required by the employee. Although this method may be used independently, it is most frequently found in combination with others. It is extremely useful in filling information gaps about the employee that often occur in the more highly structured methods.

The strength of the essay method depends on the writing skills and analytical ability of the appraiser. However, many supervisors have writing difficulties; they become confused about what to say, how much they should state, and the depth of the narrative. The essay method can consume much time because the appraiser must collect the information necessary to develop the essay and then must write it. The essay method also depends on the strength of recall by the appraiser.

A problem arising with this method is that appraisers may be rated on the quality of the appraisals that they give. The quality standards for the appraisal may be unduly influenced by appearance and grammar rather than content. Thus, a "high quality" appraisal may provide little useful information about the performance of the appraisee.

## The Critical Incident Method

The critical incident method requires the appraiser to maintain a log, containing observations of what the supervisor considers to be successful and unsuccessful work behavior, on each employee. This method demands continuous and relatively close observation. Many employees consider this type of constant surveillance a threat that is damaging to workplace relationships. Time elapsing between the observed behavior and its description has a definite impact on the accuracy of the description of what occurred. Here again, recall ability strongly influences the accuracy and validity of the review.

An example of a positive critical incident is:

4/18   Employee demonstrated a broad range of job knowledge in uncovering the cause of a quality problem with product "A" that Quality Assurance had been working with for over a month.

An example of a negative critical incident is:

7/28   Employee responded impulsively and with little tact when employee "Z" refused to work overtime in order to complete a prior assignment.

Like the essay method, the critical incident method is time consuming, costly, and requires that the appraiser have good analytical skill and the ability to provide straightforward, honest descriptions. An appraiser who is an extremely competent writer and analyst may provide an impression to those reviewing the description that can bias the review either in favor of or against the appraisee. This is not to imply that competent writing skills are undesirable but simply that good writers have an advantage using these methods.

Although the critical incident method was designed to overcome subjectivity, it has had little effect in reducing rater bias. Raters hesitate to describe an event that they consider to be detrimental to a particular individual or that possibly casts a doubt on their own managerial skills or makes them look bad. They may also tend to be inconsistent; for example, they may attack one individual by blowing a situation completely out of proportion and then protect another individual by deciding that the demonstrated workplace behavior is not worth the time and effort it takes to describe it.

Workers frequently develop anxiety and hostility when they know that their supervisor is keeping a log on them. To protect themselves, they may hide their actions and keep information from their supervisor that, if known, could lead to a poor performance appraisal. On the other hand, knowing that the supervisor is keeping a log could lead to performance improvement.

The critical incident method is valuable in that it focuses on actual job behavior, not on impressions of ambiguous traits. Although the incidents do not lend themselves to quantification, they can be very useful when the appraiser counsels the employee or provides feedback on performance. The most valuable contribution of this method to the performance appraisal process is the likelihood of increased accuracy in appraisal ratings because of documentation of critical behaviors.

## The Field Review Method

In the field review method, the appraiser, normally a representative of the personnel department or a staff member of the specific work unit, interviews the employee's immediate supervisor. Based on the supervisor's responses to a series of questions, the employee is rated. This method does not use forms or rating factors. The appraiser provides a simple "outstanding," "satisfactory," or "unsatisfactory" rating.

Appraisers making field reviews normally receive training in how to conduct the interview and have developed their writing skills. Being independent of the work scene, they normally have less bias (for or against the appraisee) than the immediate supervisor. Even though the supervisor supplies biased information, the appraisers may be able to pinpoint areas requiring training and development assistance. Requiring the use of an additional person in the process increases the cost of the appraisal, but it may focus greater attention on the process by both the immediate supervisor and the unit conducting the interviews.

## Ranking Technique

The simplest, least costly, and possibly one of the more accurate appraisal techniques (especially in small groups in which the appraiser intimately knows each member) is the ranking technique. This technique requires the appraiser (normally the immediate supervisor) to rank from best to poorest all members of a work unit or workers performing the same job. The strength of ranking lies in the fact that the human ability to discriminate improves when comparing (ranking) one item with another. Its basic weakness is that many ranking techniques use a minimum number of performance dimensions, thus oversimplifying an extremely complex relationship, employee job performance.

### Straight Ranking

Straight ranking normally appraises employees relative to one factor, such as performance or effectiveness. This appraisal method gives very good results when appraisers are familiar with the members of their work units, have intimate knowledge of the job and employee inputs and outputs, and are able to suppress biases related to personality differences and to focus on work behavior. The straight ranking method can provide a high degree of interrater reliability (different raters giving the same results). A major problem, however, is that rankings are difficult to justify to those ranked, especially those who fall in the bottom half of the rated group. This type of ranking results in a zero-sum game, meaning that somebody wins and somebody loses. Since a basic intent of the entire process is to improve the performance of the organization, a zero-sum game is neither desirable nor valid. The goal is to allow everyone to be a winner. This is possible when performance appraisal leads to improved productivity. In this situation, most members gain increased rewards, including satisfactory recognition of performance.

Research indicates that practically *all* employees consider their own performance to be average or above average. Thus, from an employee's point of view, a below average ranking is unacceptable and, in most cases, is considered unjustified. Ranking can stimulate intragroup hostility, resulting in lowered productivity and more worker dissatisfaction. Ranking is weak in relating the members of one group to those of another. A relatively low-ranked employee in a high-performing unit may be superior to a highly ranked employee in an average or moderately performing work unit. Within the same unit, there may be considerable difference between the workers ranked fourth over fifth whereas workers ranked seventh, eighth, and ninth may be essentially the same in performance.

## Forced-Distribution Ranking

A slight variation of the straight-ranking method is forced distribution. This method requires the appraiser to allocate a certain percentage of work group members to certain categories, such as superior, above average, average, below average, and unacceptable performance. The distribution of employees to be placed in each category usually approximates the bell-shaped curve or normal distribution. Five percent fall in each of the top and bottom categories, 15 percent in each of the next two, and 60 percent in the middle category.

| Categories of Performance | Percentage of Employees to Be Allocated |
|---|:---:|
| Superior | 5 |
| Above Average | 15 |
| Average | 60 |
| Below Average | 15 |
| Unacceptable | 5 |
| | 100 percent |

Both the number of categories and the percentage of employees to be allocated to each can vary according to the design considerations of a specific business.

Similar to all types of ranking, the problem that develops is not the validity of the ranking, but the use of the ranking and what it means. It is certainly possible to take a group of employees in a particular unit and to assign one-third to the top group, one-third to the middle, and one-third to the bottom. If, for example, the bottom third are performing acceptably and are, in fact, more productive than the middle third of another group, of what value is the forced-distribution or, for that matter, any ranking?

An associated problem that arises when using any type of ranking concerns the merging of various ranked groups within an organization. Each rater must defend his or her rankings. This leads to defensiveness and hostility and makes it extremely difficult to perform the merger.

## Paired-Comparison Procedures

A number of paired-comparison procedures are available for ranking employees. They include the deck-of-cards, stub selection, paired-comparison ranking table, card-stacking, and alternative ranking procedures.

*The Deck-of-Cards Procedure.*   One of the simplest yet most effective of the paired-comparison procedures used for ranking a group of items is the deck-of-cards procedure. In this procedure, the rater:

1   Places each name or item to be compared on a separate card and into a pile.
2   Chooses two cards from the pile, compares them, and selects the best.
3   Holds the best in his or her hand and discards the loser into a new pile.
4   Selects another card from the first pile, compares it with card in hand, chooses the best, and discards the loser in the new pile.
5   Continues with this step, until the original pile has been depleted.
6   Places the card in his or her hand in a second new pile. This is the top selection.
7   Repeats all steps, using the first new pile as the replacement for the original pile for the eventual second choice.
8   Continues the process until all remaining names have been placed in the pile with his or her first choice. This gives the ranking for the group.

An additional step that may be included in this process to exclude rating bias is to perform the entire process a second time. Beginning in Step 2, the rater identifies the lowest or least important item and then builds to the highest by always returning to the pile that item rated higher. This reversal process should provide the same order of rank. Any discrepancy becomes an area for further investigation.

*The Stub Selection Procedure.*   The stub selection procedure attempts to overcome two basic weaknesses of other paired-comparison procedures: (1) the inability of the human brain to store and compare a large variety of items (in fact, it is difficult for most brains to compare more than five items at one time), and (2) the halo effect (i.e., once an item is judged to be superior to a number of items, it begins to carry an inborn superiority over items that follow.) In the following procedure, each number represents a name or term of items to be compared. In this case, the largest number circled represents a specific choice. The rater:

1   Cuts out the stubs.

2   Circles the largest number of each stub (the circled item is considered a vote).

3   Makes a pile for each circled item.

4   Counts the stubs in each pile upon completion of all comparisons.

The pile with the largest number of stubs is the highest ranking item, the next largest number is second, and so on. The lowest ranking item is the one that received the fewest votes.

***The Paired-Comparison Ranking Table.***   An adaptation of the stub selection procedure is to develop a matrix in which all the items to be compared are listed in both the rows and the columns of a table known as a paired-comparison ranking table. In the boxes formed by the intersection of the rows and columns, the appraiser places an "X" where the item in the row is more important, valuable, or some other characteristic than the item in the column. The item receiving the highest score (i.e., number of "X"s) is the most important item.

***The Card-Stacking Procedure.***   In the card-stacking procedure, the rater receives a deck of cards. Each card contains the name of one employee who is an immediate subordinate.

1   The rater is asked to make three stacks. Stack 1 contains the cards of all employees who are above-average performers. Stack 2 contains the cards of all employees who are average or acceptable performers. Stack 3 contains the cards of all employees who are marginal, below average, or unacceptable performers.

2   The rater counts the number of cards in each stack to see whether there are 30 percent in the above average stack and 30 percent in the below average stack. If Stack 1 contains more than 30 percent, the rater must identify the least effective performer(s) of this stack and place them in Stack 2 until Stack 1

## PAIRED-COMPARISON RANKING TABLE

| Columns \ Rows | Mes-sen-ger | Data Proc. Mgr. | Data Entry Opr. | Exec. Sec. | Com-puter Opr. | Sys. Anal. | Con-trol Clk. | Pro-gram-mer | File Clk. | Asst. Dir. | Total |
|---|---|---|---|---|---|---|---|---|---|---|---|
| Messenger | — | | | | | | | | | | 0 |
| Data Processing Manager | X | — | X | X | X | X | X | X | X | X | 9 |
| Data Entry Operator | X | | — | | | | | | X | | 2 |
| Executive Secretary | X | | X | — | X | | X | X | X | | 6 |
| Computer Operator | X | | X | | — | | X | | X | | 4 |
| Systems Analyst | X | | X | X | X | — | X | X | X | | 7 |
| Control Clerk | X | | X | | | | — | | X | | 3 |
| Programmer | X | | X | | X | | X | — | X | | 5 |
| File Clerk | X | | | | | | | | — | | 1 |
| Assistant Director | X | | X | X | X | X | X | X | X | — | 8 |

144

contains only 30 percent. Then Stack 3 must be checked for the 30 percent quota, and the same process is performed. If Stack 3 contains more than 30 percent, the excess is placed in Stack 2. If Stack 3 (or Stack 1) contains less than 30 percent, then the rater takes the best performers of Stack 2 and places them in Stack 1, or takes the poorest performers of Stack 2 and places them in Stack 3. Upon completion of Step 2, 30 percent of the employees will be in the above average stack, 40 percent in the average stack, and 30 percent in the below average stack.

3   The final step is to review Stacks 1 and 3 and place one-third of each stack in the best of the above average performance group and in the poorest one-third of the below average stack in a separate stack. There are now five stacks, containing the superior 10 percent, the above average 20 percent, the average 40 percent, the below average 20 percent, and the least effective or poorest 10 percent. Each stack of employees can be rated using the paired-comparison, deck-of-cards procedure to give a final ranking of all employees.

Paired comparison is unwieldy when one is comparing large numbers of items, as shown by the following formula. This formula determines the number of comparisons to be made for a given number of comparison items:

$$\frac{N(N-1)}{2}, \text{ where } N = \text{the number of comparison items}$$

For example:

$$\text{Comparing 7 factors, } \frac{7(7-1)}{2} = 21 \text{ comparisons}$$

$$\text{Comparing 15 jobs, } \frac{15(15-1)}{2} = 105 \text{ comparisons}$$

**The Alternative Ranking Procedure.**   Another available approach is alternative ranking. In alternative ranking, the appraiser has a list of all employees to be ranked. The first selection is the employee whom the appraiser considers to be the best performer. The name of this employee is placed on the first line of a sheet of paper that has numbered lines, one for each employee to be ranked. The appraiser then strikes the ranked employee from the list. The second selection is the employee considered to be the lowest rated performer; this employee's name is placed at the bottom of the list and is also crossed out of the original list. The third employee ranked is the highest remaining in the original list; fourth is the lowest rated remaining employee, whose name is placed on the rank-ordered list and stricken from the original list. This process continues until all unit members are ranked.

An alternative ranking list with 20 employees to be ranked is shown below:

1   Highest rated employee

2   Next highest rated employee

3   Next highest rated employee

•

•

•

18   Next lowest rated employee

19   Next lowest rated employee

20   Lowest rated employee

## Checklist Technique

A series of more sophisticated methods uses some form of checklist for measuring employee performance. This approach requires the development of a list of traits, behaviors, or other job characteristics that are useful for identifying successful or unsuccessful job performance. Normally, inputs from a large number of individuals familiar with the job provide the statements to be analyzed. These statements are standardized or scaled and cover a complete range of incumbent job-related behaviors. Raters select from these statements those that best describe the workplace performance of the appraisee. The checklist approach includes the simple checklist, the weighted checklist, and the forced-choice checklist.

### The Simple Checklist

The simple checklist method uses a collection of traits, behaviors, or other job characteristics. These lists may include from 15 to 50 different items. The rater reviews the lists and checks those statements that best identify the performance of the employee being rated.

Some typical checklist items are:

1   Maintains systematic and orderly records.

2   Instructs new employees in a manner that encourages learning.

**3**   Provides clear and detailed instructions to subordinates.

**4**   Uses company property only for business-related use.

## The Weighted Check List

The weighted checklist method adds a degree of sophistication by assigning a weight to each item, thus permitting a numerical score in the rating process. Normally, experts trained in testing and evaluation procedures review the items and, by using various psychological and statistical procedures, weight the items and assign a numerical value to each. The items may include those that identify both positive and negative job performance characteristics. Raters select those that best fit the demonstrated performance of the employee during the appraisal period. Generally, the rater does not know the weight or numerical value assigned to each item.

## The Forced-Choice Checklist

An even more sophisticated checklist method uses forced choice. This method involves combining checklist items into groups containing between two and five statements. There may be as many as 50 groups from which the rater makes selections. The design of the groups is usually such that each item appears to have equal desirability or to be of equivalent value. However, the items differ in their ability to differentiate between the more and the less successful performer.

The ability to discriminate rests on the fact that employees demonstrate a wide variety of behaviors in performing job assignments. Some behaviors are acceptable; others are unacceptable. Some acceptable behaviors relate directly to high-quality performance, whereas other acceptable behaviors have little or no impact on the quality of performance. On the other hand, some unacceptable behaviors relate directly to poor performance, whereas other unacceptable behaviors that may be distasteful to some raters have little or no influence on job performance.

In using the forced-choice checklist, the rater selects the one item that best identifies the workplace behavior of the appraisee. In cases where the group includes from three to five characteristics, the rater may be asked to select the item that best describes the performance of the appraisee and also the item that is least descriptive.

A simple forced-choice selection may require a rater to choose between the words *energetic* and *trustworthy*. Since both words refer to socially acceptable characteristics, it is difficult, if not impossible, for the rater to make a selection that has an intent other than to provide the most accurate description of the appraisee. A more complex forced-choice selection requires a rater to select from a list of statements those most descriptive and least descriptive of the employee's behavior. For example, a list may be set up in the following way:

| *Most Descriptive* | *Least Descriptive* | *Item* |
| --- | --- | --- |
| ☐ | ☐ | Reviews work of subordinates and provides assistance as needed. |
| ☐ | ☐ | Follows up on all delegated assignments to ensure conformance with operating procedures. |
| ☐ | ☐ | Requests employee opinions and uses them when conditions permit. |
| ☐ | ☐ | Meets deadlines on work assignments. |
| ☐ | ☐ | Praises those whose workplace behavior has earned recognition. |

Upon completion of a forced-choice checklist, the items selected as most and least descriptive (when requested) are grouped together. From these final groupings, "index of discrimination" and "index of desirability" scores are developed; these scores purport to identify the degree of successful job performance. (Discrimination refers to the ability of the rating technique to differentiate the effective from the ineffective employee; desirability refers to the degree to which the quality is valued.)

The major goal of the checklist technique is to minimize bias. In theory, the rater acts as a recorder of observed behavior, not as a judge. In this manner, he or she will not demonstrate typical patterns of rater bias. In reality, however, individual perceptions of actual behavior are still an unresolved issue.

The development of a weighted checklist and, to a far greater degree, a forced-choice checklist requires the effort of skilled professionals. Such checklists are extremely costly to design. Raters are also very leery of using any system in which they do not know the final determinations of their efforts and the effect that their ratings will have on the future of their subordinates (whether for pay adjustments or future career opportunities). The evidence available at this time does not indicate that the forced-choice method provides more accurate measurements of employee performance. This method also provides little opportunity for identifying areas of employee improvement or assisting through employee counseling.

## Rating-Scale Technique

The rating scale is commonly used and is probably the easiest to administer of all performance appraisal techniques. It uses a list of qualities that in some manner relates to job performance. Raters use scales to indicate the degree of the quality of performance demonstrated by the employee and observed by the rater. This technique is also known as a graphic rating scale.

Rating scales use words or phrases as labels to identify the degree or quality demonstrated. Each point on a rating scale must be meaningfully different. Although identification points on a scale can vary from two to more than fifteen, a scale of values that is applicable to most performance appraisal instruments ranges from five to nine. The description of George Miller's work in Chapter 2 about the processing of information and the magical number 7 plus or minus 2 also relates to scale design.

To provide effective distribution of scores, the scale must have an adequate number of intervals. When there are few intervals (fewer than five), there is a good chance that the scale omits valid measures of performance. When the scale contains too many intervals (normally, more than nine), the descriptors are repetitious and make it very difficult for a rater to distinguish between interval points. Weber's law of "just perceptible differences" is also valuable for understanding how many intervals to use on a rating scale. Weber's law resulted from investigations conducted in the early nineteenth century by Ernst H. Weber (1795–1878).[1] It states, "The increase of stimulus necessary to produce an increase of sensation in any sense is not an absolute quantity but depends on the proportion which the increase bears to the immediate preceding stimulus." More simply stated, the small perceptible difference in two objects is not absolutely the same but remains relatively the same; that is, it remains the same fraction (percentage) of the preceding stimulus. For example, if we can distinguish between 16 and 17 ounces, we should be able to distinguish between 32 and 34 ounces, but not necessarily between 32 and 33.

$$\frac{17 - 16}{16} = \frac{1}{16} = C_1$$

$$\frac{34 - 32}{32} = \frac{2}{32} = \frac{1}{16} = C_1$$

$$\frac{33 - 32}{32} = \frac{1}{32} \neq C_1$$

[1]*Encyclopaedia Britannica:* Micropaedia Vol. X, 15th edition (Chicago, IL: Encyclopaedia Britannica, Inc., 1974), p. 593.

Later in the nineteenth century, Gustav Fechner continued to work in this area and laid the groundwork for an area of study now called *psychophysics*. Psychophysics investigates the relationships between the magnitude of physical qualities and the magnitude of the corresponding subjective considerations. Current investigations now focus on complex situations in which there is no simple relationship between the stimulus as physically measured and the observer's judgment. This area of study may be extremely useful for the designing and developing of performance appraisal systems.

In the 1940s, Edward N. Hay conducted a series of studies based on Weber's law of just perceptible differences. He noted that a 15 percent or approximately 1/7 difference in the importance of one factor as compared with the preceding factor was discernible by trained raters at least 75 percent of the time.[2] This 15 percent difference provides a valuable criterion, index, or rule of thumb for a variety of uses when just observable magnitudes of difference are a basic input. In review, it appears that there must be at least a 15 percent difference between any two objects or factors in the compensation–reward area before they have a workable recognition or discrimination value.

With rating scales, the issue of *odd* and *even* numbers of interval points also arises. When an odd number is used, raters are inclined to use the average or central tendency values. This is not necessarily unacceptable because most employees do behave in an average manner, but all too often the appraiser uses a mid-value for rating a quality in order to escape making a decision. An even number of interval scales does not permit the rater to use an average value; rather, it forces a decision that differentiates among the large group in the middle—slightly above or slightly below average.

The typical appraisal instrument that uses a rating scale lists or describes a particular performance-related quality (e.g., job behavior, job duty, employee trait) and then provides some type of scale for the rater to identify the degree to which the employee has demonstrated that quality. For example, one of the qualities selected for appraising performance may be the trait "effort."

**Effort:**   Considers accuracy, neatness, and attention to detail; is industrious.

The next step is to develop a scale that measures the degree of the trait that best characterizes the appraisee. When the scale is a continuum with terminal anchors, such as

[2]Edward N. Hay, "The Application of Weber's Law to Job Evaluation Estimates," *Journal of Applied Psychology*, 34 (1950), 102–104.

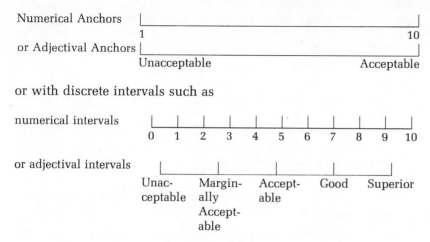

Numerical Anchors

1            10

or Adjectival Anchors

Unacceptable         Acceptable

or with discrete intervals such as

numerical intervals

0   1   2   3   4   5   6   7   8   9   10

or adjectival intervals

Unac-    Margin-   Accept-   Good   Superior
ceptable  ally      able
          Accept-
          able

the appraiser receives instructions to place a check along the line at the point or within the interval that most accurately identifies the degree of the quality or trait as demonstrated by the employee. A point score can be identified by the location of the check on the continuum. An interval scale provides the appraiser with more specific reference points when rating.

Another approach to scaling may be to provide a discrete or multiple-step rating scale in which the rater ranks the trait according to its importance in the performance of the job and checks the box that most adequately describes the trait characteristics of the appraisee. For example:

|  | *Not* | | | *Very* |
|---|---|---|---|---|
| *Effort* | *Important* | *Marginal* | *Average* | *Important* |
| (1) | ☐ | ☐ | ☐ | ☐ |

| (Considers accuracy, neatness, and attention to detail; is industrious.) | Provides less than acceptable effort. | Maintains minimum acceptable standards of effort. | Provides reasonable effort. | Consistently provides superior effort. |
|---|---|---|---|---|

(2) ☐☐    ☐☐☐   ☐☐☐    ☐☐

In (1), the appraiser rates the trait according to importance in the performance of the job. In (2), the appraiser indicates the appropriate degree of the trait for the appraisee.

Two widely used procedures for labeling scales are those using single words or short adjective phrases, simple adjective rating scales, and those using lengthy phrases or sentences that describe a specific observable behavior, behavioral-anchored rating scales (BARS).

## Simple Adjective Rating Scale

A simple adjective rating scale is one that measures a quality by descriptors such as *unsatisfactory, marginal, satisfactory, above average,* and *superior.* These descriptors may be defined as follows:

*Unsatisfactory:* performance clearly fails to meet minimum requirements.

*Marginal:* performance occasionally fails to meet minimum requirements.

*Satisfactory:* performance meets or exceeds minimum requirements.

*Above average:* performance consistently exceeds minimum requirements.

*Superior:* all aspects of performance clearly and specifically exceed stated job requirements.

## Behavioral-Anchored Rating Scales

Behavioral-anchored rating scales (BARS) are descriptions of various degrees of behavior between the most negative and most positive behavioral positions. These interval descriptions are critical if job-related behaviors are to be an essential part of performance appraisal. They identify in behavioral terms a complete range of behaviors relative to a performance dimension or performance element of a single job or group of jobs. Because of the number of behaviors that must be identified and the work involved in determining the levels of performance as related to a particular behavior, BARS are both difficult and expensive to develop.

Each behavior from most negative to most positive provides intervals for the assignment of specific numbers or points or is useful for setting some rating or ranking order for demonstrated behavior. By having the descriptors represent equal or nearly equal intervals, the behaviorally described performance appraisal can provide a point score for tying performance appraisal to salary administration and for assisting in implementing a pay-for-performance or merit program. By using BARS, instrument designers avoid the use of vague, universal descriptors, such as *always, excellent,* and *average.* They also minimize the use of vague concepts or terms.

**JOB DIMENSION: TRAINING**
**Ensures effective crew training.**

130

Ignores agreed upon training procedures.

Doesn't have sufficiently trained back-up on key jobs.

When crew member calls in sick or is pulled off job, foreman has no immediate replacement—has to train someone to fill in.

Doesn't check knowledge level of trainee before starting the training.

New people assigned to crew stand around waiting for instructions.

Has no written plans or schedule for crew training and upgrading.

Doesn't follow up on newly trained operations and check job knowledge.

Foreman tells someone on crew "here is new man, show him the ropes," does not set training guidelines to follow up.

105

Tells person how to do job, shows them when done wrong, but doesn't explain why or check whether person understands what he is doing and reason for method.

Replacements filling in for vacations/sickness cause drop in production/quality.

Expects understanding by "telling".

No follow up on training—does it once.

Does not have all jobs covered with back-up people.

Spends little time with crew in operating area—"expects but doesn't inspect" correct control.

Does some training but no skills inventory taken for department upgrading.

Has key position covered but not others.

80

Has crew fully trained for normal job functions and adequate back-up for all jobs.

Uses slack periods for training if people are spare.

When crew member calls in sick or is pulled off job, foreman is able to cover job with trained person in crew.

Foreman delegates training of new person to crew member who is a good coach, knows job well, and rechecks new or reassigned crews.

Foreman uses J.I.T. approach to structure skills training.

Instructor who is crew member uses J.I.T. approach in training new operator.

65

Foreman encourages crew members to take outside courses related to industry.

Has clear objectives for crew training and keeps abreast of changes in the operation which will require operator retraining.

Cross-trains crew where feasible to increase overall effectiveness or crews.

50

Foreman promotes and organizes upgrading program for crew (e.g., grading course).

Foreman determines training needs for each person on crew and sets up plan and schedule to complete this training by specified date.

Understands various training techniques (e.g., learning curves) and uses them.

Looks for more efficient training methods and upgrading programs.

Influences others in achieving a high level of crew training and assists with training in other departments.

0

FIGURE 8-1    BEHAVIORAL-ANCHORED RATING SCALE (COURTESY, D. H. LAWSON, CROWN ZELLERBACH CANADA LIMITED)

**153**

When the BARS that relates to a particular dimension or performance element is analyzed, there are at least two methods for identifying employee behavior. First, the rater selects that behavior statement that best identifies employee behavior. Secondly, the rater identifies a minimum threshold (i.e., no behavior listed below it describes the employee's behavior) and a maximum threshold (i.e., no behavior listed above it describes the employee's behavior). A combination of the two methods is possible.

The accuracy of the ratings increases when the rating scale relates to work activities maximally controlled by the appraisee, is relatively easy to observe, and adequately describes behaviors that assist recall.

Figure 8-1 describes a behavioral-anchored rating scale for a particular performance dimension—training. There is a further discussion of BARS and their development later in this chapter within the section related to performance dimensions.

## Mixed Standard Scale

The mixed standard scale was designed to minimize halo effect and leniency errors. This scale consists of three statements that describe good, average, and poor performance relative to a specific dimension or trait. The three statements describing a number of different performance dimensions or traits—Friedrich Blanz and Edwin E. Ghiselli identified 18 traits—are grouped together in a random order.[3] The Blanz and Ghiselli example has a list of 54 statements (18 traits × 3 statements for each trait). An appraiser then treats each statement independently of all other statements and appraises the employee relative to the statement. A "+" indicates the appraisee is better than the description; a "0" means the appraisee fits the statement and a "−" indicates the appraisee is worse than the statement.

The relatively large number of statements—in the example, 54—and their random order mix minimizes the chance that the appraiser will identify the designed order-of-merit of each set of descriptors. This in turn reduces the opportunity of the appraiser to rate the statements with regard to their designed order rather than honestly relating the statement to the appraisee's demonstrated workplace behavior. This type of scale permits a 7-point score for each dimension or trait being rated.

[3]Friedrich Blanz and Edwin E. Ghiselli, "The Mixed Standard Scale: A New Rating System," *Personnel Psychology*, Summer 1972, pp. 185–199.

## STATEMENTS FOR A
## DIMENSION OR TRAIT

| I | II | III | Point |
|---|----|-----|-------|
| + | + | + | 7 |
| 0 | + | + | 6 |
| − | + | + | 5 |
| − | 0 | + | 4 |
| − | − | + | 3 |
| − | − | 0 | 2 |
| − | − | − | 1 |

An example from the dimension:

*Ensures Effective Crew Training*

Good Performance Statement: Looks for more efficient training methods and uses them.

Average Performance Statement: Has crew fully trained for normal job functions and adequate back-up for all jobs.

Poor Performance Statement: Ignores training procedures and does not have trained back-up on key jobs.

The mixed standard scale, similar to BARS, requires a detailed job analysis to identify the basic or primary activities, functional areas, or responsibilities or performance dimensions of each job. Supervisors of those intimately familiar with the job are then asked to recall critical incidents which provide examples of good and poor job behaviors. Behaviors further identified as critical job behaviors are then related to the previously identified job activities, etc. The behaviors are again scored on a scale, e.g., 1 to 7, or 1 to 9, with 1 representing a very poor performance behavior and the highest value representing a very good behavior. From this list, the three statements for each activity or dimension are identified.

### Rating Scale Analysis

Rating scales are useful for measuring three general categories of performance-related qualities: job behaviors, responsibilities and duties, and incumbent traits. These categories of performance qualities are discussed in detail later in this chapter. A weakness in the use of any rating scale is its ability to be faked. If an appraiser consciously wishes to fake a rating, no system, method, or process will stop such behavior. Scaling techniques like BARS or the Mixed

Standard Scale, however, will minimize subconscious efforts to fake a rating. The strengths of practically all rating scale techniques are that they: (1) are relatively easy to administer, (2) translate directly to quantitative terms, (3) permit standardization thus allowing for comparability across various organization lines (departments, functions, occupations, jobs), and (4) relate to various types of qualities or dimensions.

## The Goal-Setting Technique

The performance appraisal technique known as goal setting can be accomplished by having goals set for a subordinate by a higher level authority or through a form of participation in which the subordinate has a voice in setting the goals. Chapter 5 discusses this technique in detail.

## Performance-Related Qualities

This chapter has included a discussion of various techniques, methods, and procedures available for identifying, describing, and measuring employee performance. When describing these various techniques and methods, terms such as job behaviors, responsibilities and duties, and traits have been mentioned but not defined in specific terms. Chapters 3 and 4 focus considerable attention on the identification and description of responsibilities and duties, and some attention is also placed on performance dimensions. We will now return to these qualities and add to the previous discussion.

### Job Behavior

With the advent of the Equal Employment Opportunity Commission (EEOC), concern intensified over developing testing instruments (performance appraisal in most cases must be considered a test) that do not discriminate against any group and that can be validated as being related to the job. In the performance appraisal area, attention focused on the development of instruments with a firm foundation in actual job behavior. Gathering and analyzing data and information necessary for the development of performance appraisal processes based on behavior follow the path described in Chapter 3.

The measurement of performance-relevant behavior requires intensive analysis of job requirements and extensive review of potential job behavior of employees. These efforts assist in identifying and describing the array of behaviors that employees are able to demonstrate when performing a specific job. A job content and job behavior analysis provides the following:

1   Identification of performance dimensions (factors);

2   Definition of performance elements—subdimensional or sub-factor criteria;

3   Determination of behavioral anchors for performance dimensions or performance elements; and

4   Development of behavioral-anchored rating scales (BARS).

In 1949, John C. Flanagan identified an approach that would improve the quality of performance appraisal by providing appraisal information based on actual job performance.[4] It uses the critical incident technique (CIT) developed by the American Institute for Research. This approach requires the systematic observation of actual job performance and behavior. These observations provide information that helps to identify and define *critical* job requirements. Flanagan defines such a requirement as a duty that the jobholder must perform in order to be considered effective or successful (or ineffective or unsuccessful) in job performance. This definition differs from the definition of a duty in Chapter 3. In Chapter 3, a duty is simply defined as a job requirement—an organizational demand for an observable work activity—and does not take into consideration how well or how poorly an incumbent performs it.) Individuals observing and reporting these incidents are normally supervisors or associates of the employee involved in the incident. The incident must relate to an important aspect of the work and must describe an *actual* behavior "which is outstandingly effective or ineffective with respect to the specific situation."[5]

Critical incident information may be obtained through personal interviews or in writing. G. P. Latham and R. R. Scott identify three questions that must be answered to establish incident quality:[6]

1   What were the circumstances surrounding this incident? (Background or context)

2   What exactly did this individual do that was so effective or ineffective? (Observable behavior)

---

[4]John C. Flanagan, "A New Approach to Evaluting Personnel," *Personnel*, January–February 1949, 35–42.

[5]Flanagan, "A New Approach," p. 42.

[6]G. P. Latham and R. R. Scott, *Defining Productivity in Behavioral Terms* (Tacoma, WA: Weyerhaeuser Company, 1975), p. iv.

3 How is this incident an example of effective or ineffective behavior? (So what?)

In one study, Latham and Scott interviewed 28 operators and 5 supervisors.[7] These 33 individuals were asked to reflect about the past six to twelve months and to describe specific incidents that they had actually observed. Latham and Scott defined an effective behavior as one that the observer considered to contribute significantly to accomplishment of the objective. Ineffective behavior, if occurring repeatedly or even once under certain conditions, would cast doubt on the competency of the individual performing the assignment.

A less rigorous procedure available for identifying critical incidents is to have experienced employees review a list of job activities and to identify examples of "good," "average," and "poor" behavior.

Critical incidents relating to a specific job can be collected over time. They can be classified under more general categories that relate closely to major job performance requirements. These major categories are often called performance dimensions, which are sets of related job behaviors or distinctive features necessary for job performance. An example of a performance dimension is:

*Application of Knowledge:* Analyzes work and sets initial work priorities before involving others in work process. Identifies critical work issues, information needed, whom to contact, and when to make requests to complete assignments on schedule.

There should be enough performance dimensions to cover completely all essential behaviors of the job.

Performance dimensions should be independent of every other dimension, but collectively all of them should cover the major behaviors required in successful job performance. This coverage is essential if an appraisal instrument using performance dimensions is to have content validity.

The identification of performance dimensions is derived directly from analysis of job content and job behavior. An analysis of goals set in the performance of a job may also be a valuable source for identifying performance dimensions. The analysis of job content focuses on identifying the responsibilities and duties of the job. This analysis also identifies the education, experience, and skill necessary to perform the job and the environmental conditions existing at the workplace. The analysis of job behavior, however, focuses on specific employee behavior that can be observed, defined, and mea-

[7]Latham and Scott, *Defining Productivity*, p. 2.

sured while the job is being performed. These types of analyses identify those behaviors that are critical to effective job performance and that comprehensively describe job requirements.

Jobholders and supervisors who are familiar with the job identify those performance incidents and critical behaviors required for performance. From a broad list of such incidents, knowledgeable job performers, supervisors, or skilled staff specialists identify those job behaviors that are similar in content, and they cluster them under specific performance dimensions. An issue that arises when any group of either job evaluation or performance appraisal factors is listed is whether they are equal in importance or should be weighted differentially. Resolving the weighting issue is one of the problems facing designers and administrators of the performance appraisal program.

In 1949, J. C. Flanagan identified six performance dimensions.[8] In a study conducted from 1972 through 1976, psychological researchers of Sears, Roebuck and Co. identified seven dimensions that relate closely to those established by Flanagan.[9] G. P. Latham and R. R. Scott identified four dimensions in 1975.[10]

| *Flanagan (1949)* | *Sears (1976)* | *Latham and Scott (1975)* |
|---|---|---|
| 1 Proficiency in handling administrative detail. | 1 Technical knowledge. | 1 Work performance. |
| 2 Proficiency in supervising personnel. | 2 Application of knowledge. | 2 Job commitment. |
| 3 Proficiency in planning and directing action. | 3 Administrative effectiveness. | 3 Interactions with others. |
| 4 Proficiency in technical job knowledge. | 4 Work relations. | 4 Planning, organizing, and setting priorities. |
| 5 Acceptance of organizational responsibilities. | 5 Response to superiors. | |
| 6 Acceptance of personal responsibility. | 6 Directing subordinates. | |
| | 7 Personal commitment. | |

[8]Flanagan, "A New Approach," p. 42.

[9]Robert H. Rhode, *Development of the Retail Checklist Performance Evaluation Program* (Chicago, IL: Sears, Roebuck and Co.), pp. 26–37.

[10]Latham and Scott, *Defining Productivity*, pp. 13, 14.

A performance dimension that validly relates to a job should be useful in the following four personnel areas: Selection, Training, Appraisal, and Rewarding (STAR). If a performance dimension is not appropriate or useful in any one of the four functional areas, its validity is highly questionable.[11]

Through the use of the critical incident technique (CIT) or a modification of it, employees identify performance elements. These are identifiable, observable, and measurable behaviors described in one sentence or a single paragraph. Information for writing these performance elements may be gained through personal interviews, a questionnaire, or both. By analyzing all job responsibilities, employees identify those behaviors that lead to job success or failure. From these lists of behaviors, specialists identify those that cover or fully describe a specific performance dimension. Behavioral analysts collect performance elements; then, through the use of factor analysis, a statistical procedure, they analyze these elements and group them with those having similar content in the more global performance dimensions.

When supervisors or specialists review performance elements for validation purposes, they answer questions such as the following:

1   How important is this element in your unit of authority?
2   Is it observable to the degree that you can rate an employee on it?
3   Does it contribute to effective job performance?
4   Does each employee have a relatively equal on-the-job probability of demonstrating the described element?

The acceptance or rejection of performance indicators depends on a review by two or more sets of qualified observers who are knowledgeable about the job and who are observing the same job behavior. These raters must agree about the importance of the behavior and the frequency of its occurrence.

The identification, validation, and weighting process may take the following approach:

Step 1.   A group of jobholders and their supervisors identify performance incidents (job-related behavior) required in the performance of the job under review.

---

[11]The STAR concept was developed by A. Daniel MacIntosh, Director of Management and Organizational Consulting, Southeastern Region, Towers, Perrin, Forster & Crosby, Atlanta, GA.

Step 2.    A second group of jobholders (performing the same job) and their supervisors review the performance incidents and assess the degree of job relevancy of each incident. The resulting relevancy rating scale may take this form:

*Relevancy Rating Scale*      *(Lowest Number = Highest Relevancy Rating)*

| | |
|---|---|
| 1 | Extremely Relevant |
| 2 | Very Relevant |
| 3 | Somewhat Relevant |
| 4 | Irrelevant |

Step 3.    A third group reviews and analyzes relevant performance incidents, combining those that identify the same behavior or that are so similar as to be difficult for most people to perceive as being different. The performance incidents now become the performance elements.

Step 4.    The elements are weighted as to their worth in the performance of the total job.

Step 5.    A final review ensures that each identified, relevancy-scored, and weighted performance element ties directly to the responsibilities, duties, and accountabilities of the job.

When performance appraisal instruments use a list of performance elements for describing a performance dimension, the list of elements is called a performance profile. In Fig. 8-1, the performance dimension is "training," and the groups of performance elements that describe various levels of the quality of training form a performance profile.

A review by experts of employee-defined behaviors that are critical to both superior and unacceptable job performance leads to the establishment of behavioral anchors. The behavior considered most negative or unsatisfactory and that considered most positive or extremely acceptable become the two behavioral anchors for the performance dimension or performance element. An example of behavioral anchors is:

*Most Positive:* Solves problems affecting job performance no matter how complicated or time consuming the resolution may be.

*Most Negative:* Fails to identify the critical issue when attempting to resolve workplace problems.

The middle-out approach is also valuable for setting behavioral anchors. This approach starts by identifying and defining standard behavior. The scales are incrementally defined in moving away from standard behavior. This allows for an open-ended setting of the most and least desirable behaviors.

The CIT is again most valuable for identifying and defining these anchor points.

This entire technique, using performance dimensions, performance elements, and BARS, is the easiest of all performance appraisal techniques to substantiate and justify. It comes directly from demonstrated workplace behavior. The potential for gaining face, content, and concurrent validity (see discussion on validity in Chapter 11) is far greater than in a technique based on worker traits.

### Job Responsibilities and Duties

The job responsibilities and duties technique directly concerns the responsibilities and duties listed on the job description. The rater appraises employee performance by using these specific responsibilities and duties as basic appraisal criteria. Because the technique uses these work requirements, a separate appraisal form must be developed for each job. The appraisal form lists the responsibilities and duties and criteria for identifying how well the jobholder performs each one. Responsibility and duty appraisal forms may also include space for the rater to indicate the relative importance of each requirement.

This type of appraisal often fails to recognize employee contributions that are crucial to work group and organizational success. In addition, this approach may fail to recognize environmental issues—situational demands—that have an impact on modifying performance relative to certain responsibilities and duties. Examples include willingness to accept additional responsibilities, adaptability and innovativeness in solving problems at the work station, and willingness to assist other members achieve acceptable performance standards.

Chapters 2 and 3 identify and describe the establishment of responsibilities and duties.

### Employee Traits

Performance appraisal instruments that use employee traits were introduced into industry along with the "scientific management" movement at the turn of the century. The traits used in these instruments are those characteristics firmly anchored in human behavior—distinguishing qualities of character—that manifest themselves on the job and that influence performance. To minimize differences in interpretation, each trait requires careful definition.

Even with such care, human perception will vary significantly among individuals. Another weakness of all trait-rating instruments is that a high rating does not necessarily correlate with good performance.

Traits have traditionally been the most common category of qualities used to appraise employees. Although trait-rating techniques have traditionally been accepted by management as being worthwhile indicators of performance, federal legislation and court rulings of the past 10 years have cast a dark shadow over their credibility. The integrity of trait-rating performance techniques and their ability to reflect actual performance have been questioned. There has been a minimal amount of success in validating a causal relationship between traits and performance. The many different ways in which people interpret traits and the potential for bias in any trait-rating appraisal technique have caused doubt about the worth and value of all trait-rating techniques.

Although there are literally hundreds of traits available for appraising performance, most techniques include from 10 to 15. The following are some of those commonly used:

| Punctuality | Cooperation | Personality | Industriousness | Loyalty |
|---|---|---|---|---|
| Attendance | Dependability | Judgment | Leadership | Application to |
| Effort | Initiative | Attitude | Self-Control | duty |
| Conduct | Intelligence | Adaptability | Resourcefulness | Acceptance of |
| | | | | responsibility |
| | | | | Concentration |
| | | | | on work |

In most cases, relevant worker traits can be described in behavioral terms and thus can be converted into identifiable job-related behaviors. For example:

Honesty (trait). Employee can be trusted and does not steal, lie, or in any manner attempt to deceive.

Honesty (job related behavior). Employee entrusted with valuable technical information and maintained confidentiality when competitor offered valuable inducements to divulge such information.

Honesty (job related behavior). Employee does not use company property and materials for personal use.

## Summary

The combinations possible from the various methods and techniques available for appraising performance are almost limitless. The pressure is on the designers and implementers to analyze their situations, identify the requirements they wish to satisfy, and select those methods, techniques, and processes that will meet both organizational and employee demands. Somewhere within the array of performance measurement instruments and tools lie one or more devices that will adequately and effectively perform the appraisal assignment. Unlocking the mysteries of performance appraisal requires knowledge of: (1) the measurement tools that are available, (2) who is to be measured, (3) the intended uses of appraisal information, and (4) how conflicts among these potentially conflicting areas may be minimized.

# 9

## Appraisers and Timing of Appraisals

Appraisal programs that meet business demands may require not only different instruments, techniques, and methods but also different appraisers who appraise performance and review appraisals at various times. Gaining credible performance information about employees who work at numerous jobs requiring a wide variety of knowledge, skills, and responsibilities in an almost limitless number of settings is a monumental assignment. It is difficult to conceive of a place or situation in which one instrument or one set of appraisers will be adequate to achieve performance appraisal objectives and goals for the business at one specific point in time.

A major barrier to effective appraisal of performance is quite often human, not technical. Measurement and appraisal of performance, in most situations, require analysis that depends on the human eye and brain. However, as Jacob Bronowski states, the eye and the brain provide an *interpretation* of reality, not a view of *absolute* reality. Related to the perceptual problems are problems that involve the human brain in storing, recalling, processing, and disseminating information. In addition to human intellectual and perception problems are those that relate to personal aspirations and expectations.

To overcome deficiencies related to these issues, many businesses develop appraisal systems that link the appraisee, various appraisers, and other review authorities into an integrative process. A first step in identifying ways to improve the inefficiencies and ineffectiveness resulting from human limitations is to review those persons involved in the appraisal process.

## Who Are the Appraisers?

Appraisers, raters, superiors, and supervisors are names that often identify those who appraise the performance of other individuals. At times, the process may involve members of the business other than the appraisee and a single appraiser. In fact, research indicates that the use of more than one appraiser is advantageous in reducing bias resulting from differences in appraiser perception and demonstrated employee behavior. Some researchers favor including appraisers who are superiors at levels above the immediate supervisor as long as the appraisers have adequate knowledge of the performance of the individual being rated. In addition to the immediate and higher level supervisors, some businesses promote self-rating and permit peers, co-workers, subordinates, staff personnel specialists, and at times, even external consultants to input data into the rating process. In addition to minimizing bias through the use of more than one appraiser, involving appraisers at different levels provides a variety of rating considerations from different points of view.

### Immediate Supervisor

Because of close contact, most businesses feel that immediate supervisors are best able to appraise subordinates. The immediate supervisor is the one person who should know the responsibilities and duties of the jobs within his or her domain and how the outputs of these jobs assist in the attainment of unit goals. Furthermore, an effective supervisor is aware of subordinate strengths and weaknesses and is able to relate demonstrated subordinate performance to specific individual capabilities. Among all possible appraisers, it is the immediate supervisor who has the greatest opportunity to observe the appraisee's performance and to provide feedback on how well the employee performed relative to specific performance criteria or job standards. The immediate supervisor is the one person from whom most subordinates want to receive performance-related feedback. They feel confident that the immediate supervisor knows job requirements, established workplace procedures, and expected outputs. Because of the supervisor's knowledge and better understanding of unique personal qualities, the appraisee feels more comfortable in discussing with the supervisor improved or preferred methods or changes in behavior required for satisfactory or superior performance. It is the immediate supervisor who establishes a workplace environment that makes it possible for subordinates to gain a sense of satisfaction from the work that they do and to feel that their efforts have been recognized and that they have made valued contributions.

Most organizations want four major pieces of information from appraisals:

1   How well is the employee performing?
2   Is the employee ready for a vertical promotion or lateral transfer into a job with different knowledge, skill, and responsibility requirements?
3   What kinds of training and development programs could be provided to improve overall present and future employee output?
4   Should the employee be demoted or terminated?

In most cases, the immediate supervisor is able to provide relevant information for each of these four critical areas.

It must now be apparent to the reader why over 90 percent of businesses having performance appraisal programs use the immediate supervisor as one, if not the only, appraiser of employee performance.

The major weaknesses of having only the immediate supervisor appraise performance relate to the personal issues that contaminate the appraisal process. In the beginning of Chapter 6 appears an extensive discussion of the types of appraiser errors and the forces that introduce bias to the appraisal ratings and impact on practically all human beings. Personal factors not discussed there that assist in contaminating appraisals are friendships, stereotypes, and irrelevant or poorly understood performance standards. These factors can bias any rating.

*Friendship.*  It is always possible for interpersonal relationships to bias a performance rating. In many cases, it is almost impossible to see a glaring deficiency in the performance of a friend. However, when someone we do not particularly like does one little thing slightly out of line, we are all too ready to initiate termination procedures. The friendship issue relates not only to specific individuals but also to groups. There is the possibility that the appraiser relates personally to a specific unit or group. (It may be a group that has always been particularly helpful and can be counted on to provide assistance when requested, a group the appraiser was once a member of, and so on.) The appraiser who has a group affinity may rate members of that particular group higher than individuals in other groups who perform equally well.

*Stereotypes.*  Like friendships, stereotypes are a typical personal bias that can contaminate appraisals. Most people develop an opinion about other people very shortly after meeting. Sometimes these first impressions are correct, and sometimes they are completely wrong. The issue facing appraisers is of not allowing first impressions to block out completely true recognition of what the person is and how he or she performs. Stereotypes can bias a rating either favorably or unfavorably.

*Irrelevant or Poorly Understood Performance Standards.*  This issue becomes increasingly important the further removed one is from the job site. Although it is entirely possible for an immediate supervisor to appraise an employee on criteria that have lower or minimal weightings as compared with other criteria or not even to know or understand just what the performance standards are, this situation is more likely to occur with appraisers other than the immediate supervisor. Frequently, employees establish, with the approval of their immediate supervisors, certain workplace behaviors that are not in line with standing orders or operating procedures. When individuals other than those having knowledge of the changes see what appears to be an unacceptable behavior, they may rate the employee improperly because of their lack of knowledge of what the workplace standards or performance criteria actually are.

*Other Contaminating Factors.*  Other factors that influence appraisal ratings even though they have little or no relationship to actual job performance are:

1  Membership in an elite unit;

2  Incumbent in a highly prized job; and

3  Appraisee's sex, (male), race (white), age, (30 to 35), tenure, (5 to 15 years in organization). Even height (over 6 feet), weight (slender), and other physical characteristics.

## Supervisors of the Immediate Supervisor

Some organizations require supervisors at levels higher than the immediate supervisor to review and, at times, to rate performance. (A discussion of review responsibilities follows this section.) A major reason for involving the appraiser's supervisor(s) in performing the actual appraisal is the thought that these individuals may have an even better understanding of what the employee should be doing and of the processes that the employee should be using to achieve a certain output. Supervisors on one or more levels above the immediate supervisor may be more aware of suboptimizing behavior and, by active involvement in the actual appraisal, may identify such activities and implement necessary changes.

From their vantage point, higher levels of management may focus on goal integration, methods used to achieve goals, unintended side effects from goal achievement, acceptance of responsibility, and job knowledge. On the other hand, the immediate supervisor may concentrate on accomplishment of responsibilities and duties and employee behaviors with which he or she agrees or disagrees but not necessarily those most desired by the organization.

## Self-Appraisal

Self-appraisal has received support in recent years as more businesses have become involved in participative goal setting. A valid participative goal-setting program requires the business to identify and subdivide objectives and goals and involved employees to develop their own goals that assist the group and organization to achieve theirs. Setting goals and then analyzing successes and failures gained in goal achievement provide participating employees with valuable opportunities for self-appraisal. Self-appraisal is especially valuable for self-development and the identification of training and development needs. It permits the employee to assess personal potential and to verbalize his or her desires for lateral transfer or future promotions. On the other hand, individuals who have high dependency requirements or low self-esteem are poor candidates for involvement in self-appraisal programs.

A major problem related to self-appraisal is that the great majority of employees feel that they are average or above average performers. From a literal definition of the word "average," half of those being appraised are above average, and half are below average. Thus, when a supervisor appraises an employee as performing below average, there is a great likelihood of a conflicting situation. Having employees appraise their own performance enhances or at least encourages employees to verbalize actively their discontent with the appraisal. Although this is a problem frequently related to self-appraisal, in reality, it is a problem that relates to all appraisals. If self-appraisal brings into the open differences in appraisee and appraiser perceptions, it is a valuable addition to the appraisal process. It is far better for employees to be able to voice their discontent than for them to suppress their feelings or to agree to a rating that they feel to be unjust and incorrect.

Regarding the issue that the "great majority of employees feel that they are average or above average," there are some legitimate answers to this problem. If an organization has existed for an extended period of time ("extended" must be defined by each organization), has done a careful job of screening job applicants, and has through performance requirements or normal attrition eliminated most individuals who have not met minimal job requirements, the words "average employee" may be misleading. Many organizations have large groups of acceptable employees (possibly 80 to 90 percent of the work force) and a group of superior employees that may range from 5 to 15 percent of the work force; the unacceptable performers may be as few as 1 to 5 percent of the work force. (This type of calculation would normally exclude new hires or those in a probationary situation.)

## Peers and Co-Workers

Although seldom used as appraisers, peers and co-workers may possibly have excellent insight into identifying leadership skills and future potential. However, some very definite problem areas limit or even negate the use of peer appraisals.

It must be remembered that the basic and overpowering need for security exists among practically all employees. Frequently, behaviors related to satisfying this need are not readily apparent, but they are demonstrated as soon as an individual feels that his or her security is threatened. Many individuals do excellent jobs of hiding security-satisfying behaviors even when they demonstrate such actions. The point here is that employees work for employer-provided rewards. Some great competition for current and future employer rewards exists among members of a work group. Employees see employer-provided rewards as a very discrete package, and, if someone else receives a desired reward, then it may be quite likely that these rewards will be unavailable to them. Employees have a very long-term perspective when it comes to working for employer-provided rewards. Reward aspirations and expectations may cloud how one employee perceives or identifies the performance of another.

Because of the above-listed reasons, it is quite possible that intra-group competition for employer rewards can raise individual levels of stress, accentuate the demand for self-protection, and encourage anxiety and hostility. Even though the high-performing organization needs some competition, activities that result in intra-group hostility and fears must be avoided if at all possible.

If an organization accepts the idea that peers can identify and analyze the personal strengths and weaknesses of their co-workers with considerable accuracy, and if that organization uses this information for reward purposes, problems may quickly arise. Once employees recognize that the organization is using information that they provided to make reward decisions that discriminate among its members, the informal organization will stop the flow of this kind of information. In retaliation, they may institute job-related behaviors that block the achievement of organizational goals.

An interesting observation about peer appraisals is that peers can provide information that is valuable for predicting workplace successes. However, research does not indicate that peers provide accurate assessment of workplace performance. A major reason for co-worker inability to judge performance accurately is that they look at a job and employee outputs differently from the supervisors of those jobs. Peers frequently do not have sufficient information on co-worker job requirements and actual performance to determine level or quality of performance. In fact, the very reason that businesses expend the time and energy to write and disseminate up-to-date and valid job descriptions, to promote goal setting, and to have the supervisor and subordinate sit down and mutually discuss goal attainment is to ensure that the supervisor and subordinate know and mutually agree on job requirements and performance criteria. If businesses need to expend this much effort for the supervisor and subordinate to understand and agree to performance requirements, why should peers be expected to understand them? And, if they do not, how can they accurately identify performance?

Because of the competition for rewards and the opportunity for friendship and stereotypes to bias ratings, one idea that has been promoted may make it possible to use peer appraisals in a relatively nonthreatening manner. Many employees recognize that peers can identify personal strengths and weaknesses (most likely, weaknesses) better than any other members of the business. There is a great likelihood that employees will accept peer analysis of particular deficiencies and will implement behavioral changes aimed at minimizing or overcoming these weaknesses. The issue is how peers can identify co-worker characteristics and how organizations can transmit this information to the affected individual without jeopardizing the employee's opportunities in the organization.

Telling employees that peer appraisal information is to be used only for counseling purposes by the supervisor is so much trivia. The more weaknesses are identified by peers, the greater are the chances that the supervisor will lower his or her esteem of that particular individual. Thus, this information has the opportunity of unfavorably biasing the supervisor.

A possible, though not fool-proof answer is the use of an in-house or external professional counselor as the only person to receive and review peer appraisals and to discuss them with each respective employee. The purpose of peer appraisal is strictly to assist the employee to become a more effective member of the organization. This approach will minimize the need to appraise a peer unjustly because of common, desired rewards or to overrate a peer because of friendship. In fact, true friendship within this type of a system may foster constructive criticisms that would never be identified under any other type of situation. Co-workers who would tend to be unjust appraisers would say nothing because their accusations could only hurt their cause, not help it. (If a criticism is unjust and is recognized as such in an open counseling session, the appraisee realizes some individual in the group has these feelings. Although this may put an employee on guard, he or she at least knows what feelings are present in the workplace.)

## Immediate Subordinates

Other seldom used but possible additions to the appraiser group are immediate subordinates. Although they tend to overrate their supervisor, they do identify his or her effectiveness in communicating job knowledge, interest in subordinates as individuals and team members, and skill in coordinating the subordinates' efforts into effective team work.

The major weakness of subordinate appraisal is lack of information regarding acceptable performance standards. Not understanding what their supervisor should be doing may bias the appraisal. Additionally, subordinates hold supervisors whom they perceive to have more influence throughout the organization in higher esteem. If subordinates find that their supervisor can gain special treatment either for themselves or their work units, there is the likelihood that they will appraise the supervisor's performance relative to this influencing ability rather than according to other and possibly more important demonstrated workplace behaviors (the halo effect in action).

## Committee

Using a committee for appraisal permits more than one person to have an immediate input. This approach allows various perspectives to be considered at one time. A strength of multiple raters is their ability to observe different behaviors. Committee members are usually managers one level above the employee being appraised and have had contact with the employee during the past appraisal period. The committee may also consist of managers at various levels who are aware of the employee's performance. However, just as committee appraisal may result in fair and just treatment, it may result in a "kangaroo court." A committee appraisal can be influenced by the same contaminating factors that bias individual appraisals. Another weakness in using committees is excessive use of time.

## Staff Personnel Specialists

Well trained specialists from the personnel department often assist in the employee appraisal. In most cases, when they are part of the appraisal process, they work together with individuals who have had the opportunity to observe the appraisee's performance directly (e.g., in the field review method of appraisal discussed in Chapter 8).

A 1977 study by The Conference Board revealed that almost 95 percent of the respondents stated that the *immediate supervisor* was an appraiser. Others identified as appraisers were *self* (about 13 percent of the time), *groups or committees* (about 6 percent), and *representatives of the personnel department* (about 6 percent). Representing less than 1 percent each were consultants (internal and

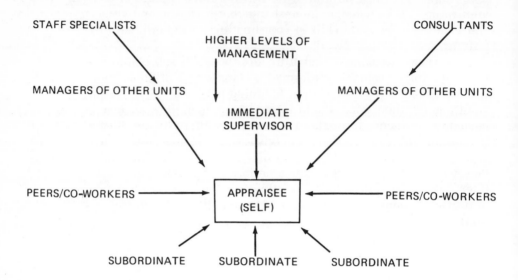

FIGURE 9-1    THE APPRAISERS

external), peers or co-workers, and subordinates (zero percent by this study).[1]

This study also found that the appraiser's immediate supervisor was a reviewer about 70 percent of the time, with the personnel department performing reviews about 30 percent of the time, and the appraiser's immediate supervisor's superior about 20 percent of the time.[2]

## Reviews and Checks and Balances

From the first pages of this book, concern and interest have been expressed regarding the barriers blocking successful implementation of an appraisal program. Complex interactions, perceptual differences, natural conflicts among uses, and human frailties are some of the more crucial issues that require constant analysis and review. Because of the quality and pervasiveness of problem areas relating to performance appraisal, it is unlikely that any program has a chance for long-term success without a review that includes various sets of checks and balances. These reviews and checks and balances must be incorporated into the initial design of

[1] Robert I. Lazer and Walter S. Wikstrom, *Appraising Managerial Performance: Current Practices and Future Direction.* Conference Board Report No. 723, (New York: The Conference Board, Inc. 1977), p. 26.

[2] Lazer and Wikstrom, *Appraising Managerial Performance,* p. 28.

the appraisal system. The major components of the review and check and balance subsystem are auditing and monitoring.

## Auditing

Auditing is a formal examination that reviews and verifies degree and quality of actual accomplishment. Auditing serves to identify how well the program is working, whether or not the program is meeting its objectives, and whether or not there are better ways of performing certain assignments. Systematic and methodical reviews analyze identified components of the appraisal system. The audits may occur at specific points in time or at irregular intervals. Areas or components to be audited may receive prior notice of an audit or the audit may be performed without any prior warning. Auditing responsibilities are normally contained within one especially designated unit of the organization. The auditing unit will normally be independent of any operating unit. After performing an in-depth analysis of a particular problem, the unit usually issues a final document that identifies the purpose of the audit, its findings, and recommendations for future actions to be taken.

## Monitoring

Performance appraisal monitoring is an integral part of the appraisal system. Some parts of the monitoring system operate continuously while others become active only when triggered by certain events. The monitoring process observes specific activities and, through a reporting mechanism, keeps tract of certain kinds of results. The monitoring process identifies such deficiencies as ineffective raters, unfair or inaccurate ratings, inadequate or poorly designed appraisal components, and so on.

*Higher-Level Review.*    A fundamental part of any appraisal process is higher-level review of approval ratings. As identified in The Conference Board study and in the discussion on supervisors of the immediate supervisor, many businesses require higher level managers to review the appraisals conducted by their subordinates. Through this review, more senior levels of management monitor and control the appraisal process. (Review authorities may be more than one level above the immediate supervisor.) Although this individual may disagree with the rating of the appraiser, the reviewer will seldom, if ever, change the original rating.

A major reason for review is to ensure the use of the same standards and to achieve consistency in appraisal ratings among the various supervisors performing appraisals. This type of monitoring and review assists in providing fair and equal rating treatment to all employees.

Active involvement and commitment on the part of the review authority can reduce rater bias. In most cases, even when the appraiser's superior actually does appraise the subordinate's performance, little difference is found in the two ratings. The secret of effective review is real involvement, not merely bureaucratic "rubber stamping."

Review by higher levels and members of the personnel department aids in linking performance appraisal to salary administration and pay-for-merit incentive programs. (This is the major focus of Chapter 12.)

*Appraisee Review.*   Many appraisal forms require the appraisee to sign the form upon completion of the review with the appraiser. Normally, there is a statement above the signature line that states that the employee's signature only indicates that the review has taken place and has no bearing on employee agreement with the appraisal rating. Many employees, however, will not verbalize a disagreement with a rating although they may feel very strongly that it is incorrect. Frequently, when appraisees have such feelings and sign the appraisal form, they feel that they are being forced into agreement with the rating and may harbor resentment against the organization.

*The Appeals Process.*   Possibly the most powerful check on an appraisal system occurs with the establishment of an appeals process. An open, participative appraisal system must allow employees to appeal to higher levels of authority those decisions or actions that they feel to be unfair, unwise, or unnecessary. The most critical component of an appeals process is the employee's right to appeal a particular rating. The process must be so designed and administered that an employee who does appeal a rating is not immediately branded as a troublemaker or complainer. An appeal must be thoroughly researched and properly adjudicated. The employee should be able to recognize employer concern and interest even when the appeal is lost. The appeals process provides base information for both the monitoring and auditing systems.

*The Attitude Survey.*   Another input to the monitoring and auditing systems develops through the use of the attitude survey. More and more organizations are using this valuable communication tool to improve their understanding of employee desires and concerns. It may not be necessary to design an attitude survey specifically to obtain performance appraisal related information; a number of questions in practically any kind of attitude survey could focus on the performance appraisal system. The anonymity of the wide variety and large number of employees who can participate underscores the value of this approach.

*The Computer-Based Information System.* An essential part of the monitoring system includes a computer-based information system that stores, analyzes, and disseminates appraisal data to appropriate parties. Because of the wide array of data collected, the various individuals who must have access to this data, and the need for the data to be quickly and easily accessible and available when needed, it is difficult to see how an appraisal system would be able to perform its many missions without computer assistance.

# Who Are the Appraisees?

A performance appraisal method used in the early stages of the Industrial Revolution was a rectangular piece of wood approximately two inches long and one inch wide that was painted a different color on each side and hung over the work station of each employee. Each day, the supervisor would turn the wood to the color that he thought denoted the employee's performance for the preceding day—black for bad, blue for indifferent, yellow for good, and white for excellent.[3]

Performance appraisal in the early part of the twentieth century also focused on operative employees. However, in the past two decades, there has been a notable trend toward eliminating performance appraisal among nonexempt employees and focusing on performance appraisal at the executive, managerial, and professional levels of the business.

One reason for the lack of interest in appraising nonexempt employees is the inability of businesses to develop valid and workable measuring instruments. Another reason is the strong allegiance of the operative levels to seniority. Many businesses consider their nonexempt, operative jobs to be highly procedural and technically oriented, and they think that all that is necessary to appraise performance of the operative is to measure output. If this were true, the idea of not appraising the performance of lower level employees might be valid. Often, however, this is not the case; even when the

---

[3] Robert Owen, "The 'Silent Monitor'" in E. C. Bursk et al. eds., *The World of Business*, Volume III, New York: Simon and Schuster, 1962, pp. 1350–1352.

job requires that the employee follow specific procedures, 100 percent performance goes far beyond the faithful performance of a list of activities.

Acceptable employee performance- at all levels has elements that are difficult to specify. Employee contributions that affect output quality, reduction in costs, and the identification and solution of nagging problems are evident at every level. Measurement of these contributions requires some form of appraisal. Acceptance of seniority as the only criterion for rewarding performance is not only unacceptable but also wrong. This does not mean that seniority should not be recognized; it does mean that seniority and on-the-job performance are not the same thing and may not have a direct relationship. It is almost impossible to operate a business that places a high value on human talent and individual differences without having a system for appraising performance.

## Appraiser Contributions

The various types of appraisers identified in this chapter provide different kinds and levels of inputs into the appraisal process. Table 9-1 analyzes the strengths and weaknesses of appraiser contributions to the appraisal process. This table assists the reader in recognizing what different types of appraisers can contribute, how their ratings can be joined to produce more effective appraisal ratings, and just where their interest and attention should be focused. Those involved in designing an appraisal process may find that their own scoring of this guidechart will aid in developing an appraisal system most useful for their respective organizations.

### Factors that Tend to Improve the Accuracy of Appraisal Ratings

1   Appraiser has observed and is familiar with behaviors to be appraised.
2   Appraiser has documented behaviors to improve recall.
3   Appraiser has a check list to obtain and review job performance-related information.
4   Appraiser is aware of personal biases and is willing to take action to minimize their effect.
5   Higher levels of management are held accountable for reviewing all ratings.
6   Rating scores by appraisers are summarized and compared with those of other appraisers.

**Table 9-1**
**INFLUENCE OF APPRAISER CONTRIBUTIONS AND PERSPECTIVES***

| Variables in the Appraisal Process / Types of Appraisers | Knowledge of Job Requirements, and Job Standards | Identification of Demonstrated Work-Related Behaviors | Provision of Job Performance Feedback | Assessment of Individual Capabilities | Identification of Behavioral Traits/Qualities | Identification of Transfer, Promotion, and Termination Qualifications | Identification of Merit Pay Adjustments | Influence of Behavioral Changes | Integration of Organizational, Unit, Individual Goals |
|---|---|---|---|---|---|---|---|---|---|
| Immediate Supervisor | 5 | 5 | 5 | 3 | 4 | 5 | 5 | 4 | 3 |
| Managers at Levels Higher than Immediate Supervisor | 3 | 3 | 3 | 2 | 2 | 4 | 3 | 3 | 5 |
| Self | 5 | 4 | 4 | 4 | 3 | 2 | 3 | 5 | 2 |
| Peer/co-worker | 3 | 2 | 2 | 3 | 4 | 2 | 2 | 4 | 1 |
| Subordinate | 3 | 2 | 1 | 2 | 2 | 2 | 1 | 2 | 1 |

5 – Extremely High
4 – Noticeably High
3 – Moderate
2 – Somewhat
1 – Little to None

* Ratings based on subjective judgment of author.

7   Appraiser focuses attention on performance-related behavior over which appraisee has greatest control.

8   Appraiser ratings are tied to quality of rating given and performance of units.

## Factors that Tend to Decrease the Accuracy of Appraisal Ratings

1   Appraiser rates appraisee only at times when administrative actions are contemplated.

2   Appraiser tends to inflate ratings when appraisees receive scores and results of appraisals.

3   Appraiser tends to recall more behaviors known to be of particular interest to higher level managers, whether or not they are pertinent, when his or her ratings are reviewed by such authorities.

4   Appraiser is unable to express himself or herself honestly and unambiguously.

5   Appraisal systems, processes, and instruments fail to support appraiser.

## The Timing of Appraisals

It has been common practice to perform a formal performance appraisal once a year. The proponents of the annual appraisal state that, if held more frequently, formal appraisals tend to become mechanical, worthless procedures. A semantics problem arises here regarding the meaning of the term *formal appraisal.* If it means completion of a special form, then this consideration may have some validity; however, if it applies to the entire process, then it is probably incorrect.

The appraisal process should be continuous. In order to identify successfully employee performance, potential, strengths, and weaknesses, formal elements may require consideration at least bimonthly or quarterly.

An intensive study conducted by the General Electric Company into the effectiveness of its appraisal system resulted in a Work Planning and Review (WP&R) report.[4] Among its conclusions were that comprehensive annual performance appraisals are of questiona-

---

[4] Herbert H. Meyer, Emanuel Kay, and John R. P. French, Jr., "Split Roles in Performance Appraisal," *Harvard Business Review,* January–February 1965, 123–129.

ble value and that coaching should be a day-to-day, not a once-a-year activity.

Some of the appraisal techniques and methods described in Chapter 8 lend themselves to frequent use and to certain forms (of a fairly simple nature) that require completion on a monthly, bimonthly, or quarterly basis. These forms by themselves or combined with other instruments, promote the on-going requirement as described in the General Electric WP&R report.

The bimonthly or quarterly appraisal process permits an averaging of a number of reports, thus deemphasizing the importance of any one appraisal or any one set of activities. Furthermore, the once-a-year appraisal may over-emphasize recent activities and thus distort their actual value.

In line with the General Electric study, research indicates that performance feedback is most effective when it closely follows the behavior to which it relates. Employees should not receive feedback solely on unacceptable or below-par performance. Feedback that recognizes above-standard performance is appreciated by most employees. Most people like to know that their supervisors are aware of what they are doing and to consider that their efforts are worthwhile and are making a valuable contribution to the achievement of group goals. Feedback on performance is the basic ingredient of the day-to-day coaching responsibilities of a supervisor.

Performance reviews in a well designed performance appraisal system include daily feedback sessions relative to specific workplace behaviors or at other appropriate times. Progress reviews that analyze performance goals that may lead to redefinition of goals or redirection of work activities may range in frequency from monthly to quarterly. They vary according to the type of work performed and the job knowledge of the incumbent. Finally, there is the annual review in which there is an analysis of performance for the year.

Some experts believe that annual performance appraisal should be separated from salary review. They feel that the annual review should focus on what has happened during the past year and where the future will lead. Coaching and counseling inputs relative to desired behavior changes and possible training and development activities should not be tarnished with discussions regarding change in pay or other compensation incentives.

It may be desirable to have two annual reviews with the annual salary administration and incentive pay session coming after the review and development session. However, almost always, the appraisee is taking into consideration everything that is said during this developmental review and is figuring out what it means relative to future reward opportunities (in-job pay increases, desired lateral

*Predetermined Time Periods:*

1   Daily or weekly performance reviews.

2   Monthly, bimonthly, quarterly performance or goal achievement reviews.

3   Semiannual or annual formal performance audit.

4   Formal audit upon anniversary date of employment or entry to job.

5   Specified periods during probationary period:

    **a**   30 days after entry into job;

    **b**   90 days after entry (may include next level of management at interview); and

    **c**   180 days (or near end of probation period). Identify retention, separation, or request extension for further training or job experience.

*Work-Related Time Periods:*

1   Upon completion of observable and measurable work cycle.

2   During a period of declining performance.

3   Upon conclusion of an exceptional performance.

FIGURE 9-2     GUIDECHART FOR TIMING APPRAISALS

transfers, or promotions with pay increases). Figure 9-2 identifies the various times for conducting a performance appraisal.

## Putting It All Together

An analysis of performance appraisal underscores its failures. Experience has proved the limitations of any one process, method, tool, appraiser, set of appraisers, or specific time for appraisal. The situation,[5] conditions, and organizational contingencies[6] may limit the use and effectiveness of performance appraisal.

[5] Mary Parker Follet, *Creative Experience* (New York: Longman's Green and Co., 1924). The author points to the *situation* and develops a social philosophy of management that calls attention to three factors in social situations: what the persons concerned are doing, what they think they are doing, and what they say they are doing. Recognizing the powerful impact of the situation on improved human relations requires a vast interweaving of ideas. It is not compromise but coordination that makes for organizational success.

[6] Paul R. Lawrence and Jay W. Lorsch, *Organization and Environment* (Homewood, IL: Richard D. Irwin, Inc., 1969). The *contingency theory* proposed by these authors asserts that organizations develop to meet contingencies forced upon them by their environments. In another article by the same authors, "Differentiation and Integration in Complex Organizations," *Administrative Science Quarterly*, June 1967, 1–47, the hypothesis is developed that organizations achieve various levels of *differentiation* because of task and environmental conditions that in turn have an impact on the education and experience of their managers, which affect their work styles and mental processes. Organizations also achieve *integration* of these diverse elements in order to gain unity of effort in accomplishing organizational goals.

Whether it is the wide variety of personal aspirations and expectations, the increasing series of interactions necessary to produce an output, the unending pressures from government regulations, or external social forces, the contingencies under which businesses operate require a broad range of managerial skills. The ability to combine a variety of processes, methods, and tools contributes significantly to business success. This applies particularly to performance appraisal.

Although businesses have been drifting away from the appraisal of nonexempt, operative employees, it is time to turn the tide by involving all members in the process. However, it may be necessary to design a different procedure for different groups because of changing situations and conditions.

It is possible that the traditional completion of an imposing appraisal form will continue to be an annual event, but on-going appraisal activities will support the annual report and assist in making it fair, accurate, and objective.

# 10

# Designing A Performance Appraisal System

A useful performance appraisal system must be a working example of the basic architectural design concept that *form* follows *function*. The functions of performance appraisal are the identification and description of employee performance and the assessment of individual potential. Job performance information is used to make decisions that include changes in base pay, awards of incentive pay, and promotion to more desired jobs (lateral or vertical), demotions, layoffs, and termination. From assessment information, businesses make decisions regarding training and development and potential for transfer and promotion for the employee. The instruments, forms, methods, and procedures must all provide valid and useful information for these vital employee-related decisions.

Information from performance appraisals must assist in obtaining the quality of decisions that will result in a more productive work force. It is most unlikely that any organization is able to generate information of sufficient quality and quantity to justify various compensation and staffing opportunity decisions without a disciplined, formalized performance appraisal system. Here lies one of the keys or basic building blocks for ensuring the efficient and effective use of human resources.

This chapter focuses on performance appraisal processes of five organizations: the Forest Service of the U.S. Department of Agriculture, Delaware County Community College, Southern Bell Telephone and Telegraph Company, the city of Greensboro, North Carolina, and Lincoln Electric Company. No attempt is made to describe the appraisal system of each organization completely, but a definite effort is made to describe through words and examples the major components of each plan, its purposes, and how it operates. Again, a warning: it is unlikely that an appraisal system developed by one organization can be transferred without modification to another organization and achieve the results desired by the transferring unit. One purpose of this book is to present ideas and examples of various appraisal systems and their components, but previous experience emphasizes the need to tailor what is presented to fit individual requirements.

## Forest Service of the U.S. Department of Agriculture

After years of effort, in the late 1960s the Forest Service devised a performance and career progress appraisal system to rate performance and promotability more accurately. The personnel specialists responsible for developing and designing the appraisal system used the critical incident technique (CIT), discussed in Chapters 6 and 8, to generate the needed appraisal information. Thousands of Forest Service employees contributed to the identification and weighting of the job-related information. From the CIT-generated information, job behavior elements and performance dimensions were identified and defined. The final design of the appraisal system includes 16 performance dimensions (called performance appraisal elements by the Forest Service), a profile of performance subdimensions that normally includes five to six behaviors that identify a specific degree or level of performance (behavior) of the performance dimension, and five rating levels—outstanding, superior, satisfactory, needs improvement, and unsatisfactory. Figure 10-1 is the appraisal instrument; Figure 10-2 provides a descriptive sketch of each performance dimension; Figure 10-3 is a behaviorally anchored rating sheet that provides examples of five different levels of behavior related to the performance dimension, maintaining quantity of work.

The system design does not require the appraiser to rate the appraisee on all 16 performance dimensions although an appropriate number of dimensions have been identified for each occupation. Lower level, unskilled and clerical jobs may require only four dimensions for adequate rating whereas a professional or manager may require nine performance dimensions. In no case are more than nine dimensions used because the instrument designers felt that nine or fewer dimensions are adequate for rating job performance.

One of the design features that provides individual tailoring for this system occurs when the appraiser and appraisee independently rank the importance of each factor in the performance of the job (New Profile column in Figure 10-1). After ranking the dimension, each party compares, discusses, and agrees to a final rank (Joint column in Figure 10-1). The accepted performance dimensions to be used for the next annual appraisal are called the Job Profile by the Forest Service. An inspection of Figure 10-1 shows that the Job Profile can change from one year to the next. The first column, Present Profile, identifies those performance dimensions to be rated during the current appraisal period. The Rating: Present Profile column provides space for the final rating of each accepted dimension. A rating of 1 is unsatisfactory and 9 is outstanding.

Figure 10-3 comes from the appraiser's Performance Rating and Discussion Guide. The appraiser, prior to the appraisal session, checks those specific statements (performance subdimensions) that describe the appraisee's performance during the review period (the four blocks in the check-off columns permit the appraiser to use the guide for four appraisees). A review of the distribution of checks

USDA-FOREST SERVICE

# JOB PROFILES AND PERFORMANCE RATINGS

INSTRUCTIONS: <u>JOB PROFILE</u>: Help your work supervisor decide which work activities are most important in accomplishing your job. Assign "1" in the NEW PROFILE; EMPL. column to the most important element, "2" to the second most important, and so on. You are required to rank at least four important elements and for most jobs there is value in ranking 9. Your work supervisor will follow the same procedure, completing the NEW PROFILE; SUPVR. column on another copy. Then you and he will meet. Look at each other's most important selection. Help your work supervisor decide which should be top for your job. He will assign a "1" in NEW PROFILE; JOINT column, then continue, assigning ranks 2, 3, etc.

<u>PERFORMANCE RATINGS</u>: Work supervisors must rate and discuss employee performance on <u>at least</u> the elements in his <u>present</u> profile (established at least 90 days ago). The ratings are N/A - not applicable; "1" - unsatisfactory; "3" - needs improvement; "5" - satisfactory; "7" - superior; "9" - outstanding, as described in the <u>Rating and Discussion Guide</u>.

| NAME (Last - First - Initial) | | 0 | 8 | 0 | SOCIAL SECURITY-NUMBER | AGCY. 1 1 | ORGANIZATION | R C |
| --- | --- | --- | --- | --- | --- | --- | --- | --- |

| DUTY STATION | NEW PROFILE PERIOD FROM: UNTIL: SUPERSEDED | PERFORMANCE RATING PERIOD FROM: TO: |
| --- | --- | --- |

| PAY PLAN (GS, WB, etc.) | SERIES | GRADE | POSITION TITLE | POSITION NUMBER |
| --- | --- | --- | --- | --- |

| PRESENT PROFILE | PROFILE ELEMENTS (See over for descriptions) | RATINGS: PRESENT PROFILE | | | | | | NEW PROFILE | | |
| --- | --- | --- | --- | --- | --- | --- | --- | --- | --- | --- |
| | | N/A | 1 | 3 | 5 | 7 | 9 | EMPL. | SUPVR. | JOINT |
| | 1. MAINTAINING QUANTITY OF WORK | | | | | | | | | |
| | 2. MAINTAINING QUALITY OF WORK | | | | | | | | | |
| | 3. FOLLOWING POLICIES AND PROCEDURES | | | | | | | | | |
| | 4. EXERCISING PROFESSIONAL, SCIENTIFIC, TECHNICAL OR CLERICAL SKILLS | | | | | | | | | |
| | 5. COMMUNICATING ORALLY | | | | | | | | | |
| | 6. COMMUNICATING IN WRITING | | | | | | | | | |
| | 7. ACCEPTING RESPONSIBILITY AND INITIATING ACTION | | | | | | | | | |
| | 8. RESPONDING TO NEED FOR EXTRA EFFORT | | | | | | | | | |
| | 9. ADAPTING TO NEW OR DIFFERENT SITUATIONS | | | | | | | | | |
| | 10. SHOWING CREATIVITY ON THE JOB | | | | | | | | | |
| | 11. EVALUATING FACTS AND MAKING DECISIONS | | | | | | | | | |
| | 12. PLANNING AND ORGANIZING OWN WORK | | | | | | | | | |
| | 13. RESEARCH LEADERSHIP; LEADERSHIP IN NON-SUPERVISORY SITUATIONS | | | | | | | | | |
| | 14. GETTING ALONG WITH OTHER WORKERS | | | | | | | | | |
| | 15. DEALING WITH PERSONS OR GROUPS OUT-SIDE FOREST SERVICE | | | | | | | | | |
| | 16. SUPERVISING OTHERS | | | | | | | | | |

| Summary: "X" one below ____ Satisfactory * ____ *Outstanding * ____ *Unsatisfactory (*See Personnel Office before checking) | **EMPLOYEE GRIEVANCE AND APPEAL RIGHTS:** An employee who is dissatisfied with the final rating (Satisfactory, Unsatisfactory, Outstanding) has the right to appeal the rating. Full information about appeals is included in DPM 430, and is available by contacting the Personnel Officer. | Position Accuracy: Is position description accurate? IF NO SEE FSM 6151.14c | YES | NO |
| --- | --- | --- | --- | --- |

**CERTIFICATION:** I certify that the above performance ratings and profile have been discussed.

| EMPLOYEE'S SIGNATURE | SUPERVISOR'S SIGNATURE | DATE | REVIEW |
| --- | --- | --- | --- |
| | | | |

(OVER)

6100-8 (4/70)

FIGURE 10-1     APPRAISAL INSTRUMENT

## DESCRIPTIVE PARAGRAPHS OF PROFILE ELEMENTS

1. MAINTAINING QUANTITY OF WORK: This element involves (1) amount of work completed in a day, week or month, (2) flexibility in accommodating work interruptions and changes in priorities, (3) dealing with difficulties and barriers to work accomplishment, (4) relationships with other work in the unit (like helping, hindering, or having no effect upon others getting their work done).

2. MAINTAINING QUALITY OF WORK: This element involves (1) the accuracy with which tasks are performed, (2) appropriate attention to work details that lead to "craftsmanship," or acceptance by the scientific community, (3) alertness to methods for boosting quality, (4) checking own work for adherence to standards (quality control).

3. FOLLOWING POLICIES AND PROCEDURES: This element involves (1) the knowledge of instructions, procedures, rules, and regulations and their appropriate use, application and purpose; (2) use of judgment and common sense in when and how the policies and procedures apply to a specific situation, and (3) advising others on policies and procedures.

4. EXERCISING PROFESSIONAL, SCIENTIFIC, TECHNICAL OR CLERICAL SKILLS: This element involves (1) the possession and application of specific knowledges and skills learned through schooling or experience, (2) keeping skills and knowledges current, and (3) acceptance (or nonacceptance) of beneficial new knowledge or techniques to appropriate work programs and problems.

5. COMMUNICATING ORALLY: This element involves (1) expressing information and instructions; (2) understanding replies or requests of others to enable completion of the exchange; (3) maintaining an attitude of willingness to listen and share information.

6. COMMUNICATING IN WRITING: This element involves (1) composition of reports of scientific findings; directives; letters; memos; proposals; and other official documents, and (2) use (or lack) of good principles of writing, such as clarity, brevity, yet with sufficient detail, etc.

7. ACCEPTING RESPONSIBILITY AND INITIATING ACTION: This element involves (1) the amount of personal responsibility taken for the completion of work, (2) the amount of work progress made without complete supervisory direction, (3) the willingness to think through work barriers, and risk making mistakes occasionally, to keep work going toward priority goals, (4) the conception of and movement on work that seems necessary to achieve priority job or unit goals, (5) the amount of action taken for self-improvement.

8. RESPONDING TO NEED FOR EXTRA EFFORT: This element involves (1) how one responds when emergency help is needed, (2) the depth of commitment to goals when barriers arise requiring extra effort, (3) the quality of the extra effort given, and the results produced, (4) attitude toward requests to expend extra effort.

9. ADAPTING TO NEW AND DIFFERENT SITUATIONS: This element involves (1) the amount of acceptance of, or resistance to, changing practices, policies, procedures; (2) the appropriateness of techniques used to respond and adapt to these situations; (3) the recognition of opportunities as well as problems in new or different situations.

10. SHOWING CREATIVITY ON THE JOB: This element involves (1) recognition of a problem, goal or enigma not yielding to present methods of solution and requiring creative effort; (2) identification of the relationships between key elements involved; (3) identifying a solution or answer and sharing it with others; (4) following through or implementing the solution to be sure it truly solves problem.

11. EVALUATING FACTS AND MAKING DECISIONS: This element involves (1) assembly of available information, data, or facts, (2) review, analysis and evaluation of those information, data or facts, (3) application of logic and decision making principles to the information, (4) selecting a decision from among the options available, and (5) sharing the decision with others as appropriate.

12. PLANNING AND ORGANIZING OWN WORK: This element involves (1) anticipation or clarification of the requirements of tasks or projects and their expected results, (2) planning, scheduling of the work to get expected results within budgeted time, (3) coordination of own plans with others when interrelationships exist, (4) advanced anticipation of problems.

13. RESEARCH LEADERSHIP; AND ASSUMING LEADERSHIP IN NON-SUPERVISORY SITUATIONS: Research leadership involves (1) the amount of one's contribution to basic and applied knowledge, (2) the amount of influence one exerts in the research community because of his research knowledge and experience. Assuming leadership. . .involves (1) amount and type of influence upon fellow workers or formal leadership, (2) amount of influence upon work standards, task accomplishment or outside groups.

14. GETTING ALONG WITH OTHER WORKERS: This element involves (1) amount and quality of cooperation offered to other workers, (2) contribution toward a productive, friendly atmosphere in the unit, (3) reactions to the inevitable personal pressures and stress put on the unit or its members.

15. DEALING WITH PERSONS OR GROUPS OUTSIDE THE FOREST SERVICE: This element involves (1) the image one projects of the Forest Service, (2) the amount of assistance given to outside persons and groups; (3) the honesty, tact, and courtesy extended to outsiders, (4) the amount of courage displayed when difficult confrontations are required.

16. SUPERVISING OTHERS: This element involves (1) scheduling and assigning tasks to and getting results from subordinates, (2) their training and development by self or others, (3) the morale and tenure of subordinates (4) setting or influencing standards of work and work pace. (5) This element also involves, when appropriate, supervisory responsibility in furthering equal employment opportunity.

## DEFINITIONS OF SUMMARY RATINGS

Satisfactory-Overall performance is acceptable. One or more, but not all of the employee's present profile elements may be at the "Outstanding" level. One or more, but not all of the employee's present profile elements may be at the "Unsatisfactory" level provided the performance in any one or more of the elements so marked does not seriously impair the work.

Outstanding-Employees rated outstanding on all present profile elements must be rated outstanding following endorsement by the appropriate reviewing body. Employees with 75% or more present profile elements rated outstanding may be considered for an outstanding rating by reviewer(s) so long as all aspects of performance exceed normal requirements and deserve special commendation.

Unsatisfactory-Performance in one or more of the employee's present profile elements is at the "Unsatisfactory" level and seriously impairs the work. The employee has been given the required 90 days warning notice and has failed to bring his performance up to an acceptable level after full and fair trial during such warning period.

GPO 898-842

FIGURE 10-2    DESCRIPTIONS OF PERFORMANCE DIMENSIONS

**1**

MAINTAINING QUANTITY OF WORK: This element involves (1) amount of work completed in a day, week or month; (2) flexibility in accommodating work interruptions and changes in priorities; (3) dealing with difficulties and barriers to work accomplishment; (4) relationships with other workers in the unit.

**1**

General Statement: The "1" employee is unsatisfactory. Often he is in passive or open rebellion to the established work quantity goals. He often fails badly in meeting quantity goals. He requires a good deal of supervisory prodding for even marginal performance, and without such prodding may spend his time on low priority or non-work Forest Service activities.

Specific Statements:
Lets outside interests interfere and decrease quantity of work  . . . . . .
Does not do work in terms of priorities, responsibilities, etc. . . . . . . .
Sometimes sleeps on job if left alone . . . . . . . . . . . . . . . . . .
Assignments are not completed unless he is prodded . . . . . . . . . . .
Does not boost quantity of work after requests by work supervisor . . . . .
Spends too much time on phone or writing personal letters during work hours
. .

**3**

General Statement: The "3" employee needs to improve. His quantity of work often drops below expected standards because of minor conflicts in priorities or small difficulties, or other things that normally are readily overcome. However, he exceeds the "1" because he accepts and works toward quantity goals. With a little more effort he could meet them consistently.

Specific Statements:
Not very flexible in switching from task to task . . . . . . . . . . . . .
Keeps busy but may select wrong priorities . . . . . . . . . . . . . . .
Usually does enough to complete jobs, seldome anymore . . . . . . . . . .
Mind isn't on work; just goes through the mechanics of the job . . . . . .
May do o.k. maintaining short range quantity, less well over long periods .

**5**

General Statement: The "5" employee is fully satisfactory. He can be counted on to give the Forest Service a full, honest days work. He exceeds the "3" because of the very few occasions that he fails to maintain quantity of work.

Specific Statements:
Work is turned out on time . . . . . . . . . . . . . . . . . . . . . .
Flexible in accommodating and coordinating the demands of the job . . . . .
Knows what tasks to do next . . . . . . . . . . . . . . . . . . . . . .
Uses "slack" periods to maintain quantity in other areas . . . . . . . . .
Chooses priorities correctly . . . . . . . . . . . . . . . . . . . . . .
. .

**7**

General Statement: The "7" employee exceeds the "5" by his consistency in meeting or exceeding quantity goals, the priority he gives to overcoming quantity barriers and the energy he expends in devising ways to raise output quantity even higher.

Specific Statements:
Completes own work and helps others maintain quantity of their work . . . .
Sets a work pace others try to achieve . . . . . . . . . . . . . . . . .
Keeps assignments and jobs organized for high production . . . . . . . . .
Wastes no time going to next task . . . . . . . . . . . . . . . . . . . .
Sticks to the job and sometimes gets bothered when others come to visit . .
Works rapidly . . . . . . . . . . . . . . . . . . . . . . . . . . . . .
. .

**9**

General Statement: The "9" employee exceeds the "7" by meeting or exceeding production standards under more difficult conditions; or, if the conditions and requirements are the same, by producing more work or by making more effective use of himself or his staff to combat existing or future problem sources.

Specific Statements:
Consistently completes all jobs in work plan, maintaining high output . . .
Recognizes his limitations and abilities and prepares ahead to maintain
high quantity of work . . . . . . . . . . . . . . . . . . . . . . . . .
Willing to work long hours and forego breaks to maintain high production
level . . . . . . . . . . . . . . . . . . . . . . . . . . . . . . . . .
Carries heavy quantity load but accepts extra projects as a challenge and
accomplishes them promptly . . . . . . . . . . . . . . . . . . . . . . .
Organizes all tasks for highly efficient and effective production . . . . .
. .

FIGURE 10-3     PERFORMANCE DIMENSION RATING GUIDE

then indicates the appropriate rating for the appraisee relative to that specific dimension.

The Forest Service system requires employee participation beginning with the ranking of important performance dimensions. It provides an opportunity for appraiser–appraisee two-way communications when they agree to a final ranking of the dimensions. At this step, both the appraiser and appraisee have the opportunity to see how the other party perceives the job and to gain insights into job priorities.

The behaviorally anchored ratings on the Rating Guide provide the appraiser with specific behaviors for both rating and discussion purposes. These dimension rating profiles not only provide examples of behaviors for each level of performance but also minimize the opportunity for the appraiser to use traits instead of observable and identifiable behaviors as measures of performance for discussion purposes.

The appraiser may use the Rating Guide as a critical incident check list during the entire appraisal period, identifying and even dating observed behaviors as they occur; the Guide is also helpful in providing the appraisee with feedback on the specific behavior. During the appraisal review session, the guide sheet is open for discussion purposes, and both the appraiser and the appraisee can see how the behaviors distribute over the rating scale for the dimension. By identifying behaviors when they occur, the appraiser does not have the traumatic experience of recreating the performance of the year in a brief preappraisal session review period.

Another interesting part of this system requires the establishment of the profile for the coming year before reviewing the appraisee's performance of the past year. This allows both parties to become involved and refreshed in job requirements and to start the session in a nonthreatening manner.

Although the appraisal system of the Forest Service has many strong and fine qualities, like all other systems, it has some weaknesses. One of the more notable is that some of the profile statements (subdimensions) are more trait related than behavior-oriented. A review of the profile example for all nine performance dimensions indicates a need for improved relationships between identified levels of behavior and activities performed in job assignments. It is apparent that appraisers can use this system and still inflate ratings unless their ratings are closely reviewed by the appraiser's immediate supervisor or superiors at higher levels. (The average rating of subordinates should relate to the overall rating that the unit receives from higher levels of management.)

Another potential weakness in the appraisal system relates to one of its basic strengths. Since the appraiser and appraisee select up to 9 from 16 dimensions for appraisal purposes, there is no one standard appraisal form for relating the performance of employees in the same job in various settings and geographic locations.

## Delaware County Community College

A community college in southeastern Pennsylvania, Delaware County Community College (DCCC), developed a performance appraisal system in the late 1970s. Their plan borrowed ideas, concepts, and forms from various sources. The result of their efforts is a system that uses objectives (goals, as used in this book) that relate to specific job responsibilities for rating employee performance. In addition to the individualized performance responsibilities— objectives and standards rating (Figure 10-4), they incorporate a standardized ten-dimension, annual appraisal form that permits the assignment of rating scores that allow for the comparison of employees performing a wide variety of jobs (Figure 10-5).

A strength of the DCCC plan is that it joins together the mission (broad organizational objectives) of the college with the objectives or goals of the individual members. The design of the appraisal plan attempts to focus on objective performance criteria related to the expectations of the *position* and attempts to minimize subjective elements of personality.[1] The system also contains training and orientation programs that identify the mission of the college and how to perform an appraisal, including performance review with the employee. The appraisal forms are completed annually, but each supervisor reviews the performance of each subordinate on a quarterly basis. At the quarterly review, objectives are reviewed, modified, or restructured if circumstances identify such a need.

The performance responsibilities (first column in Figure 10-4) are taken from the responsibility–duty section of the job description. They are selected and mutually agreed upon (supervisor and subordinate) as those responsibilities on which the subordinate will focus attention and are the basis for the objectives to be achieved. After the objectives have been identified, standards are set for appraising the degree of objective accomplishment.

The use of a standardized appraisal form is an excellent addition to the plan, but the use of personal attributes (traits) makes it suspect. Traits would be more acceptable if they were described in terms of the work accomplished. The issue in this case is to define

---

[1] Delaware County Community College, *Annual Performance Appraisal Process Executive/Administrative/Managerial Employees*, p. 3.

Employee: _____
Area or Unit: _____
Fiscal Year: _____
Quarterly/Final Review: _____
(specify one)

PART II—ANNUAL OBJECTIVES

| PERFORMANCE RESPONSIBILITIES | OBJECTIVES AND STANDARDS | COMMENTS RELATED TO PERFORMANCE ACHIEVED (Quarterly and/or final) | PERFORMANCE ACHIEVED (Place an "X" against the scale for each objective) (If "O," note under comments) 1  2  3  4  5 |
|---|---|---|---|
| | | | |

0 – Objective modified or delayed by mutual agreement (explain under comments, if applicable)
1 – Far below standard
2 – Below standard

3 – Meets standard
4 – Above standard
5 – Well above standard

FIGURE 10-4    ANNUAL PERFORMANCE APPRAISAL EXECUTIVE/ADMINISTRATIVE/MANAGERIAL EMPLOYEES DELAWARE COUNTY COMMUNITY COLLEGE

## PART III—PERFORMANCE FACTORS

### APPRAISAL TERMINOLOGY:

*0 = NOT OBSERVED/NOT RELEVANT*—This factor in question is either not applicable to the position being evaluated, or the rater simply cannot make a judgment concerning the particular attribute.

*1 = INADEQUATE*—Inadequate performance is performance that leads one to consider an employee a liability rather than an asset. This rating is to be used when an employee clearly fails to meet the minimum requirements of the area being appraised.

*2 = BELOW NORMAL*—This is performance that is below what can reasonably be expected of an employee after a reasonable period of time and training. It is nonsatisfactory performance.

*3 = NORMAL*—Is that which you can reasonably expect of a competent person. It is performance that is "Satisfactory."

*4 = ABOVE NORMAL*—Above normal performance is performance that exceeds the requirements of the job. It is performance above that which you would expect of a normal, fully competent person in this position.

*5 = OUTSTANDING*—Genuine outstanding performance is all you can possibly expect for the area described. It is performance that conspicuously stands out. It is performance that is uncommonly excellent.

| | | | | | |
|---|---|---|---|---|---|
| 1. Job Knowledge (Depth, currency, breadth) | 0 | 1 | 2 | 3 | 4 | 5 |
| 2. Judgment and Decisions (consistent, accurate, effective) | 0 | 1 | 2 | 3 | 4 | 5 |

FIGURE 10-5   ANNUAL PERFORMANCE APPRAISAL EXECUTIVE/ADMINISTRATIVE/MANAGERIAL EMPLOYEES DELAWARE COUNTY COMMUNITY COLLEGE

*PART III—PERFORMANCE FACTORS* (continued)

| | | | | | | |
|---|---|---|---|---|---|---|
| 3. Plan and organize work (Timely and creative) | 0 | 1 | 2 | 3 | 4 | 5 |
| 4. Management of Resources (Manpower and material) | 0 | 1 | 2 | 3 | 4 | 5 |
| 5. Leadership (Initiative, human relations, accept respon- sibility) | 0 | 1 | 2 | 3 | 4 | 5 |
| 6. Adaptability to Stress (Stable, flexible, dependable) | 0 | 1 | 2 | 3 | 4 | 5 |
| 7. Oral Communication (Clear, concise, confident) | 0 | 1 | 2 | 3 | 4 | 5 |
| 8. Written Communication (Clear, concise, organized) | 0 | 1 | 2 | 3 | 4 | 5 |
| 9. Professional qualities (Attitude, cooperation, bearing) | 0 | 1 | 2 | 3 | 4 | 5 |
| 10. Human Resource Participation (Sensitivity, treatment) | 0 | 1 | 2 | 3 | 4 | 5 |

FIGURE 10-5 (cont'd)

## PART IV—OVERALL PERFORMANCE

1. **CHECKLIST SUMMARY** (Reflects the total appraisal results covered in Parts II and III of the appraisal document. Primary emphasis should be given to the achievement of objectives under Part II

### APPRAISAL TERMINOLOGY:

0 = *NOT OBSERVED/NOT RELEVANT*—This factor in question is either not applicable to the position being evaluated, or the rater simply cannot make a judgment concerning the particular attribute.

1 = *INADEQUATE*—Inadequate performance is performance that leads one to consider an employee a liability rather than an asset. This rating is to be used when an employee clearly fails to meet the minimum requirements of the area being appraised.

2 = *BELOW NORMAL*—This is performance that is below what can reasonably be expected of an employee after a reasonable period of time and training. It is nonsatisfactory performance.

3 = *NORMAL*—is that which you can reasonably expect of a competent person. It is performance that is "Satisfactory."

4 = *ABOVE NORMAL*—Above normal performance is performance that exceeds the requirements of the job. It is performance above that which you would expect of a normal, fully competent person in this position.

5 = *OUTSTANDING*—Genuine outstanding performance is all you can possibly expect for the area described. It is performance that conspicuously stands out. It is performance that is uncommonly excellent.

---

### SUMMARY OF OVERALL PERFORMANCE

| 0 | 1 | 2 | 3 | 4 | 5 |
|---|---|---|---|---|---|

FIGURE 10-5 (cont'd)

traits in job content-related terms that are general enough to cover the variety of executive, administrative, and managerial employees of DCCC.

## Southern Bell Telephone and Telegraph Company

In the mid 1970s, Southern Bell Telephone and Telegraph Company implemented the Management Development and Evaluation Plan (MDEP). The purpose of MDEP is to help develop skills and job knowledge in the manager, to provide useful and valid performance-related information for salary treatment, to evaluate a manager's potential for advancement, and to provide feedback to the manager. Recognizing the importance of their human resources, the Bell system feels that it is imperative that all employees be given the opportunity for a fair and valid appraisal of their performance. The MDEP requires the identification of major job responsibilities, the setting of objectives, and the identification of results. Figure 10-6 is the MDEP Performance Worksheet that ties together and documents responsibilities, objectives, and results.

Since development is an essential part of the plan, attributes or dimensions that are valuable indicators of an individual's potential for successfully performing a higher level job are included within the MDEP. (Chapter 13 discusses in detail the development by American Telephone and Telegraph Company (AT&T) of the dimension for assessing potential.) MDEP uses eight of these dimensions that are observable and measurable by an appraiser. Southern Bell (an AT&T operating company) recognizes however, that a major factor in determining potential for promotion to a higher level in the system is current performance. To be considered for promotion, an employee must be performing in his or her current job at an above-average level.

Appraisal of job performance is a means of determining a management employee's effectiveness in fulfilling job responsibilities. The appraisal process includes orientation of subordinate, objective setting, progress reviews/documentation, formal review, and formal evaluation. Figure 10-7 is an Appraisal Cycle Flow Chart that lists and briefly describes the timing of performance and potential activities.

One of the first steps in the appraisal process is the identification and description of major responsibilities. These responsibilities relate to the job itself, self-development, and Affirmative Action. These responsibilities provide the foundation for establishing objectives. Because of the dynamics involved in the setting and achieve-

The form contains:

- Southern Bell
- **MDEP Performance Worksheet**
- Form 3098-A (3-78)
- Front
- Page_____ of_____ Pages
- Name
- Title
- Period Covered
- From:
- To:
- PDN
- Salary Class
- A — Major Job Responsibilities
- B — Objectives
- C — Results
- Supervisor's Comments

FIGURE 10-6    MDEP PERFORMANCE WORKSHEET

| PHASE | TIME FRAME | STEP | PERFORMANCE | STEP | POTENTIAL |
|---|---|---|---|---|---|
| I | Within First Week | 1 | Conduct Orientation On Performance, And | 1 | Conduct Orientation On Potential |
| II | Within First Month | 2 | Set Performance Objectives 3098-A & 3098-E | 2 | That Potential Dimensions Can Be Seen |
| III | Throughout Appraisal Period | 3 | Progress Reviews (Check Interim Objectives) | 3<br>4<br>5 | Observe, Classify, Document, And<br>Feedback Info. On Potential |
| IV | Eleventh Month | 4 | Formal Review · · · · · · 3098-A Col. C | 6 | Rate Dimensions And Evaluate Potential *3098-B 2* |
| V | Eleventh Month | 5 | Formal Evaluation · · · 3098-A 1 / 3098-B 1 | 7 | Evaluate Potential (Yes or No) |
| VI | Eleventh to Twelfth Months | | Establishing Composite Appraisal Rating on Performance and Potential (10, 20, 30, or 40) *Group Review* *3098-B 3* | | |
| VII | Twelfth Month | | *Feedback* Information On Performance, Potential, And Composite Rating Career Counseling | | |
| | First Month Of Following Appraisal | | RECYCLE—BEGIN WITH PHASE II STEP 2 | | |

FIGURE 10-7   APPRAISAL CYCLE FLOW CHART

ment of objectives, the MDEP includes the setting of interim or short-range objectives. Through informal reviews, the appraiser and appraisee provide feedback on progress toward achievement of both the interim objectives and the associated major objective. The appraisee has the responsibility of documenting ongoing interim objective-related performance; this, in turn, provides information for documenting objective-oriented performance. Changes in interim-oriented performance requirements may cause changes in the associated major objective.

To assist appraisers in determining the value of appraisee accomplishment, Southern Bell has identified six factors to use as measurement criteria. These factors are:

Difficulty of the accomplishment.

Amount of supervision and/or manager support required.

Other circumstances outside employee's control that facilitated or inhibited the achievement.

Effectiveness of the employee in reducing barriers to future achievements.

Employee's efforts to facilitate the achievement of others.

Contribution to organizational goals.

One of the great strengths of these six factors is that they assist in overcoming or minimizing a critical weakness inherent in any goal-setting performance appraisal process. This weakness is the judging of relative performance of subordinates—the comparison of goal achievement between and among employees. These six factors serve as guidelines that can be clearly understood by an appraiser and communicated to appraisees. This addition to the appraisal process further strengthens mutual understanding and acceptance.

To help appraisers improve their decisions regarding appraisee achievement, these six factors are further defined as follows:

### Difficulty of the accomplishment

What barriers had to be handled in the course of accomplishing the result?

What was the nature of these barriers and how difficult to handle were they?

Were the barriers avoidable? Were they a result of how the employee pursued the goal?

Did the achievement involve the employee's efforts alone or did it require cooperation and interrelating with others? How many others? What was the quality of the cooperation gained and interrelationships achieved?

How controversial was the goal, or activities required to achieve it? How did this affect achievement?

How did the employee's approach to the problem affect difficulty?

### Supervision and/or manager support required

How much of the supervisor's time was used in supporting the accomplishment?

How appropriate was the amount of time?

When the employee requested assistance, had he/she identified the problem, some alternative solutions, and the advantages and/or disadvantages of each?

### Circumstances outside employee's control that facilitated or inhibited the achievement

What happened to inhibit or facilitate achievement besides the employee's efforts?

What affect did such occurrences have on the overall achievement?

How appropriate was the employee's handling of the occurrence, given the specific situation?

What other problems, if any, were created by the employee's handling of the circumstances that arose?

### Effectiveness of the employee in reducing barriers to future achievements

How effective was the employee in establishing working relationships that will facilitate work in the future with the same people or groups of people?

How will procedures be established and, in the course of this achievement, facilitate further work in this area?

If the accomplishment was the solution to a problem, what other problems, if any, did its solution create? What other problems were solved in addition to the original one?

### Employee's efforts to facilitate the achievement of others

What did the employee do to avoid creating barriers for others or, in fact, to facilitate the work of others?

What kinds of things did the employee do in the course of achieving this accomplishment that contributed in some way to the organization as a team? Recall compromises, changes in methods, modes of interaction with other team members, and innovations to increase compatibility of his or her goal to group/team goals.

### Contribution to organizational goals

Did the employee make a special contribution to the organization beyond what is considered his or her normal responsibilities? (e.g., changed a method of obtaining and distributing printed material that saved money).

Which organizational goal was impacted?

How much was it affected?

Dollars, hours, or manpower saved, index improved.

Critical working relationship significantly improved.

If the achievement can't be quantified, then describe the impact.

The use of these six factors in no way eliminates the need for appraiser judgment. It does, however, provide a framework for minimizing personal biases. As the Bell system manual states, "A significant step toward objectivity can be taken if the appraiser takes care to be sensitive to points when his or her pet peeves, or personal likes or dislikes, start to impact the process inappropriately."

Bell system managers seldom use all six factors for measuring achievements. They have found that the first three factors apply more frequently than do the last three. It is quite likely that a certain factor may be weighted more heavily in a certain situation by an appraiser than at another time. The strength of the six factors is that they stimulate the appraiser to be more aware of the context of the situation and the total worth of the goal accomplishment. The six factors permit a look at the whole situation.

In addition, the six factors also assist in comparing the value of achievement of different goals. Responding to the following questions derived from the six factors allows the appraiser to identify significant achievements:

Which single achievement stands out as the most significant? Of the remaining, which is the next most significant? And so on.

Of all the achievements documented, which one seems to represent the person's most *important* work? His or her *best* work?

Which of the achievements will the employee see as most valuable?

How might supervisors of other organizations see the value of the employee's achievement?

How much of the employee's time was devoted to each accomplishment? For example, an achievement which consumed 50% of the employee's time might be most significant by this fact alone. Its mere overshadowing of other activities and goals in terms of time spent might strongly influence its significance.

On which achievements was the most positive feedback received? Negative feedback?

It is the major achievements, which best represent or indicate total performance, that should be documented.

In this process goals or expectations not met, or only partially met, should also be considered. Again, these non-achievements should be viewed in light of the six factors. However, non-achievements should enter further into the total performance decision only if their impact outweighs that of the achievements.

The entire performance-review process is one in which feedback provides the information necessary to improve objective-oriented performance and encourages and assists employees to develop and grow to the fullest of their potential. At the end of the appraisal period, the appraiser assigns a rating based on the demonstrated performance of the appraisee. Figure 10-8 is the Supervisor's Proposed Ratings form used by Southern Bell. The MDEP requires the appraiser to provide salary performance, potential, and composite appraisal ratings. In addition to demonstrated performance, the composite rating considers breadth of knowledge, company experience, and overall comparison to others in the same level.

After the appraiser (normally, the immediate supervisor) completes the MDEP ratings, a group of supervisors who work in the same department join together to perform a Group Review. The chairperson for the Group Review is normally the supervisor of the managers participating in the review. This Group Review meeting has the responsibility for verifying the salary performance potential and composite appraisal ratings. The Group Review also considers allowable percentages of salary performance rating distribution as applicable to the specific group, the comparability of similar jobs at the same level, and the appraisee's contribution to company goals. The Group Review can accept or modify the ratings of the original appraiser.

After completion of the appraiser and Group Review ratings, the appraiser and appraisee hold a formal feedback and career counseling session. At this meeting, there is a review of the various ratings, including a discussion of the Group Review decision. The

Form 3098-G
(11-78)

**Southern Bell**

**MDEP**
**Supervisor's Proposed Ratings**

| Name | Title | Salary Class |
|------|-------|--------------|

## Salary Performance Rating (SPR)

☐ Highly Proficient (HP)  ☐ Marginal (M)

☐ Fully Proficient (FP)  ☐ Unsatisfactory (U)

☐ Satisfactory (S)  ☐ Not Rated (NR)

## Potential Rating

☐ Yes – Potential to perform effectively at the next higher management level now evident.

☐ No – Potential to perform effectively at the next higher management level not now evident.

☐ Not Rated (NR) – less than 6 months in present level.

## Composite Appraisal Rating

☐ Should not consider for promotion at this time (NC)

☐ Consider for promotion within same level now (SL)

☐ Consider for promotion to next level now (NL)

☐ Outstanding candidate to consider for promotion to next level now (ON)

## Supervisor's Rationale for Composite Rating

| Supervisor's Signature | Title | Date |
|------------------------|-------|------|

FIGURE 10-8    PROPOSED RATINGS FORM

204

session provides the appraiser with the opportunity to request feedback on specific issues and to discuss developmental ideas. This is not, however, an in-depth developmental session; the most appropriate time to discuss developmental issues is in phase two of the MDEP, when objectives are identified and set and activities and behaviors necessary for achieving them are identified.

## City of Greensboro, North Carolina

In order to improve communications regarding employee performance between supervisors and subordinates, the city of Greensboro implemented a Performance Planning and Appraisal system (PPA) in the mid 1970s. The system was designed to encourage employee inputs throughout the entire appraisal process. The system integrates individual job requirements with unit objectives, which support the objectives of the city government.

The first step in the development of the PPA is the establishment of a performance work plan for each employee. The work plan identifies the job responsibilities of each employee and then requires the supervisor and subordinate mutually to project desired results for the appraisal period, courses of action to follow in order to achieve these results, and standards to be used for measuring the degree of success. Developing the work plan provides a forum for the supervisor and subordinate to specify expectations concerning desired results from the job and how they perceive it.

Figure 10-9 is a Performance Work Plan used for keeping a written record of the objectives and a brief explanation of work performed to achieve these objectives. The Greensboro system classifies objectives into three categories: new project or program objectives, routine task objectives, and personal professional development objectives. These objectives tell what the employee will do. The standards column tells when, how much, or how well it will be done and the resources necessary to do it. Priorities may be set as 1, 2, or 3, or as a percentage of 100 (see weighting section in Chapter 4).

The system calls for the supervisor to provide regular feedback to employees with quarterly performance reviews and an annual appraisal. For the annual appraisal conference, both the supervisor and subordinate review the activities of the past year and document reasons for successes and failures in achieving objectives. The annual appraisal form requires the supervisors to rate their subordinates' overall performance as Above Standard, Standard, or Below Standard. If, for some reason, the supervisor feels unsure about the rating to be given to a particular employee, he or she may delay for up to 90 days the actual rating and, at the normal time, give a rating

| Priority | Work Objective | Standards | Performance Notes |
|---|---|---|---|
| Weight Established For Each Objective | Target or Result to Be Accomplished in One Year Period | Time, Quantity, Quality or Resources Required | |
| | | | |

FIGURE 10-9      GREENSBORO PERFORMANCE WORK PLAN

of Extended. The extended rating should be used sparingly and only when it is in the best interests of both the city and the employee.

## Lincoln Electric Company

For many years, the Lincoln Electric Company of Cleveland, Ohio, has been using a relatively simple appraisal system that ties directly into their unique and world-famous annual bonus plan. In this system, supervisors appraise their subordinates twice a year on four performance dimensions: quality, output, dependability, and ideas and cooperation. Figure 10-10 provides an example of the report cards used for appraising the performance of production workers at Lincoln.

This appraisal system uses a forced distribution for rating employee performance. Each supervisor receives 100 points for each

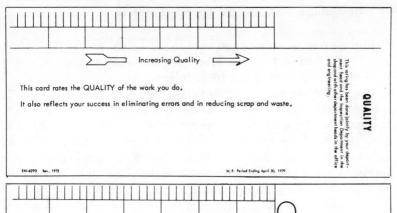

This card rates the QUALITY of the work you do.

It also reflects your success in eliminating errors and in reducing scrap and waste.

QUALITY

This rating has been done jointly by your department head and the Inspection Department in the shop and with other department heads in the office and engineering.

EM-629D  Rev. 1975                    M. R. Period Ending April 30, 1979

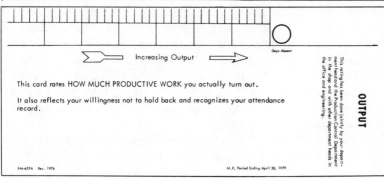

Increasing Output

Days Absent

This card rates HOW MUCH PRODUCTIVE WORK you actually turn out.

It also reflects your willingness not to hold back and recognizes your attendance record.

OUTPUT

This rating has been done jointly by your department head and the Production Control Department in the shop and with other department heads in the office and engineering.

EM-629A  Rev. 1976                    M. R. Period Ending April 30, 1979

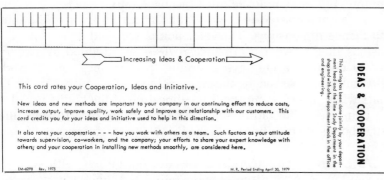

Increasing Ideas & Cooperation

This card rates your Cooperation, Ideas and Initiative.

New ideas and new methods are important to your company in our continuing effort to reduce costs, increase output, improve quality, work safely and improve our relationship with our customers. This card credits you for your ideas and initiative used to help in this direction.

It also rates your cooperation - - - how you work with others as a team. Such factors as your attitude towards supervision, co-workers, and the company; your efforts to share your expert knowledge with others; and your cooperation in installing new methods smoothly, are considered here.

IDEAS & COOPERATION

This rating has been done jointly by your department head and the Time Study Department in the shop and with other department heads in the office and engineering.

EM-629B  Rev. 1975                    M. R. Period Ending April 30, 1979

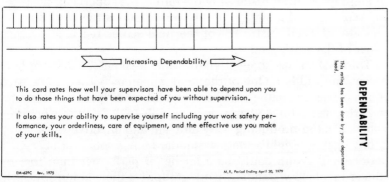

Increasing Dependability

This card rates how well your supervisors have been able to depend upon you to do those things that have been expected of you without supervision.

It also rates your ability to supervise yourself including your work safety performance, your orderliness, care of equipment, and the effective use you make of your skills.

DEPENDABILITY

This rating has been done by your department head.

EM-629C  Rev. 1975                    M. R. Period Ending April 30, 1979

FIGURE 10-10    LINCOLN ELECTRIC CO. PERFORMANCE REVIEW REPORT CARDS

subordinate, e.g., a supervisor having 10 subordinates has 1,000 points (10 subordinates × 100 points per subordinate = 1,000 points) to allocate among the 10 members.

The supervisor must distribute the 100 points for each subordinate among the four appraisal rating dimensions. On the average, each dimension for each employee receives a rating score of 25. It is entirely possible for a given employee to receive a score of 28 or 30 on a particular dimension, but this means that other employees in the supervisor's work group will receive less than 25 points, permitting the overall average for the group on the specific dimension to be 25.

For example, a supervisor ranks 10 members of his work group relative to the performance dimension quality and decides that the top-ranked employee performed excellently. He decides to allocate 30 points to employee 1. Employee 2 has done a job beyond expected standards in quality, and the supervisor rates this employee at 27. Employee 3 is slightly over expected, and the supervisor assigns this person 26 points. Four employees are right at acceptable and are assigned 25 points each. Three employees remain to be rated with 67 points to be distributed among them. One member performed just below expected and receives a score of 24. Employee 9 is rated at 22. Therefore, the last employee must receive a rating of 21.

All employees receive two ratings a year on each of the four performance dimensions. The total points received in all four dimensions in the two performance reviews are divided by two in order to obtain the employees' annual performance rating. Each additional point earned in the final rating can mean hundreds of dollars when determining the final allocation of the bonus pool for each employee. The rating scores at Lincoln tie directly into the annual bonus distribution, which, in 1978, was in excess of $41 million.

At Lincoln, the supervisors discuss the ratings with each of their employees. After discussing the rating, the supervisor posts the rating scores for all members of the work group at the work site. No names are attached, just a list of the final scores received by each member of the work group.

This system has some strengths and weaknesses that are both apparent and hidden. One of the more apparent is that, since each group receives the same number of points (100 per employee for each performance review), how is it possible to differentiate between members of a top-producing, very efficient and effective work group and one that is slightly below standard? A good producer in a superior work group could be a far better performer than the top producer in a below-standard work group, yet the good producer in the superior work group could receive a rating of 96 while an acceptable producer in the below-standard work group could receive a rating of 102. Although this is frequently encountered when there is a forced distribution among work groups and each group is considered to be equal in performance, it has not been a serious problem at Lincoln.

Another issue that relates to a forced distribution such as this one is that new members of a work unit may permit an escalation of ratings for the other members. This occurs since new members may receive lower ratings because of less experience and thus more points are available for older members.

An additional issue may arise when a poor performer terminates. This situation may result in the lowering of an employee's rating even though that employee's performance actually improved during the rating period. For example, a 90-point employee is terminated; the replacement is a good performer who receives a rating of 100. The supervisor now has 10 less points to allocate among the better workers. If the terminated employee was the only "bad apple," the rating of some other members must drop.

In the Lincoln Electric system, a superior performer is an employee who receives more than 110 points at any one rating session. When an individual receives more than 110 points and this superior rating has been approved by higher levels of management, additional points are allocated to the group with the superior performer(s). This additional pool of points permits a distribution of points to other members of the group, thus not requiring the ratings of other members to be unduly suppressed in order to allow for the superior ratings.

Even with these issues, requiring supervisors to rank employees is not an illogical or irrational consideration. Employees should know where they stand. There is nothing so definite as an employee's being told that he or she ranks 10th in a group of 10, or, even worse, 26th in a group of 26.

As one executive of Lincoln said, "This Merit Rating System is not perfect. We know it is not completely accurate, but it is done fairly and honestly. And we know that our people in the Lincoln Electric Company *believe* that it is fair and honest."[2]

No performance appraisal system designed by man to appraise the performance of other men will ever be perfect. The goal for which to strive is acceptance and belief by those appraised of the

---

[2] William Irrgang, *The Lincoln Incentive Management Program*, Lincoln Lecture Series (Scottsdale, AZ: Arizona State University, 1972), p. 21.

accuracy and integrity of the entire process. Lincoln is achieving this mission.

Although forced-distribution ranking may lead to some hostility between supervisor and subordinate, it may require that these two talk to each other so that the supervisor can explain what strengths and weaknesses he or she perceives and what both of them can do in order to improve the subordinate's performance.

The critical issue here is that the supervisor absolutely require "hard" data for ranking. The supervisor must be able to justify and *support* the ranking. In one way or another, businesses that pay employees differently according to their performance actually do some form of ranking, clustering, or banding (where individuals who perform similarly are grouped together). The issue that still must be faced is "Why was I ranked below acceptable and am receiving only a 4 percent pay increase while Helen received an above acceptable rating and a 10 percent pay increase?"

A problem that appears to be widespread among employees performing all types of jobs and from low-level, relatively unskilled work to the ranks of management is the feeling that "No one really cares what or how well I am doing." Whether it be immediate supervisors, other managers, personnel specialists, or outside consultants who do it, appraising performance and providing counseling support regarding employee strengths and weaknesses is certainly one way in which to combat this cancer of the workplace. In regard to an issue discussed in earlier chapters, people want to be appraised; they want rewards commensurate with their contributions; but the great majority of employees feel that they are "average" or "above average" workers. If businesses are to treat all employees as individuals and to provide equitable (not equal) reward treatment, it becomes absolutely essential that the technologies used to determine standards of performance and to identify actual performance be improved. Performance measurements must stand up under the toughest employee scrutiny, and at no time do employees scrutinize work standards more closely and carefully than when their paychecks are affected. It should be remembered that a demotion or termination is a paycheck consideration; termination is a $0 paycheck.

Requiring supervisors to do some form of forced ranking or forced distribution has its positive and negative sides. Done poorly, it can have as destructive an effect on morale and productivity as possibly anything that management can do. Yet, if businesses truly want to operate a pay-for-performance program, this may be the strongest approach possible. The issue here is truly not whether it is good or bad, but rather what must a business do to generate the data and information to support such a plan.

# Summary

These six appraisal systems do not provide examples for the use of peer–co-workers and subordinates as appraisers. (Southern Bell and Lincoln Electric do, however, provide for ratings by other supervisors or at least for their review.) They also do not provide examples of forced-choice type appraisal methods. A review of Chapters 8 and 9 in conjunction with the approaches presented in this chapter provides those interested in developing their own appraisal system with information that may be extremely helpful in pursuing such a venture.

In the 1980s, more organizations will develop and implement performance appraisal systems that identify and measure observable job behaviors. The outputs of these appraisal systems will permit employers to reward employees commensurately with their performance. The systems will also permit organizations to hold supervisors accountable for the efficient and effective use of their human resources. Employees will receive clearly articulated job requirements and performance standards and will understand that these requirements and standards will be used to measure their performance. They will recognize that productivity improvement is not only in the best interests of their employers, but also in their own best interests. To achieve these results, appraisal systems must be comprehensible and acceptable to appraisers, appraisees, and administrators.

The performance appraisal systems of the 1980s will be more complex than the six examples presented in this chapter. Employees will receive performance appraisal information continuously throughout the appraisal period. The appraisal process will use a number of appraisers for various purposes, ranging from measurement of performance to assessment of potential. Multi-appraisers will be used as checks and balances and to provide insights that one pair of eyes is incapable of viewing or identifying. The instruments used in the appraisal process will be both behavior and trait based. However, traits will be as valid an indicator of future performance as demonstrated behavior is of current performance.

To permit greater use of computer-based information systems (CBIS), appraisal instruments will use some kind of scale or scoring procedure to permit quantitative measurement for comparison purposes. Businesses with large numbers of employees must have available some kind of index that provides single or usable measures of performance for needed comparisons. These indexes (quantitative data related to well defined measures) would be used for pay-related decisions (base-pay adjustments and various kinds of monetary and in-kind incentives) and for training, promotion, and other types of desired advancements.

It should not be a surprise or unusual for effective appraisal systems to require continuous appraisals with multiraters that use multiple instruments consisting of various kinds of dimensions (variables or elements). The unique qualities of human beings are well known. Human nature is a multidimensional variable, as is job performance. It is unlikely that any simple or single method or procedure will adequately or accurately identify and measure human potential and behavior. For these reasons, a well-designed appraisal system will require auditing and monitoring processes.

In addition to the unique qualities of individual employees, each business must analyze the various groups included within the total organization. Appraisal processes and approaches must relate to variables in organizational structure and job requirements.

Organizational levels that may require different types of appraisals are:

Executives

Senior Managers

Upper level operating managers

Lower level operating managers

Operative employees

Occupational groups that may require different types of appraisals are:

Staff specialists/administrators

Professionals

Technicians

Skilled craftworkers

Equipment operators (moving and stationary)

Skilled assemblers

Routine assemblers

Maintenance workers

Clerical and administrative personnel

When an appraisal system for efficiency and effectiveness is analyzed or reviewed, it is easy to become overpowered by the techniques, methods, procedures, and instruments used for gathering, reviewing, measuring, reporting, monitoring, and auditing appraisal information. Everyone involved in the appraisal process must resist such temptations and recognize that the only valid measure of system efficiency and effectiveness is how well employee performance is measured and potential is assessed.

11

Government Involvement,
Validation Processes,
and Training Opportunities

With the passage of the Civil Rights Act of 1964, the federal government began taking an active interest in employment/personnel practices that discriminate unfairly against any individual because of race, religion, sex, color, or national origin. The Equal Employment Opportunity Commission (EEOC), the federal agency responsible for administering and enforcing the Civil Rights Act of 1964, as amended, looks with extreme disfavor on any employer who measures job performance and uses the measurement data to make personnel decisions in such a manner that job-relatedness cannot be demonstrated. To be in compliance with the Act, to avoid costly lawsuits, and to demonstrate good personnel practices, employers are reviewing the various instruments that they use for test purposes to ensure their validity and reliability. (A test is any method, process, or procedure used in making employment decisions that sort individuals on relative capability to perform important job functions.)

Court rulings and EEOC's interpretations and guidelines that relate to Section 703(h) of Title VII of the Civil Rights Act of 1964 have made organizations very cautious about implementing any personnel-related action that may be considered discriminatory. Section 703(h) states:

It is not an unlawful practice for an employer to give and act upon the result of any professionally developed ability test provided that such test, its administration or action upon the results is not designed, intended or used to discriminate because of race, color, religion, sex, or national origin.

### Government Regulations, Court Rulings, and Performance Appraisal

Employees constantly exert pressure on supervisors to learn where they stand and on managers to provide an equitable relationship between pay and performance. As if these internal pressures were not enough for management to face, legislation and court rulings make the entire appraisal process more complex and difficult to manage.

Title VII of the Civil Rights Act of 1964 and EEOC guidelines state that:

1   Employers must take affirmative action not to discriminate because of race, color, religion, sex, or national origin when making employment decisions.

2   Employment decisions include those involved in the selection, training, transfer, retention, and promotion processes.

3   Any paper-and-pencil or performance measure used in making employment decisions is a test.

4   A test must be fairly administered and empirically validated. (A test is any selection device used to hire, promote, demote, provide merit increases, or permit entry to training programs.)

Most formal performance appraisal techniques rely on paper-and-pencil methods to identify employee work behavior. The information provided by these techniques assists management in making employment decisions. The EEOC and the courts recognize the impact that the appraisal process has on employment opportunities and the possibility of inherent bias in many parts of the process. The EEOC and the courts have played and will continue to play an important role in the development of the process of performance appraisal.

*Uniform Guidelines On Employee Selection Procedures (1978).* To accomplish a coordinated approach to federal requirements regarding employee selection, the EEOC issued the *Uniform Guidelines on Employment Selection Procedures (1978).* These guidelines have an impact on performance appraisal because appraisal continues to be viewed as a selection procedure. The guidelines provide detailed standards regarding minimum validation requirements, with particular emphasis on content and construct validation efforts. To assure compliance with the Uniform Guidelines, those involved in selection procedures may either validate the selection instrument or use a system of quotas. Quotas, however, are difficult to implement and cause an almost unacceptable amount of discontent within the work force. Additionally, recent Supreme Court rulings on quotas [*Regents of The University of California v. Baake*, 97 S. Ct. 2733 (1978); 17 FEP Cases 1000] and [United Steelworkers of America v. Weber, 99 S. Ct. 2721 (1979); 20 FEP Cases 1] have failed to clarify a legally acceptable approach to quotas. Validation also is easier said than done. If performance appraisal is truly a system, a validation process may require that all components of the system and the system as a whole be validated. At this time, validation of performance appraisal instruments has been slow and has achieved minimal success. Little effort has been directed toward validating performance appraisal systems.

The 1978 *Uniform Guidelines* states that a selection procedure must not adversely impact on any group protected by Title VII of The Civil Rights Act of 1964. The *Guidelines* further defines adverse impact as a selection rate for any Title VII group that is less than 80 percent of the rate for the group with the highest rate. This is known as the "rule of thumb" or 4/5ths rule. When the overall selection process does not adversely impact on protected groups, EEOC will normally not examine the individual components of the selection process for evidence of validity. The *Guidelines* calls this approach the "bottom line."

A review of some of the court rulings that have identified and defined the responsibilities that management must accept in designing and managing appraisal programs indicates the direction that organizations must take with performance appraisal.

*Albemarle Paper Company v. Moody, 95 S. Ct. 2362 (1975); 10 FEP Cases 1181.*   Supervisors must use some criteria in making employment decisions. Performance ratings that do not have a job-content base have a built-in bias, and such tests must be validated statistically.

*Allen v. City of Mobile, 331 F. Supp. 1134 (1971); 3 FEP Cases 1226.*   Service ratings of black police officers were discriminatory. Special performance appraisal programs outlined by the court must be implemented.

*Brito v. Zia Company, 478 F.2d 1200 (1973); 5 FEP Cases 1207.* Performance appraisal ratings resulted in the layoff of a disproportionate number of Spanish surnamed employees. The court concluded that the practice was illegal because (1) the ratings were based on subjective supervisory observations, (2) the ratings were not administered and scored in a controlled and standardized fashion, and (3) some appraisers had little daily contact with the appraisees.

*Davis v. Washington, D.C., 426 U. S. 229 (1976); 12 FEP Cases 1415.*   Face validity is sufficient for validating police officer selection and training tests.

*Douglas v. Hampton, 512 F.2d 976 (1975); 10 FEP Cases 91.* Content validity is to be employed only in those instances where criterion-related validity is proven to be infeasible.

*Dowdell v. Dun & Bradstreet, Inc., 14 EPD ¶7797 (U.S. Dist. Ct., Ala., 1977).*   An employee claiming discrimination in an employment decision lost the case when the business provided detailed, comprehensive information on the quality and quantity of work done by individuals involved in the promotion decision.

*Flowers* v. *Crouch-Walker Corporation, 552 F.2d 1277 (1977); 14 FEP Cases 1265.* The employer had not expressed displeasure with an employee's performance prior to dismissal and the employee was subsequently replaced by a white employee. This resulted in a prima facie case of racial discrimination as the employee was qualified for the job and met normal job requirements.

*Griggs* v. *Duke Power Company, 91 S. Ct. 849 (1971); 3 FEP Cases 175.* In this landmark case, the central issue was that an educational restriction on an employment decision is useless unless it can be proven that there exists a bona fide occupational qualification (BFOQ) between the test and actual job performance. The burden of proof is on the employer to show nondiscrimination in any employment decision related to discrimination.

The decision in the *Griggs* case also states that "The Equal Employment Opportunity Commission having enforcement responsibility has issued guidelines interpreting Section 703(h) to permit only the use of job related tests. The administrative interpretation of the Act by the enforcing agency is entitled to great deference."

*James* v. *Stockham Valves and Fittings Company, 559 F.2d 310 (1977); 15 FEP Cases 827.* A program for selecting individuals for an apprenticeship program was discriminatory since selections were made by predominantly white supervisors without any formal written guidelines and a disproportionately low number of blacks were selected for the program.

*McDonald* v. *Santa Fe Trail Transportation Co., Inc., 96 S. Ct. 2574 (1976); 12 FEP Cases 1577.* Reverse discrimination is illegal. The Civil Rights Act covers all employees.

*McDonnell Douglas Corporation* v. *Green, 94 S. Ct. 31 (1973); 5 FEP Cases 915.* Simple proof is enough to prove nondiscrimination, but tests must be job related.

*Rogers* v. *International Paper Company, 510 F.2d 1340 (1975); 10 FEP Cases 404.* The use of subjective considerations was considered when a court ruled that in all fairness to applicants and employers alike decisions about hiring and promotion in supervisory and managerial jobs cannot be made realistically using only objective standards.

*Rowe* v. *General Motors Corporation, 457 F.2d 348 (1972); 4 FEP Cases 445.* All-white supervisory recommendations were based on subjective and vague standards leading to a lack of promotions and transfers for black employees that in turn led to discriminatory practices.

***Wade v. Mississippi Cooperative Extension Service, 528 F.2d 508 (1976); 12 FEP Cases 1577.***  Trait-rating systems can be subjective and biased and are usually not based on job content. There must be a BFOQ between the trait and the work performed. Data must be provided that show a relationship between appraisal instruments and job analysis and show that the appraisal instrument is a valid predictor of job performance.

Although EEOC guidelines and court rulings leave much to be desired, they do provide a significant amount of useful information regarding actions to be taken by performance appraisal designers and administrators. Duane E. Thompson, Charles R. Klasson, and Gary L. Lubben make the following 11 recommendations to assist in complying with EEOC guidelines and court rulings:

1   The overall appraisal process should be formalized, standardized, and, as much as possible, objective in nature.

2   The performance appraisal system should be as job related as possible.

3   A thorough, formal job analysis for all employment positions being rated should be completed.

4   Subjective supervisory ratings should be considered as only one component of the overall evaluation process.

5   Evaluators should be adequately trained in the use of appraisal techniques.

6   Evaluators should have substantial daily contact with the employee being evaluated.

7   If the appraisal involves various measures of performance, the proportion which each measure carries with respect to the overall assessment should be fixed.

8   Whenever possible, the appraisal should be conducted independently by more than one evaluator.

9   The administration and scoring of the performance appraisal should be standardized and controlled.

10   Opportunities for promotion or transfer should be posted and the information made available to all interested individuals.

11   An employee initiated promotion/transfer procedure should

be established which does not require the immediate supervisor's recommendations.[1]

Three additional recommendations may also be useful to designers and administrators of performance appraisal systems:

1   Criteria used for appraising performance must not unfairly depress the scores of minority groups.
2   Appraisal forms and instructions to evaluators are an essential part of the process and require validation.
3   Criteria such as regularity of attendance, tenure, and training time are usually not considered part of actual work proficiency. Because they are frequently used as performance appraisal criteria, they require validation evidence.

## Validity and Reliability

For performance predictors to be acceptable to the EEOC and the federal courts, they must be valid and reliable.

### Validity

*Validity* is an index of the extent to which an instrument actually measures what it purports to measure when it is compared with an acceptable criterion. Thus, index of validity is the ratio of performance as rated by the appraisal system to actual jobholder performance.

The principal kinds of validity are as follows:

*Concurrent Validity.*   This is an "existing status" statistical correlation between predictors of performance (appraisal item on form) or test factors and actual job performance or present indicators of job performance. Individuals receiving high ratings on form perform better than those receiving low ratings.

*Content Validity.*   This is a showing through documentation of job data and methodology that the content of a testing procedure is representative of all important job behaviors or outputs required in the performance of a job. This is a pragmatic or empirical-based

[1] Duane E. Thompson, Charles R. Klasson, and Gary L. Lubben, "Performance Appraisal and the Law: Policy and Research Implications of Court Cases," pp. 5–6. A paper presented at the 39th Annual Meeting of the Academy of Management, Atlanta, Georgia, August 9, 1979.

validity and, in the case of performance appraisal, must be an easily identifiable relationship between appraisal form items and job-related activities, situations, and outputs.

*Criterion-Related Validity.*   This is a statistical statement based on empirical data that describes the relationship between scores on a predictor (a selection procedure) and scores on a criterion measure. For example, measures of job success as identified by various factors on a selection instrument must be relevant and critical to the job and must relate either positively or negatively to employee job performance (criterion) or some set of performance subfactors (criteria) as may be identified in a performance appraisal instrument.

*Predictive Validity.*   This is a "future status" statistical correlation between test factors and subsequent indicators of performance. Predictions made by reviewer are confirmed at a later date. An appraiser rates a subordinate as promotable; the employee receives a promotion and does well on the job. This may be an indicator that the appraisal instrument has predictive validity.

*Face Validity.*   This is the practical, job-directed relationship between the predictor of performance and actual job performance.

*Construct Validity.*   This is the degree to which scores obtained through a test may be interpreted as measuring a hypothesized or synthesized trait or property (the construct—motivation, intelligence, leadership.) The issue involved in measuring a psychological quality in performance appraisal is the ability to obtain an objective measure of the quality. The appraisal instrument designer must clearly identify and describe what constitutes the psychological quality of the construct. For example, cooperation is a trait or construct on the form, and employees rated high on cooperation actually are more cooperative than employees rated low. The measure has construct validity. The problem is how to get an objective measurement of cooperation. (Construct validity is also often called synthetic validity.)

*Convergent Validity.*   The correlation between the same traits as rated by different raters should be significantly different from zero.

*Discriminant Validity.*   (a) The correlation between the same traits as rated by different raters should be higher than the correlation between different traits rated by the same rater. (b) The correlation between the same traits as rated by different raters should be higher than the correlation between different traits rated by different raters.

The basic assumptions underlying both concurrent and predictive validity are:

1　The job is static.

2　There is a large influx of applicants with similar characteristics.

3　There is a large number of candidates seeking jobs.

4　Motivational determinants for all taking the test are the same.

5　Scores on the test are not related to experience.

　　These assumptions identify weaknesses in these two types of validity.

## Reliability

*Reliability* is a measure of the consistency or stability of a "test" over time or with its use by different raters. A reliable test is one that provides similar or comparable results regardless of when it is used or who uses it.

There are basically three different methods used for determining the reliability of a performance appraisal test. They are the test–retest method, the subdivided test method, and parallel test method.

*Test–Retest Method.* The test–retest method requires administering the same test at two different points in time. This method is the easiest to use of the three, but its ability to determine reliability is questionable. The first time that an individual takes a test (completes a performance appraisal instrument), a learning effect occurs. When the same individual uses the same test instrument a second time, the responses to certain questions may be influenced by the learning experience from the first time that the instrument was used. When the test–retest method is used for determining consistency, it is difficult if not impossible to separate change in the job performance that the test is determining from the effect of learning on the appraiser.

*Subdivided Test Method.* The subdivided test method requires that a test be split into two equal parts (equal in that they both cover the same performance behaviors). The test can be administered as one test. The comparable test items are split into equivalent halves for scoring purposes. If the test is reliable, each half will give the same or comparable ratings. The division can be by odd-even numbers, and the actual test items can be randomly placed or placed by any other method. It is only necessary that each part represent all types of test questions asked in the original instrument.

*Parallel Test Method.*   The parallel test method uses two completely comparable or equivalent performance appraisal instruments. The items or appraisal dimensions included in each form do not have to be identical, but they must cover the same performance behaviors and have a measuring scheme that permits a comparison of the behaviors. The parallel tests may be administered consecutively or after a lapse of a period of time. If the tests are reliable, they will provide the same results. The major problem with this method is the development of two tests that are truly equivalent.

Performance appraisal tests must also meet intrarater and interrater reliability standards:

*Intrarater Reliability.*   Intrarater reliability means that the same rater using the same instrument at different times produces the same test results. The performance appraisal issues here are that the test subject's behavior may have changed and that the rater forces the result to be the same as those provided the first time by remembering the ratings given the first time.

*Interrater Reliability.*   Interrater reliability means that different raters produce the same results using the same instrument over a period of time. The same issue of actual changes in employee behavior over time must not be misconstrued as an inadequacy in the design of the instrument.

## Developing Valid and Reliable Implementation Procedures

The introductory pages of this chapter emphasize the importance of having skilled professionals design and develop the performance appraisal system. Gathering sufficient and accurate information that completely describes job requirements and then processing this information into responsibilities and duties, knowledge and skills, performance dimensions and standards, and objectives and goals is neither easy nor inexpensive. Once the professionals have developed the approaches, techniques, methods, and procedures for appraising performance and have identified who will be involved, the design of the instruments to be used, and the timing of the appraisal(s), successful operation lies primarily in the hands of the appraisers. There is no reason not to believe that the primary appraiser in the future will be the same person who today is responsible for appraising—the immediate supervisor.

A major reason for a business to expend the effort and to incur the cost necessary for developing a valid and reliable appraisal system is to support the appraiser. Very few people like to play "God" with other people, and making judgments on individual behaviors that have an impact on current and future pay, retention, transfer, demotion, and promotion is a large responsibility. If businesses want their supervisors to make decisions or to assist in making decisions in the critical human resource areas, they must support these individuals in every way possible.

In the final analysis, if appraisal systems are to be valid and reliable, the immediate supervisors must be willing and capable of implementing their areas of responsibility in a valid and reliable manner. Validity and reliability from the point of view of the appraiser mean that this person must know how to (1) collect sufficient and accurate job-content and performance data, (2) process identifiable and observable behavior information, and (3) communicate this information in a nonthreatening manner that keeps levels of anxiety, hostility, and fear to a minimum.

These requirements provide organizations with one of the finest opportunities to design and implement training programs that can make supervisors into "good" managers. Training in understanding and implementing performance appraisal covers a wide range of knowledge and skills required of all managers. It permits linking management and behavioral science theory to the practical application of a difficult managerial assignment. The remainder of this chapter reviews some training areas that will benefit most supervisors. The major training areas to be discussed are (1) analyzing job content; (2) developing observation and measuring skills; (3) improving interviewing and counseling skills; (4) linking organization, unit, and individual objectives and goals; and (5) understanding human behavior.

## Analyzing Job Content

Throughout this book, there have been discussions relating to the importance of tying performance appraisal directly to job content. This chapter continues to reinforce this view by identifying legal requirements and court cases that mandate such linkages. It is neither necessary nor wise to use only staff specialists for analyzing and reanalyzing job content. Much of the analysis can be done by the incumbent and the supervisor. Although these individuals have the most intimate knowledge of the job, it does not mean that they automatically have the knowledge or skills to analyze the job, to develop responsibility and duty statements, and to identify required knowledge and skills.

With some well designed training programs, most supervisors can learn how to do these shunned and frequently neglected activities. (In my experience in this field, I have seldom, if ever, found a person who likes to write responsibility and duty statements or to develop job descriptions—this includes requesting a personnel specialist to write his or her own job description).

A training program to develop these skills may start by defining precisely what responsibilities and duties are and then showing how to obtain a list of job activities and to establish their order of importance. (Job content analysis is described in detail in Chapter 3.) A training program may require supervisors to complete a job analysis questionnaire, as described in Chapter 3. The next step is to exchange questionnaires and to have participants develop a prioritized listing of responsibilities and duties. At this time, they receive instruction on how to write a responsibility/duty statement (verb, modifier, etc.) and how to search for and to classify responsibilities (functional areas and knowledge and skill requirements, etc.).

In such a session lasting one or possibly two days, a supervisor develops skills not only in writing but also in observing and identifying what the members of his or her work unit are doing, what they should be doing, and how they are performing these assignments. The experience of writing about a subject or teaching others to perform an assignment quickly helps in identifying missing pieces of information in cases in which perceptions and assumptions have over-ridden reality.

Once supervisors have developed an understanding and skill in identifying and writing responsibility and duty statements, the same process can be used to expand the program to include the identification and description of performance dimensions, standards, and goals.

## Developing Observation and Measuring Skills

Before covering the area of performance dimensions, standards, and goals, the basic job-content training program should focus on the identification of critical job behaviors. This phase of the training involves the supervisor in the use of the critical incident technique or some other applicable or appropriate procedure useful for identifying and describing critical job behaviors. Here, the supervisors focus their attention on an employee(s) performing a certain job. They identify various types of behaviors that result in performance that ranges from outstanding to unacceptable. It is valuable if all the trainees are familiar with one job and are able to provide descriptions of behaviors of the same job; when this is not possible, the trainees may each do a specific job and follow the process through with the job of their choice.

In this session, the supervisor–trainee:

1   Describes a behavior,

2   Identifies circumstances leading to this behavior;

3   Describes as exactly as possible what the incumbent did that was so effective or ineffective; and

4   Specifies (1) *how* the particular behavior contributed to the overall effectiveness (or ineffectiveness) of the group, (2) *when* the behavior occurred, (3) *where* the behavior occurred, (4) *how long* the employee performed the job, and (5) *how long* the employee has been with the business.

The trainees then review the behaviors and identify which behaviors relate to specific responsibilities or performance dimensions. They identify which behaviors are essential or unessential to the performance of a job and the level of successful or unsuccessful performance that the behavior describes. This kind of training improves the supervisor's ability to discriminate among various kinds and degrees of behavior; this lays the foundation for improving the reliability of measurement and appraisal. This type of training also increases the supervisor's skills in observing and identifying workplace behavior. Even more importantly, it improves the supervisor's ability to discriminate in measuring or appraising demonstrated behaviors. Research indicates that supervisors who maintain logs or diaries of critical incidents of employee behaviors provide more accurate appraisal ratings.

This phase of the training program may include discussions of what supervisors identify as good and bad behaviors. They review what they consider to be good behavior to see whether it truly has an impact on the effectiveness of job performance. The same process applies to bad behavior. A major intent here is to have the appraiser consider the performance impact of what he or she identifies as good or bad behavior and attempt to minimize the subjective influence of normative judgments that can unfairly bias an appraisal of performance.

### Improving Interviewing and Counseling Skills

Of all supervisory responsibilities, one area that many supervisors dread is that which requires them to sit down and in a face-to-face session to tell subordinates how they have been performing for the past review period. (Chapter 6 focuses on this subject and provides information that can be used in a performance interviewing and counseling workshop.) This may possibly be the single most important training area for improving the quality of the appraisal system.

Training in these subject areas makes good use of role playing (one supervisor can be the appraiser, another the appraisee). In these role-playing sessions, skits are provided, but the students are encouraged to improvise. Audio-visual taping equipment is a powerful tool here. After taping a role-playing interview session, the appraiser and appraisee can have their performance replayed so that they can observe what they said, the tones of their voices, their nonverbal behaviors, and their skills in listening and in eliciting the other person to talk.

Under these conditions, constructive criticism becomes far more meaningful and acceptable. It is difficult to deny behavior that has just been exhibited before a camera that provides instant replays. This type of training gives supervisors the chance to learn new skills, to observe their impact on other people, and to relate criticism to behaviors that are observable on the screen or TV monitor.

### Linking Organization, Unit, and Individual Objectives and Goals

It is difficult to discuss ideas or concepts relating to the improvement of organizational productivity without the use of the words *goals* and *objectives*. The concept of goal setting and goal achievement is an almost innate part of any operation that requires the direction of cooperative human effort for some purpose. However, what is not innate is the linking or coordination of various goals that may, to some degree, be in conflict with each other but that must be achieved by individuals working together for some common purpose. All too often, unit and individual members feel that their goals must be sacrificed on the altar of supra (transcending) goals.

To overcome the individual's feeling or perception of being the victim of some monumental organizational or unit objective and also to minimize the opportunity for suboptimization, it is critical that supervisors at every level understand the overall objectives of the business. They must know how the goals of their unit interact with and reinforce the goals of other units, making it possible to achieve organizational goals. A core area of performance appraisal training is to inform supervisors about the reasons for the existence of the business and to review how these objectives become redefined in the work required of a specific unit. The supervisor must know how the performance of each job results in desired outputs of the unit. The supervisor must also know how to translate the nonpersonal, specific job responsibilities and duties set for a rather static environment into highly personal goals that must be achieved in a dynamic work situation that is constantly affected by situational or contingency variables.

This segment of the training focuses on the process that moves from responsibilities and duties to performance dimensions and standards and finally to goals. This process (discussed in detail in Chapters 2 through 5) makes it possible to develop specific means for measuring employee job-related behaviors—performance.

Using goals set in a dynamic environment as a basis for measuring performance provides measures that are observable, relate to work required (if they tie directly to job responsibilities and duties), and focus on actual results. The final appraisal must take into consideration circumstances that either assisted or blocked goal achievement.

Teaching supervisors about the goal-setting process should include these steps:

1   Reviewing with each employee his or her job description and identifying priority activity areas and resource availability;

2   Developing a common understanding of what the job is and is not;

3   Discussing performance dimensions and determining performance standards; and

4   Developing performance goals, prioritizing goals, and developing means for measuring performance dimensions and standards to be used for determining levels of performance.

The writing of goals follows a procedure similar to that discussed in Chapter 3 for writing responsibility and duty statements: a goal statement begins with an action word (verb); following the verb is a group of words that describes a desired or specific result. When possible, the goal statement should include some quantitative measure for target-setting and appraisal purposes. The goal statement focuses on *what, who,* and *when,* not *why* and *how.* For example, a goal for a sales manager may be to:

> Stabilize the minimum number of daily calls at three for ten sales representatives for the third quarter.

In this goal statement, the verb is *stabilize.* The modifying phrase describes *what, who,* and *when:* what—minimum number of daily calls at three; who—for ten sales representatives; when—for the third quarter.

When reviewing a goal, the supervisor should see whether it permits individual approaches to goal achievement and stresses individual accountability. Goals should be realistic and challenging. Finally, all goals must be agreed upon and recorded in writing. If at all possible, goal progress should be monitored, and goals used for reviewing past efforts. When necessary, efforts should be redirected when progress reviews identify unrecognized contingencies that have an impact on goal achievement. Training should also include discussions on ways and means of documenting demonstrated behaviors.

### Understanding Human Behaviors

It appears to be impossible to develop any type of management training program without including the topic of motivation. Motivation is no longer an undergraduate or a graduate school topic. It is now fair game for a serious discussion at a Brownie meeting or for a Boy Scout "merit" badge. A management or supervisory training program is just not complete without its special jargon and mystical terms: "hierarchy of needs," "Theory X and Y," "5, 5," "1, 5," or "5, 1," and on into infinity. The sound thoughts and ideas underlying many of these concepts and latest fads are particularly applicable to discussions related to appraising performance.

The beautiful part about incorporating motivational and other management-related theories into the practical application of performance appraisal is that they fit like old shoes. Abstract motivational theories become real and useful when related to performance appraisal.

The reason for implementing performance appraisal is to direct employee behavior so that it benefits the organization and, hopefully, the employees. To direct behavior in a positive, reinforcing manner requires a workplace environment in which trust permeates all levels and units of the organization. By having a trusting environment, it is easier to establish a feeling of well-being among all employees. Employees who can cope with the problems that arise in the day-to-day existence of the organization will, more than likely, have greater self-confidence and be willing and able to make the decisions that have a positive influence on improving productivity. A trusting environment also leads to a reduction in anxieties and frustration, thus minimizing the chances for hostility to arise.

The performance appraisal process provides numerous opportunities to identify and describe how open communication systems enhance understanding, which in turn leads to the development of a trusting environment. Job-content review and goal setting provide communication opportunities between supervisors and subordinates.

## Understanding Uses of Performance Appraisal

To gain supervisor acceptance and support of the appraisal system, it is imperative that each supervisor understand the uses of performance appraisal. How do appraisal ratings influence compensation decisions? What is the relationship between ratings and employee movement? How is training linked to appraisal ratings, and so on? There should be no mysteries regarding the use of the appraisal system.

If the supervisor has problems or perceives conflict among the uses of the appraisal ratings, it is during these kinds of training sessions that such concerns can be voiced and feedback provided to answer identified issues. The better informed the supervisor is, the greater is the likelihood that he or she will take a positive, proactive position regarding appraisals.

In summary, training related to the performance appraisal process grants supervisors an opportunity to understand each part of the system. The more they know, the greater is the likelihood that they will administer their areas of responsibility in a valid and reliable manner.

# 12

# Performance Appraisal and Compensation Opportunities

There are very few businesses that do not wish to attract and retain talented and capable people who are willing to become actively involved in improving the productivity and profitability of the business. One opportunity available to businesses for developing such a work force is to establish a relationship between demonstrated employee behaviors and employer-provided rewards that has both a high degree of consistency and certainty. A valid and reliable performance appraisal system is one of the most useful tools available to management for linking employee performance and employer rewards in a manner that is both consistent and certain.

Workplace *certainty* develops when both the supervisor and incumbent (1) fully understand job requirements, (2) have a similar perception of the outputs of the job and the priorities related to specific outputs, (3) are satisfied that standards of performance are well defined, (4) are confident that criteria used for measuring performance are accurate, and (5) know that specific levels of performance will result in particular kinds and degrees of rewards. *Consistency* develops when employees recognize that an accurate measurement of performance is necessary and possible and that employees performing similarly will receive similar reward treatment.

When a business does not link its rewards to employee performance, it minimizes the importance of one of its most valuable assets—human resources. If survival and growth are basic objectives of most businesses, is it not consistent and imperative to recognize how rewards influence employee behavior and to make every effort possible to communicate to employees that rewards relate to provided contributions?

It is my belief that, contrary to some popular conceptions, among all of the forms of rewards that a business provides in exchange for the services of its members, the compensation system with its many components has the greatest opportunity to influence employee behavior. To determine which components of the compensation system have the most influence on specific patterns of behavior, the modern enterprise must first critically analyze the types of behavior that it wishes its members to exhibit. It then must design and manage a compensation system that stimulates this acceptable workplace behavior. This chapter focuses specifically on those compensation components that relate in some way to workplace behavior or the results of work efforts that can, in some manner, be identified, observed, and measured and then related to the appraisal of performance.

The concept of equity has already been discussed a number of times. Satisfying equity demands requires that there be differences in kind and quantity among compensation components offered to incumbents in various jobs. It also requires that the compensation be differentiated according to incumbent performance. The degree to which compensation influences employee behavior depends as much (if not more) on relative considerations as it does on the absolute value or cost of each provided compensation component.

## Performance Appraisal and Compensation Components

The components of a compensation system take many forms. The remainder of this chapter focuses on opportunities and methods for joining performance appraisal results to compensation opportunities.

### Base Pay

Many employees have their jobs assigned to a specific pay grade. Normally, a pay grade has a minimum and maximum rate of pay. The difference between the minimum and maximum is called the range. Sometimes, the grade is divided into a number of steps with specific rates of pay. At other times, all that is identified are the first quartile (25th percentile), midpoint (50th percentile), and third quartile (75th percentile) of the pay grade.

Advancement through a pay grade may relate strictly to seniority (time on the job), to merit (performance appraisal rating), or to a combination of seniority and merit. Where there are six to ten steps within a pay grade, the incumbent's pay may increase automatically within a predetermined time period. The automatic (seniority) increases may only go to the midpoint of the pay grade, and further increases may depend on merit.

Even when increases are based primarily on seniority, the employee may receive some type of a simple appraisal rating, such as "performs acceptably" or "needs improvement." An "acceptable" rating grants the employee an advance to the next step. A "needs improvement" rating freezes the employee in the current step and can be used as a warning that termination is possible.

In recent years, the *merit guidechart* has come into favor. This procedure ties performance appraisal ratings to increases in pay. It also permits cost-of-living adjustments to be incorporated into pay increases with the percentage of the increase being determined by the incumbent's position in the pay grade (those lower in the pay grade receive larger percentage increases than those that are higher although both may receive identical performance ratings). Figure 12-1 is a merit guidechart. A review of the guidechart reveals that employees in lower levels of the pay grade receive larger pay increases for comparable levels of performance. The reasoning is that employees at the higher levels still receive more absolute dollars and also that there is a definite limit to the amount of increase granted to an employee at the upper level of a pay grade. An "X" indicates a pay grade adjustment, which may be either an increase in the top and bottom (or top only) limits of the pay grade or an across-the-board adjustment of the pay structure that is prompted, in most cases, by inflationary pressure and the desire of management to assist employees to maintain the current purchasing power of their pay. When the guidechart is used, there is nothing automatic about any pay increase. Employees who perform in a less than acceptable manner and who are currently receiving pay in the upper levels of the pay grade actually receive a pay cut in *real* income (real income relates to the purchasing power of the income).

Tying performance appraisal ratings to adjustments in pay emphasizes the importance of having valid and reliable appraisal instruments and raters who appraise validly and reliably. This also underlines a very real and important issue regarding performance appraisal: after an appraisal rating is performed, what is done with it?

There are those who feel that it is unwise and counterproductive to tie performance appraisal reviews directly to merit increases. If the business states implicitly or explicitly that it is paying for performance, there is no way to minimize the relationship between a performance rating and pay adjustments. In fact, when an organization tries to impart such a view, employees simply look upon it as another devious maneuver by management. It is entirely possible to have more than one review session. The first performance review session focuses on behaviors that should be continued, those requiring some changes, and, possibly, those that should be eliminated; its purpose is for employee development. (Chapter 14 discusses the development issue at length.) A second meeting that focuses primarily on pay review may be held four to twelve weeks later. This type of formal procedure *may* minimize the concern about pay adjustments at the first meeting, which should be developmental in orientation. However, pay adjustments may be an unspoken issue that clouds the developmental meeting.

### Direct Output (Individual)

Employees whose work output can be separated from others and can be measured accurately frequently have the amount of pay

FIGURE 12-1    MERIT GUIDECHART

| Current Position Within Pay Grade | | Performance Appraisal Rating | | | | |
|---|---|---|---|---|---|---|
| Quartile | Percentile | Superior | Good | Acceptable | Needs Improvement | Unacceptable |
| Fourth Quartile | 75 to 100 | $X + 3$ | $X + 2$ | $X$ | 0 | 0 |
| Third Quartile | 50 to 75 | $X + 4$ | $X + 3$ | $X + 1$ | $\frac{1}{2}X$ | 0 |
| Second Quartile | 25 to 50 | $X + 5$ | $X + 4$ | $X + 2$ | $\frac{2}{3}X$ | 0 |
| First Quartile | 1 to 25 | $X + 6$ | $X + 5$ | $X + 3$ | $X$ | 0 |

that they receive tied directly to their identified output. Two widely used output payment systems are piece rates for production workers and commissions for sales personnel. In both of these systems, a definite rate of pay must be set for specific output, and limiting factors that modify output-based earnings must be identified.

In many cases, all that the appraiser has to do is identify the actual output. However, some piece rate and commission plans may be modified by factors such as quality of output, resource usage, wastes incurred, machine utilization, and product mix (especially in sales where commission rates may vary according to the amount of different products or product lines sold). These variables that may change piece rate or commission earnings point out the fact that, even in one of the most simple relations between performance and rewards, factors arise that can quickly complicate the relationship.

### Direct Output (Group)

Most of the discussion concerning piecework plans normally involves individual effort, but piecework programs can be just as effective for stimulating the performance of small groups.

There are two basic approaches for developing group piecework plans. The first is identical to that used for setting individual piecework standards: Work standards are set for each member of the group and a count of the output of each member is maintained. The difference between this group approach and that related to individual piecework arises in the method of payment. The group approach may use one of the following payment methods: (1) all members receive the pay earned by the highest producer, (2) all members receive the pay earned by the lowest producer, or (3) all members receive payment equal to the average pay earned by the group.

The second and far more unique approach is to set a standard based on the final output of the group. This approach does not relieve management of the responsibility of performing a detailed analysis of the work performed by each member. Work flow and work processing information is still necessary for establishing the initial balancing of work tasks and activities among the members. Once production is underway, the group may vary any management-developed work-balancing system to meet its own demands. This approach is more useful when all members work together to complete a single product. The first approach is applicable when members are performing similar or identical assignments.

The beauty of the group approach is not only the simplification of measuring output but also the support that the individual members provide each other. A well knit, properly managed work group assists in training new and less experienced members. It sometimes rotates jobs in order to make the most effective use of its human resources. The members aid each other in overcoming both on- and off-the-job problems that affect group performance. The piecework plan provides a goal that assists in coordinating and directing group efforts for the benefit of the business, the group, and its individual members.

In most well functioning work groups, the total earnings (base pay plus any earned incentives) are split equally among the members. It is possible that the group itself may wish to grant a larger percentage to the more senior or experienced members, but this is the exceptional case and is strictly a group decision.

## Short-Term Cash Bonuses

A short-term cash bonus may be defined as a payment within the current operating year to an employee in addition to his or her regular earnings for superior performance or an above-expected achievement. Eligibility for a bonus relates to the particular contribution for which the bonus is awarded. Bonuses are usually granted for results directly influenced by the skill and effort of the employee.

The amount of the bonus normally depends on (1) the significance of the contribution, (2) the base pay of the recipient, (3) the level of job in the organization, and (4) the kind of job. Some common types of bonuses are the (1) annual (profit or other economic indicator-related) bonus, (2) award for good performance, (3) award for an unusual or exceptional contribution, and (4) part of a contract between employee and employer. In all of these examples, performance appraisal ratings have an impact on the size of the bonus and whether the employee receives or does not receive one.

*Annual Bonus.*    An annual bonus based on some type of economic indicator, such as profit sales, market shares, or return on invested capital, is usually paid to executives and senior managers. In large businesses, top operating managers may be included. Usually, employees who work for businesses that provide this type of bonus find that their base pay is less than that of those who work for nonbonus-paying companies. Comparison of performance between bonus- and nonbonus-paying businesses indicates that bonus-paying businesses frequently outperform nonbonus-paying businesses by most economic indicators.

Annual bonuses that may include large numbers of employees (possibly the entire work force) are the Christmas bonus and the

Thirteenth Month bonus. The *Christmas bonus* is usually made early in December and may equal the pay for one week or one month. When merit influences base earnings or any additional performance-related payment, the amount of the Christmas bonus may, in turn, reflect the performance influences. The *Thirteenth Month bonus* is similar to the Christmas bonus, but it provides a thirteenth monthly payment to employees. This payment is normally made in December of each year. As with the Christmas bonus, performance rating and merit pay may have an impact on the size of the Thirteenth Month payment.

*Award for·Good Performance.*   Some type of appraisal rating is vital to this process. Many businesses having this type of a bonus plan use degree of goal achievement for measuring performance.

*Exceptional Contribution.*   This type of bonus has become more widely used in recent years. Many businesses establish special committees to determine whose performance warrants special consideration. A special type of bonus is the lump sum or one-time cash bonus payment. These special awards may be made at an annual event, or they may be presented shortly after the occurrence or result of the behavior. A major reason for the popularity of the lump-sum bonus is that it recognizes a specific behavior and is not part of a permanent pay plan.

Businesses that have *suggestion plans* can use this type of bonus payment to recognize those who have made worthwhile or beneficial suggestions. The size of the bonus can relate to the appraised value of the suggestion.

*Executive Contract.*   There are times when top officials sign a performance contract with their employer. These executive contracts frequently have clauses that state that the executive will receive a certain bonus if the individual demonstrates a certain level of performance. The contract defines precisely the level of performance and the related cash bonus.

All of these performance-related cash bonus plans may, at times, include awards of stock or a combination of stock and cash. Stock-bonus plans are discussed in the following section. Long-term cash bonuses are similar in nature to short-term cash bonuses and are discussed in the section on deferred compensation.

### Stock Acquisition Plans

Ownership of stock in the employer's business is thought to be mutually advantageous to employees and employers. For employees, stock ownership is a major means for developing an estate, generating additional revenue (through stock dividends and appreciation in the price of the stock), and sheltering income or delaying the payment of taxes on income. For the employer, the market price of the stock acquired by the employee is a tax-deductible business expense. Even more importantly, there is the view that an employee who owns stock in the business will take a more active interest in seeing that the business is successful in its many pursuits. Stock acquisition by employees instills in them the same interest and incentive for business success that employers have.

There are four major types of stock acquisition plans. They are (1) stock purchase plans, (2) stock options, (3) stock grants, and (4) stock bonus plans. A lengthy discussion of each type of stock plan does not appear, but particular types of stock acquisition plans that relate directly or have close ties to performance appraisal ratings are discussed.

*Stock Purchase Plans.*   Stock purchase plans provide employees with a contract to buy stock in the business at current market prices. The number of shares available for purchase, dates when purchases can be made, and methods available for purchase are specifically described in the stock purchase contract/agreement.

Stock purchase plans may be either qualified or nonqualified. A qualified plan is one that receives special tax treatment (normally for both employer and employee) because the plan design and administration meet very specific government regulations. Qualified stock purchase plans frequently include all employees whereas nonqualified plans are usually management purchase plans.

A stock purchase plan that frequently has specific performance requirements is the *earn-out stock purchase plan*. In this type of plan, the employee receives a loan to purchase the stock; if the employee then meets certain performance requirements, he or she does not have to repay the loan (other requirements besides performance may be included within the earn-out stock purchase plan).

*Stock Option Plan.*   Stock option plans permit designated employees to purchase set amounts of stock at a specific price within a prescribed time period. These plans can also be either qualified or nonqualified. However, as a result of the Tax Reform Act of 1976, the qualified stock option plan will cease to exist as of May 20, 1981.

Normally, stock options are restricted to a select group of executives and senior managers. The concept underlying the issuance of stock options is that those who receive stock options have a direct and strong influence on the performance of the business and that the market value of the stock is an indicator or measure of their success in performing their jobs. (This is not necessarily true because many factors that have an impact on the market price of stock are beyond the control of any one or all of the senior management group of a business.) Because of the impact that senior management decisions have on the market price of shares of stock, some stock option plans have unique features tied to the market price.

A *nonqualified "yo-yo" plan* normally sets the option price at 100 percent of the fair market value. However, for each dollar increase in the market price of the stock, the option price decreases by an identical amount.

***Stock Grant Plans.*** Stock grant plans assist employees to acquire stock in the business by granting them stock at no cost. Stock grants are frequently types of deferred stock bonus plans.

Stock grants take two basic forms: stock appreciation grants and full-value grants. Stock appreciation grants entitle the recipient to receive payment that equals the appreciated value of a share of stock (or number of shares or units of stock granted) over a designated time period. A full-value stock grant entitles the recipient to receive the total value of the worth of a share (or number of shares or units of stock) over a predetermined period of time. Total value includes the base value of stock at time of initial grant, dividends, and appreciation of stock value during the period when the grant is in force.

Examples of stock grant plans that include performance criteria in the plan design are restricted stock performance plan, performance share plan, and performance unit plan.

A *restricted stock performance plan* is a special type of restricted stock plan. A restricted stock plan is one in which the business awards a prescribed amount of stock to its key managers for continued high-quality service. (With the 1981 demise of the qualified stock option, experts believe that this type of plan will once again return to prominence.) In a restricted stock performance plan, certain performance criteria are set forth, and these criteria must be achieved before the recipient receives the stock grant. This type of plan usually requires executives and senior managers to set key performance goals. These select employees only receive the stock when the business achieves these goals. A restricted stock performance plan may also set a minimum performance goal which must be achieved before any reward grant is made.

A *performance share plan (PSP)* is a stock grant plan that stipulates the achievement of certain predetermined performance goals before the recipient may have rights to the stock. Because most PSPs have earn-out periods ranging from three to ten years, they are often classified as deferred stock bonus plans.

Although performance measures can vary significantly from business to business and industry to industry, some typical measures are (1) earning per share growth rate, (2) return on invested capital (ROIC), (3) return on assets (ROA), or (4) a combination of financial measures, such as earnings per share and return on assets. A typical goal is a ten percent growth in earnings per share over the next five years.

A *performance unit plan (PUP)* has characteristics of a performance share plan (PSP) and a phantom stock plan. (Phantom stock plans grant the recipient a number of artificial units. The actual dollar payout on these units is equivalent to the value of a share of stock in the business at some stipulated future date set at the time that the grant is made.) As in the PSP, the recipient must meet certain performance measures in order to acquire the grant units. The PUP awards are made at the time of the grant, but the units only take on cash value at the end of the stipulated time period and upon meeting prescribed performance measures. Depending on their design, PUP awards may be made in a combination of stock and cash, cash only, or cash or stock.

**Stock Bonus Plans.**   In stock bonus plans, employers provide employees with shares of stock in the business. Stock bonus plans can also be either qualified or nonqualified. A stock bonus plan has characteristics similar to a profit-sharing plan except that the stock bonus distribution is not tied directly to profits and the distribution is in stock, not cash. The similarity is that stock distribution is frequently made to trusteed pension (retirement) plans. A stock bonus plan designed to receive certain tax benefits must satisfy specific Internal Revenue Service tax requirements.

One way in which performance appraisal ratings affect stock bonus contributions made to an employee is when total annual earnings are used as a measure for determining individual allocation. If a business has a merit program that varies earnings according to performance ratings, then any type of a deferred income plan that uses annual earnings as a measure for determining the amount of deferred income to be earned is affected by performance.

## Deferred Compensation Plans

Deferred compensation plans came about because of laws that tax current income. Deferred compensation plans permit employees to shelter income from immediate tax payments until some future date when the employee's projected tax payment will be less than at present. (In some cases, deferred compensation plans may permit an employee to avoid tax payment completely.) Deferred compensation usually takes the form of pension payments upon retirement, but they may be used to fund payments made to a spouse of an employee who dies, to employees who become disabled and are unable to work, or to employees who are terminated through no fault of their own.

Many deferred compensation plans are designed to meet the specific requirements of senior management personnel. These deferred plans are frequently unfunded. This means that the business makes a contractual obligation to make a payment(s) of a certain amount at a certain time, but the business does not put any money into a fund to guarantee this future payment. It is possible to fund these plans by purchasing insurance or other assets to meet future deferred compensation obligations.

Common types of deferred compensation plans are those in which employers make contributions to various types of stock acquisition, long-term bonus, and pension plans. Employer contributions are made in such a way that recipient employees are not required to pay taxes on them until they actually receive the payments (earn the contributions). Deferred income payments can be made in a number of ways. What is of interest here is the relationship between performance appraisal and the amount of employer contributions. The major impact occurs when performance appraisal ratings or the achievement of a particular goal or business performance indicator determines the amount to be contributed. In many cases, the contributions are flat or predetermined amounts that have no direct relationship to individual performance. However, more plans are being designed with a percentage of the contribution being determined by a performance rating measurement.

### Profit Sharing

Profit-sharing plans normally include all or a significant portion of the employees. These plans focus on improving the overall productivity of the business. Similar to any employer-provided reward, the reasons for implementing profit-sharing plans are to attract and retain competent employees and to establish an incentive for securing high levels of productivity by encouraging interest in the objectives of the business. Although many profit-sharing plans do not directly link appraisal rating to profit-sharing distribution, there is an implicit relationship in that improved performance by all employees leads to increased monetary rewards.

Profit-sharing plans may provide distribution in the form of cash, stock, or a combination of cash and stock. The distribution may be made in the short term or long term, or a plan may provide for both short- and long-term payments. The distribution of the profit-sharing fund among the employees is normally determined through the use of a formula. The formula may include variables such as annual earnings, years of employment, and performance appraisal ratings.

Short-term, profit-sharing payments are normally made on an annual basis although some plans provide for quarterly distribution. One of the most widely known, short-term, profit-sharing plans in the United States is that of the Lincoln Electric Company. (In Chapter 10, there is a description of the Lincoln appraisal system and how the appraisal ratings influence the amount of money that each employee receives from the distribution of the profit-sharing fund.)

Most deferred (long-term) plans make distribution to employee pension plans. A major design difference between a deferred profit-sharing plan and a pension plan is that a deferred profit-sharing plan may permit an employee to withdraw profit contributions after two years. When profit-sharing payments are deferred, the employee benefits by not having to pay income tax on the sheltered income, and the business is able to deduct any payments as a current business expense.

When profit-sharing plans are designed for individuals (the executives), the plan may be noncontractual. A noncontractual plan is one in which the size of the payment is determined by the appraisal of the employee's performance and the financial strength of the business. The more common contractual type of profit-sharing plan defines the payment according to some predetermined formula.

## Pension Plans

Pension plans take a wide variety of forms, but they all serve the major purpose of securing a satisfactory quality of life for employees after their productive working years are over. Pension plans provide a stream of income to employees after retirement. In many cases, spouses may continue to receive pension plan payments after the death of the employee.

Although the actual size of the pension payment may be a flat amount, it normally varies according to some formula that has as its major independent variables years of service and the amount of earned income. Here again, when a business varies annual earnings according to a performance rating, the size of the pension payment may be significantly influenced by the employee's appraisal ratings.

## Termination

Possibly one of the most critical influences that appraisal has on compensation occurs when a business uses performance appraisal ratings in making a decision to terminate an employee. An employee may be terminated because of continuing unacceptable workplace behavior as indicated through appraisal ratings or possibly as the result of a reduction in force (RIF) where those terminated are the lowest-rated performers. Termination is the ultimate influence on compensation; it reduces compensation to zero (with the possible exception of some severance payments).

## The Check-and-Balance System

A seldom discussed but extremely valuable use of performance appraisal is to employ it as a check and balance on the job evaluation program. If the performance dimensions, standards, and goals of the appraisal system come directly from job content and jobs are evaluated relative to content requirements, performance appraisals and job evaluations should be used as a check and balance to ensure legitimacy and credibility.

Two major problems in job evaluation are inflation of job requirements and obsolete ratings. There is the tendency for incumbents and supervisors to inflate job content and requirements so that the job receives a higher rating than deserved, thus granting employees who perform the job a higher base pay. This also increases the stature of the supervisor in the eyes of the employee. The second major problem is a failure to evaluate the job relative to current job requirements. Responsibilities are changed, deleted, or added, and knowledge and skill requirements change. There is often a failure to note these changes in the job descriptions or to have the job reevaluated.

When either or both the kind or degree of performance appraisal objectives appear to be inconsistent with job responsibilities, it is a sign that something is wrong. It may be that job responsibilities and duties have changed or that the responsibility and duty statements never truly reflected job requirements. In either case, it is a sign that the job may require reevaluation and that the pay or pay grade assigned to the job may be incorrect.

## Equity in Compensation

Throughout the book, there has been considerable attention focused on the need to recognize that each employee makes a unique contribution. However, when it comes to rewarding performance, equal and equitable treatment requires minimizing the distribution of rewards based on personality and maximizing the allocation of rewards based on well defined work standards and provided contributions. The entire subject of consistency of treatment and certainty of results is an implicit, if not explicit, part of everything that is discussed in this book.

Of the many and varied rewards that employers can offer to their employees, none may be more valuable than the compensation rewards. Even with apparently unending legislation and organized groups wielding ever-greater influence over compensation procedures, management still has considerable control over the compensation practices of the business. To ensure as far as possible that the entire compensation package is a "carrot"—highly desired by all employees—compensation system designers and administrators must make every effort possible to tie together pay, bonuses, and other compensation components to demonstrated employee performance. In some areas, the linkage is nonexistent or extremely thin; in other areas, the tie is direct and absolute. There is no doubt that many of the additions incorporated into employer-provided compensation since the end of World War II have minimal relationship to employee behaviors that further the productivity of the business. This does not mean that management must accept this as the inevitable and unending direction that compensation must take.

A compensation system that stresses pay-for-performance must have an equity base, and equity in compensation requires well identified and measured workplace performance.

In conclusion, changes in compensation rewards must eventually relate to the ability of the organization to pay. In turn, the ability of an organization to pay relates to the productivity of its employees. The importance of performance appraisal increases significantly when appraisal ratings have an effect on: (1) size and distribution of actual payroll, (2) number of employees receiving changes in pay, and (3) the percentage of change in pay as related to current pay.

The following guidelines assist in successfully implementing a pay-for-performance program:

1   Employees should understand how rates of pay are established for jobs.
2   Rules for gaining pay increases should be understood by all employees.
3   Performance measures should be known and accepted by all employees.
4   Compensation rewards should be perceived to be adequate for effort expended.

# 13

## Assessing Potential

Compensation related to current efforts, whether received now or later, has a Siamese twin in future compensation opportunities that are available through upgrading and promotion. An old adage states that hope springs eternal in the human breast, and, for many workers, a basic hope lies in changing the work that they do. The improvement made through change may initially require additional training and development that leads to a lateral transfer, to another job in the class-series, or to a job in a different occupational group. The hoped-for change may be a promotion to a higher level job in the same class or family of jobs or even into an entirely different occupational setting. When implementing action for requests for a lateral or vertical transfer, past and current performance, demonstrated skills, and identified personal traits—intellectual and mechanical qualities—have a significant impact on such decisions.

In this chapter, the relationship between performance appraisal, promotion, and manpower planning is investigated. This discussion considers issues such as promotability, training, and development. The first issues covered are assessment centers, their value in assessing potential, and the relationship between performance appraisal and assessment centers.

## Assessment Centers

With increased recognition of the importance of human resources has come the need for greater accuracy in identifying employee potential. In the past, the performance appraisal process has been a major source of information regarding employee potential. Although appraisals still provide a significant amount of such information, assessment centers have proved valuable in identifying promotable employees.

The concepts and basic procedures underlying the design of the assessment center operation were established in Germany around the start of the twentieth century. Its introduction into the world of work in the United States occurred in 1943 when the Office of Strategic Services (OSS) (the counter-subversive and espionage arm of the federal government) established a psychological–psychiatric assessment similar to that being used at that time by the British War Office Selection Boards.[1] From its inception, the assessment center had (and still has) as its primary objective the identifica-

---

[1] Joseph L. Moses and William C. Byham, eds., *Applying The Assessment Center Method* (New York: Pergamon Press, 1977), pp. 14–15.

tion of individuals who currently possess the knowledge and skills and have the required capacity for growth to perform successfully certain kinds of assignments—jobs.

The use of an assessment center for purposes other than the selection of spies received its introduction to the mainstream of American business with the Management Progress Study initiated in 1956 by the American Telephone & Telegraph Company (AT&T). This on-going study is providing management and human resource specialists with an incredible array of information that can be invaluable for improving the productivity of businesses of all sizes and kinds.

In their book, Douglas W. Bray, Richard J. Campbell, and Donald L. Grant[2] describe in detail the purposes, design, operational characteristics, and follow-up results of the assessment of 274 recruits for entry-level management jobs in the Bell system during the summer of 1956. Since the original assessment, the careers of these 274 individuals have been tracked, making it possible to relate initial assessment predictions with actual job success over a period now extending beyond twenty years.

The thousands of assessment centers spawned from the efforts of Bray, Campbell, and Grant are highly formalized structures that use a variety of examination procedures and measurement instruments for predicting the success that tested individuals will have in specific types of jobs. The various procedures and instruments used provide assessors with a multifaceted view of the individual assessees. The information generated in the assessment center measures a series of characteristics–qualities–dimensions that have a high degree of validity for predicting future success.

## Assessment Center Design

Although current assessment center operation differs from that developed by the OSS, many of the procedures and design characteristics shaped and formulated then by Henry A. Murray of the Harvard Psychological Clinic and a small group of selected psychologists are still in effect. Possibly the most important feature of an assessment center is that the work is performed in a physical site that minimizes, if not eliminates, any kind of nonprogrammed interruption. The ratio of appraisers to appraisees is extremely small. A contemporary assessment center may have 12 assessees and 6 assessors to observe, review, and measure assessee behaviors.

[2] Douglas W. Bray, Richard J. Campbell, and Donald L. Grant, *Formative Years In Business: A Long-Term AT&T Study of Managerial Lives* (New York: John Wiley & Sons, 1974).

The OSS assessment center used detailed life history, psychiatric interview, projective questionnaire, intellectual ability tests, and situational-type tests that are still very much a part of any assessment center activity.

A typical assessment center lasts from 2 to 5 days and has from 5 to 15 assessees; however, some centers may have as many as 30 assessees. The assessors are usually psychologists, other behavioral scientists, or supervisors who have been trained in such activities. These activities include job-related simulations that are designed to bring forth skills that a business has determined to be critical to job success. These simulation exercises include:

*In Baskets.*    Under specific time limitations, assessees review various incoming communiques and decide what action to take in each case.

*Business Games and Case Involvement.*    Actual business situations identify the assessee's capacity for teamwork, leadership, and other interpersonal influencing activities.

*Leaderless Group Discussion.*    Assessors develop various unstructured situations and then observe and measure the assessee's capacity to function within conditions of uncertainty.

Among the more structured information-gathering exercises are:

*Interview.*    Under a variety of interview situations, assessors analyze behavior and identify on-the-job and off-the-job interests.

*Paper and Pencil Exercises.*    These exercises uncover verbal and mathematical abilities and personality traits and aptitudes. In some exercises, assessees score themselves and then compare their scores with those developed by assessors. When involved in the comparison, assessors measure the assessee's ability to be objective.

*Projective Technique.*    The assessee analyzes and responds to a set of stimuli. A commonly used projective technique is the Thematic Apperception Test (TAT) developed by Murray. In this test, the assessee analyzes a particular scene and then answers certain questions about the personal meaning of the scene. Through a specific scoring procedure, the answers provide a behavioral profile of the assessee.

## Attributes – Qualities – Dimensions to Be Measured

The 1956 Management Progress Study of AT&T used the following 25 attributes for measuring the management potential of the 274 management recruits:[3]

1 *Scholastic Aptitude* (general mental ability)

2 *Oral Communication Skill*
How good would this man be in presenting an oral report to a small conference group on a subject that he knew well?

*Written Communication Skill*
How good would this man be in composing a communicative and formally correct memorandum on a subject that he knew well?

3 *Human Relations Skills*
How effectively can this man lead a group to accomplish a task without arousing hostility?

4 *Personal Impact*
How forceful and likable an early impression does this man make?

5 *Perception of Threshold Social Cues*
How readily does this man perceive minimal cues in the behavior of others toward him?

6 *Creativity*
How likely is this man to solve a management problem in a novel way?

7 *Self-Objectivity*
How realistic a view does this man have of his own assets and liabilities, and how much insight does he have into his own motives?

8 *Social Objectivity*
How free is this man from prejudices against racial, ethnic, socioeconomic, educational, and other kinds of groups?

9 *Behavior Flexibility*
How readily can this man, when motivated, modify his behavior to reach a goal?

---

[3] Bray et al., *Formative Years*, pp. 18–20.

10    *Need for Approval of Superiors*
To what extent is this man emotionally dependent on authority figures?

11    *Need for Approval of Peers*
To what extent is this man emotionally dependent on like and lower status associates?

12    *Inner Work Standards*
To what extent does this man want to do a good job even if a less good one is acceptable to his boss and others?

13    *Need for Advancement*
To what extent does this man need to be promoted significantly earlier than his peers?

14    *Need for Security*
To what extent does this man need a secure job?

15    *Goal Flexibility*
To what extent is this man able to change his life goals in accordance with reality opportunities?

16    *Primacy of Work*
To what extent does this man find satisfactions from work more important than satisfactions from other areas of life?

17    *Bell System Value Orientation*
To what extent is this man likely to incorporate Bell system values, such as service, friendliness, and justice of company position on earnings, rates, and wages?

18    *Realism of Expectations*
To what extent do this man's expectations about his work life with the company conform to what is likely to be true?

19    *Tolerance of Uncertainty*
To what extent does this man's work performance stand up under uncertain or unstructured conditions?

20    *Ability to Delay Gratification*
To what extent is this man able to work over long periods without great rewards in order to reach later rewards?

21    *Resistance to Stress*
To what extent does this man's work performance stand up in the face of personal stress?

22    *Range of Interests*
To what extent is this man interested in a variety of fields of activity, such as science, politics, sports, music, and art?

**23** *Energy*
How continuously can this man sustain a high level of work activity?

**24** *Organization and Planning*
How effectively can this man organize his work, and how well does he plan ahead?

**25** *Decision Making*
How ready is this man to make decisions, and how good are the decisions that he makes?

These 25 dimensions (personal qualities or assessment variables) were further grouped into 7 areas that were identified as critical to managerial success. They were:[4]

**1** *Administrative Skills.* A high-potential manager plans and organizes his work effectively, makes decisions willingly, and makes high-quality decisions.

**2** *Interpersonal Skills.* A high-potential manager makes a forceful and likable impression on others, has good oral presentation skills, leads others to perform, and modifies his behavior when necessary to reach a goal.

**3** *Intellectual Ability.* A high-potential manager learns readily and has a wide range of interests.

**4** *Stability of Performance.* A high-potential manager maintains effective work performance under uncertain or unstructured conditions and in the face of stress.

**5** *Work Motivation.* A high-potential manager finds satisfaction from work more important than those from other areas of life and wants to do a good job for its own sake.

**6** *Career Orientation.* A high-potential manager wants to advance significantly more rapidly than his peers, is *not* as concerned as others about having a secure job, and is *unwilling* to delay rewards too long.

**7** *Dependence on Others.* A high-potential manager is *not* greatly concerned with gaining approval from superiors or peers and is *unwilling* to change life goals in accordance with reality opportunities.

[4] Bray et al., *Formative Years*, pp. 78–79.

The testing procedures and instruments used to measure these seven areas were:[5]

| | |
|---|---|
| Administrative Skills | In-Basket |
| Interpersonal Skills | Group Exercises |
| Intellectual Ability | Paper-and-Pencil Ability Tests |
| Stability of Performance | Simulation Exercises |
| Work Motivation | Projective Tests, Interviews, and Simulation to some degree |
| Career Orientation | Projective Tests and Interviews |
| Dependency on Others | Projective Test |

In the years since 1956, the Bell system has developed a number of assessment centers to identify individuals considered promotable to specific kinds and levels of jobs. They have a center for assessing nonmanagement employees seeking or nominated for first-level management, one for assessing the potential of candidates for middle-level management, and a third for identifying those individuals promotable to senior management. In addition, they have developed assessment centers for sales and engineering personnel. Each of the centers uses different sets of assessment dimensions although the three management centers use some grouping of the dimensions initially identified and defined in 1956.

An important part of any assessment center is the establishment of assessment dimensions that accurately and adequately describe behaviors required for the successful performance of the job. In the Bell sales and engineering assessment centers, some managerial-related dimensions have been used for measuring assessee potential, but it has been found that the dimensions related specifically to sales- or engineering-type work are far better predictors of job success than are the basic managerial-related dimensions.

Results from the over twenty years of tracking the initial management recruits identify the possibility of incorrect prediction (false positives, those identified as promotable who did not receive promotions, and false negatives, those identified as nonpromotable who did, in fact, receive promotions). Because of the limitations of assessment center information, managers responsible for making promotion decisions are warned not to use assessment center criteria as the only or final arbiter. They must still use their judgment in

[5] Bray et al., *Formative Years*, pp. 79–80.

combining assessment center criteria with past and current performance and with other observed qualities for making a promotion or
promotion-related decisions. One of the more interesting aspects of
the promotability ratings emanating from assessment centers is that
the promotion information becomes increasingly more relevant as
the assessee moves up the managerial hierarchy, e.g., among the
original assessed recruits, those recognized as being most promotable are those within the group who have reached the highest ranks
of management in the Bell system.

Another piece of interesting information is that the intelligence
rating (as identified and measured by certain tests) has increased
over the years. Although there has not been a significant change in
the dimensions that identify managerial-related qualities, certain in-
tervening variables appear to influence promotability. These qualities are the desire to learn, to change, to grow, and possibly most
important to influence (power).

## Measuring Potential During Performance Appraisal

A side benefit to a business that has expended the effort and
costs necessary to develop a valid and workable assessment center is
the use of some of the assessment center dimensions by appraisers
during the regular appraisal of performance. It is not possible for a
supervisor to observe and measure all the dimensions normally used
in an assessment center for predicting promotability or for identifying areas needing additional training and development. Some of the
dimensions are, however, readily observable and measurable by
most supervisors.

Some Bell system companies divide the management appraisal
process into two parts. One part focuses primarily on the job output
of the appraisee, and the other part uses the following eight dimensions for appraising potential. The eight dimensions and sub-
categories are:[6]

1   *Oral Communication*

Ability to present ideas and information concisely and effectively in an oral presentation to a group.

---

[6] This type of plan has its foundation in research on assessment dimensions. The
assessment dimensions are qualitative rather than quantitative in nature and have been
selected because they are clearly visible to supervisors and information gained in over
20 years of research has made validation possible.

a   Organizes logically: presents ideas and information in a rational, logical sequence.

b   Uses appropriate terms: uses words and phrases that are appropriate to the situation and the listener.

c   Speaks clearly and concisely: presents ideas and information in simple style, without excessive explanation or irrelevant information.

d   Acts confidently: appears generally calm, confident; gives smooth presentation.

e   Obtains audience attention: audience typically appears attentive, interested, and positive.

   NOTE: Emphasis is on the manner in which ideas and information are presented.

2   *Written Communication*

Ability to express ideas and information concisely and effectively in writing.

a   Organizes logically: presents ideas and information in a rational, logical sequence.

b   Uses appropriate terms: uses words and phrases that are appropriate to the situation and the intended readers.

c   Writes clearly and concisely: presents ideas and information in simple style, without excessive explanation or irrelevant information.

d   Uses appropriate grammar and style: uses acceptable grammar, spelling and punctuation, and appropriate business format and terminology.

   NOTE: Emphasis is on the manner in which ideas and information are presented.

3   *Flexibility*

Ability to change or vary one's approach or strategy for the purpose of accomplishing a task.

a   Suits style to setting: varies manner of speaking or writing to suit different times, places or audiences.

b   Suits approach to situation needs: varies actions or behavior to suit different task or problem.

c   Tries alternatives: changes approach for dealing with a given situation when initial attempts to handle it are not fully effective.

   NOTE: Consider only actual changes initiated by the individual, not merely verbal expressions of a change of mind.

**4**   *Performance Stability* (Resistance to Stress, Tolerance of Uncertainty)

Ability to maintain a consistent level of performance under conditions of stress, uncertainty, or lack of structure.

**a**   Maintains performance under increased pressure: continues to perform at the usual level when faced with increases in work pressure.

**b**   Maintains performance under increased uncertainty: continues to perform at the usual level when given less structure or fewer guidelines for performance than are usually available.

NOTE: Consider only the ability to continue to perform at the usual level, not ability to show signs of stress or uncertainty.

**5**   *Decision Making* (Decisiveness, Quality of Decision)

Ability to make timely and effective decisions on the basis of available information.

**a**   Uses available information: bases decisions on rational analysis of all information available at the time.

**b**   Anticipates future: takes into account future needs or events that are predictable.

**c**   Recognizes interactions: takes into account, when appropriate, the effect on other business operations.

**d**   Considers situation and alternatives: bases decisions on the characteristics of the existing situation and examination of alternatives, not simply on tradition.

NOTE: Consider the quality of decisions only in the light of the information available at the time that they are made.

**6**   *Leadership*

Ability to influence others to perform a task effectively.

**a**   Shows active involvement: initiates ideas, asks appropriate questions, makes suggestions, and gives instructions or orders as appropriate without prodding.

**b**   Obtains positive response: group typically responds as desired to ideas, suggestions, or instructions.

**c**   Moves toward goal: leadership attempts are a significant factor in success of group in accomplishing goal.

NOTE: Consider the effectiveness of leadership attempts, not the style of leadership.

7   *Organization and Planning*

Ability to schedule resources and personnel and to develop systematic and effective means for accomplishing a task.

a   Sets priorities: identifies correctly critical tasks and insures that they receive adequate time and resources.

b   Anticipates needs, avoids schedule conflicts: specifies activities and schedules resources in time to meet needs; sees that personnel and materials are available when needed.

c   Delegates appropriately: sees that tasks are assigned by workload and capability.

d   Follows up: makes appropriate checks to ensure that work is correct and on time; knows the status of people, materials, and plans.

e   Gets work done: work is typically accomplished satisfactorily and on time.

8   *Inner Work Standards*

Extent to which an individual demonstrates a desire to perform at or near the limits of capability most of the time, even when a lesser effort would be acceptable.

a   Does best possible job: performs as well as capabilities permit most of the time.

b   Satisfies own criteria: typically works to satisfy own criteria for a good job, even when this means doing more than is required.

NOTE: Consider the performance exhibited in comparison with the individual's capabilities, not in comparison with the performance or capabilities of others.

It is possible to measure the demonstrated appraisee traits (qualities) relative to the eight behavioral dimensions. Figure 13-1 is a Behavior Dimension Appraisal form developed by the author using the Bell system dimensions, subdimension categories, and a Bell system five-interval rating scale.

By having the immediate supervisor appraise certain observable behavioral traits that have already been validated through assessment center efforts, it is possible to link the scores that assessees receive in the assessment centers with scores on the same qualities from demonstrated behavior in real-world situations. Combining assessment center information with management-generated appraisal information is possibly one of the most powerful employee mea-

| Behavioral Dimensions | N.A. N.O. | Ratings 1 | 2 | 3 | 4 | 5 |
|---|---|---|---|---|---|---|
| 1. Oral Communication (Emphasis is on the manner in which ideas and information are presented) | | | | | | |
| (a) Organizes logically | | | | | | |
| (b) Uses appropriate terms | | | | | | |
| (c) Speaks clearly and concisely | | | | | | |
| (d) Acts confident | | | | | | |
| (e) Obtains audience attention | | | | | | |
| 2. Written Communication (Emphasis is on the manner in which ideas and information are presented) | | | | | | |
| (a) Organizes logically | | | | | | |
| (b) Uses appropriate terms | | | | | | |
| (c) Writes clearly and concisely | | | | | | |
| (d) Uses appropriate grammar and style | | | | | | |
| 3. Flexibility (Consider only actual change initiated by the individual, not merely verbal expressions of a change in mind) | | | | | | |
| (a) Suits style to setting | | | | | | |
| (b) Suits approach to situational needs | | | | | | |
| (c) Tries alternatives | | | | | | |
| 4. Performance Stability (Consider only the ability to continue to perform at the usual level, not ability to show signs of stress or uncertainty) | | | | | | |
| (a) Maintains performance under increased pressure | | | | | | |
| (b) Maintains performance under increased uncertainty | | | | | | |
| 5. Decision Making (Consider the quality of decisions only in light of information available at the time they are made) | | | | | | |
| (a) Uses available information | | | | | | |
| (b) Anticipates future | | | | | | |
| (c) Recognizes interactions | | | | | | |
| (d) Considers situation and alternatives | | | | | | |
| 6. Leadership (Consider the effectiveness of leadership attempts, not the style of leadership) | | | | | | |
| (a) Shows active involvement | | | | | | |
| (b) Obtains positive response | | | | | | |
| (c) Moves toward goal | | | | | | |
| 7. Organization and Planning | | | | | | |
| (a) Sets priorities | | | | | | |
| (b) Anticipates needs, avoids scheduling conflicts | | | | | | |
| (c) Delegates appropriately | | | | | | |
| (d) Follows up | | | | | | |
| (e) Gets work done | | | | | | |
| 8. Inner Work Standards (Consider the performance exhibited in comparison with the individual's capabilities, not in comparison with the performance or capabilities of others) | | | | | | |
| (a) Does best possible job | | | | | | |
| (b) Satisfies own criteria | | | | | | |

NA - Not applicable.
NO - Not observable.
1 - Very little effective behavior shown compared with average behavior of persons at the subordinate's level.
2 - Some effective behavior, but less than most persons at the subordinate's level.

3 - About the same as the average person at the subordinate's level.
4 - More effective behavior than most persons at the subordinate's level.
5 - A great deal of effective behavior; more than all but a few at the subordinate's level.

FIGURE 13-1   BEHAVIORAL DIMENSIONS APPRAISAL

surements available for management decision purposes. It is also possible and highly recommended that the appraisal process require the supervisor and subordinate to be aware of such strengths and weaknesses and to develop constructive procedures and programs that relate to these and other identified traits—skill areas—that will influence future growth and promotion opportunities.

The supervisor should arrive at the rating decision by using his or her collective experience in determining what constitutes average behavior for those managers of the same level as the appraisee. No rating should be assigned to any of the dimensions if there is no documentation for support; this should be a rare occurrence.

If behavior over the appraisal period has shown a clear and consistent change, the behavior shown at the end of the period is the best indicator of what rating should be assigned.

## Linking Assessment Centers to Other Human Resource Activities

Although performance appraisal measures and identifies past performance and such performance is often an excellent indicator of future performance, it is not infallible. The possibility always exists that an individual has reached a level of incompetency (the "Peter Principle");[7] for this and similar reasons, businesses are combining performance appraisal with other techniques, such as assessment centers, in order to identify employee potential.

A valuable role that the assessment center plays is in providing information to assessees, permitting them to gain a more realistic view of themselves. Most people tend to overestimate some skills that they possess and to underestimate others. They also have difficulty in recognizing how certain characteristics that they possess limit future opportunities and how other characteristics can lead to career advancement.

Assessment center information links with and reinforces performance appraisal information. Many of the same requirements for successful performance appraisal reviews relate also to assessment center activities. Some of these are:

1   Assessor reviews with assessee results of assessment center activities.

[7] The "Peter Principle," as described by Laurence J. Peter and Raymond Hull in *The Peter Principle* (New York: William Morrow & Co., Inc., 1969), states that in an organizational hierarchy every employee tends to rise to his level of incompetency and that this is the explanation for the universal phenomenon of occupational incompetence.

**2**   Assessor identifies assessee's strengths and weaknesses.

**3**   Assessor provides assessee with specific training and development recommendations.

**4**   Assessor and assessee discuss career plans of the assessee.

**5**   Assessor and assessee discuss potential and realistic opportunities for advancement.

**6**   Assessor and assessee design training and development plans for future career growth.

**7**   Assessee receives written summary of assessment center results and recommendations.

One of the most significant contributions made by assessment centers is that the observations and measurements relate to human qualities required to perform job responsibilities and duties successfully. Assessment center outputs provide quality or trait information missing from the responsibility–duty–goal achievement procedures described in earlier chapters. The combination of job requirements (responsibilities and duties), job outputs (goal and goal achievement), and behavioral qualities that predict job success (traits) provide a very broad picture to management of their employees.

Since the primary role of an assessment center is to identify potential for higher level jobs or jobs requiring different sets of knowledge, skills, and personal characteristics, it becomes apparent that assessment centers can provide certain additional human resource information. From this kind of information, businesses can determine both individual and group training and development needs. (The words training and development have different meanings, but they do overlap, and this causes terminology confusion. *Training* provides participants with the knowledge and skills necessary to perform current assignments. *Development*, however, relates to personal growth and long-term career advancement through a series of training opportunities and varied job assignments. In the final analysis, development is still a personal choice. Each individual must make a decision regarding the acceptance and use of training, coaching, and counseling provided for growth opportunities.) Training and development can be integrated into manpower planning.

## Manpower Planning

Manpower planning focuses particularly on long-term manpower requirements. In manpower planning, businesses identify replacements or backups for managerial, professional, and other key jobs. Manpower planning also identifies the knowledge and skills required for each of these jobs, those individuals who are fully qualified, and those who have the potential for acquiring required knowledge and skills.

Accurate identification of the knowledge, skills, and responsibilities required in the performance of each job from the most senior to lower level jobs that vary according to organizational demands is a first step in manpower planning. The processes developed throughout this book fit neatly into any manpower planning operation. The precise and accurate identification of job responsibilities and duties permits the setting and weighting of goals that relate directly to job content. Valid and reliable selection and assessment of potential procedures require accurate and precise identification of job knowledge, skills, and responsibilities. Information from these sources provides those responsible for manpower planning with lists of knowledge, skills, and personal characteristics required to perform the jobs of the business successfully.

Performance appraisals and assessment center information assist manpower planners to relate available knowledge and skills to those that will be required at some future date. The identification of organizational weaknesses in the area of current employee knowledge, skills, and personal characteristics are red flags to those responsible for training and development.

Manpower planning not only identifies those who are available and qualified to perform higher level jobs but also assists in the development of career planning programs for employees. The part that counseling plays in the appraisal process is discussed in earlier chapters (specifically Chapter 7). Career development requires inputs from both manpower planning and performance appraisal. In addition, successful implementation of manpower planning and performance appraisal requires two-way communication that provides vital and useful information to both programs.

## Training

To enable the business to operate in its most efficient manner, management implements training programs. A major goal of any training program is to establish and maintain the highest standards of performance. The identification of training needs is a natural and logical part of the performance appraisal process.

It is the immediate supervisor who is in the best position to identify training requirements and is responsible for the quality and quantity of output of his or her subordinates. Successful achievement of this responsibility requires that all employees receive sufficient training so that they can adequately perform their job assignments. For these reasons, the immediate supervisor must have the primary responsibility for assuring that his or her employees receive proper training.

Training provides knowledge and skills necessary to perform the responsibilities and duties of the current job. In many cases, it also provides the knowledge and skills that an employee may be required to possess in order to perform future assignments. A prerequisite for employees receiving training in higher level jobs or in jobs in different occupational areas is that the person be considered promotable.

An output of the appraisal process should be information that identifies the kind and level of knowledge and skills currently possessed (demonstrated) by the employee. A useful training program relates demonstrated knowledge and skills with those deemed essential for successful job performance not only in the currently held job but also in those that the employee may hold in the future.

In the development of a training program from demonstrated knowledge and skills, it is important to make the determination of whether or not knowledge and skill deficiencies are the result of lack of training or because of factors such as:

1  Lack of opportunity to demonstrate the knowledge or skill(s);

2  Lack of natural ability to possess or demonstrate the knowledge or skill or a specific level of the knowledge or skill; and

3  Lack of desire or insufficient energy to demonstrate the knowledge or skill.

When one of these factors is the cause, additional training may be of minimal value although other managerial actions may be necessary.

By relating job requirements to employee job knowledge and skill deficiencies, it becomes possible not only to identify training actions but also to set training goals and to appraise how well the goals have been accomplished. The process can follow the exact same procedure for setting performance goals and measuring their achievement (Chapter 3). Figure 13-2 is a training needs work plan.

Training and performance appraisals have a very important relationship with regard to those employees identified in the appraisal process as unacceptable performers. Training is a major avenue available for bringing workers who receive such ratings to acceptable levels of performance. When training is not successful in improving levels of competency or when lack of training is not the reason for unacceptable performance, other management action may

| Major Responsibilities | Primary Duties | Level of Proficiencies | | Comments | Priority | Action or Training Planned to Overcome Deficiency | Date Imple-mented | Appraisal of Results |
|---|---|---|---|---|---|---|---|---|
| | | Satis-factory | Needs Imp. | | | | | |
| | | | | | | | | |

FIGURE 13-2     TRAINING NEEDS WORK PLAN

be necessary. Transfer to jobs in which employee knowledge, skills, and personal characteristics relate to job requirements is a possibility. The final or ultimate decision is termination; selecting this option usually occurs when all other approaches have failed.

Linking training and development programs to performance appraisal makes it possible to measure the effectiveness of such programs.

### Development

A frequently unrecognized strength of the American economy is the variety of skills and aptitudes required to fill an almost unlimited range of jobs and occupations. Many businesses themselves have so many different types and levels of jobs that they can hire and promote employees with a wide range of knowledge, skills, aptitudes, and desires. Even when employers provide limited opportunities to the employees, the mobility opportunities for employees within the United States are almost limitless. It is the wise employer who capitalizes on mobility by providing opportunities for current employment and the chance to develop knowledge and skills that will lead to better career opportunities in other businesses once the employee makes the decision to seek advancement with another employer. A key concept is that in the United States there is no such thing as a dead-end job, only dead-end employees; the decision for growth and advancement rests within the brain of each employee.

When employers assist employees to develop and expand capabilities, they not only help employees to improve current performance but also help them to recognize the talents that they do possess and how they can make better use of these talents. Employee development may appear to be of little benefit to a business that has minimum opportunities for advancement and promotion. If both employer and employee recognize that the employee possibly is not making a lifetime commitment to the current job or current employer but is using current efforts as a stepping-stone to some highly desired future opportunity, discontent and frustration will be reduced, and performance and job satisfaction increased. To develop this type of a working environment, the skills and efforts of each employee must be utilized to the fullest extent possible. When employee skills, energy, and desires outpace opportunities provided by the employer, the eternal furnace of hope can be stoked by relating aspirations to current performance. Chapter 14 further discusses the relationship between development and stress.

Upward mobility is practically a password in American society. Even employees with limited career potential possess abilities that can be developed for other jobs within most businesses. If nothing else, many jobs can be upgraded as job responsibilities and duties change, and, through training and development activities, the current incumbent can successfully perform enlarged or enriched jobs.

Active commitment by management from the executive ranks to first-line supervision to the development of employees and the promotion of career interests and opportunities is essential to the successful operation of a human resources program. The performance appraisal is a valuable source of development and career growth information. The appraisal process identifies demonstrated behavior that relates to current work activities and, through the interviewing and counseling processes, employee interest areas, aspirations, expectations, and the support that the employee can expect in meeting these self-generated demands.

*Individual Career Development Plan.*   To many employees, a very important piece of information that they want from their employers is "Where do I go from here?" and "How do I get there?" The various activities discussed in this chapter assist employees to develop their career plans.

Career counseling and career development plans identify qualifications required in higher level jobs. They also identify the knowledge and skills currently possessed, personal characteristics demonstrated in past behavior, and the individual's potential for acquiring qualities needed for future jobs.

When performance ratings and assessment center information are valid and reliable, the opportunity for making good and useful career progress decisions increases significantly. When the smoke clears away after individual confrontations and dissatisfactions with results from these activities—job requirements, performance appraisals, assessment of potential (qualifications currently possessed and those required in the future)—employees who have such information can make better decisions concerning the actions that they wish to take regarding their future.

*The Role of the Supervisor In Career Development.*   There is considerable variation in the role that the supervisor plays in organizations that have career development programs. When a business delegates authority for appraising employee performance to the supervisor, it has automatically involved that supervisor in the career progress of the employee. There is no logical reason to eliminate the supervisor from further involvement in subordinate career development other than because of lack of competence.

Lack of competence raises the issue of additional supervisory training in counseling, job requirements, and job opportunities. When a supervisor receives adequate training in these and other areas relating to interpersonal dynamics and knowledge of business opportunities and demands yet performs inadequately in career development, there is good reason to question whether the individual should be a supervisor.

A major issue that a business must face when involving supervisors in career counseling is the kind and quality of information provided about the subordinates. Some businesses employ professional psychologists for testing employees. Is it proper, ethical, or legal to provide information gathered by such sources to the immediate supervisor? The same concerns arise when assessment centers are used; should the immediate supervisors receive information regarding the results of their subordinate's performance in assessment center activities? Supervisors are held accountable for the performance of their subordinates and have the responsibility of assisting employees in their development. In achieving subordinate performance and growth goals, supervisors train, coach, and counsel their subordinates. Is it not logical for supervisors to receive verbal descriptions of the training and development needs prescribed by the assessment center? There are no yes or no answers to these questions. Each business must make its own decisions concerning the proper and acceptable approaches to these complex and critical issues.

## Promotability

Since the development of intelligence tests in the early part of the twentieth century, psychological testing has played an important role in the selection of applicants for jobs, for either entry or advancement and promotion. Although many of the standardized tests used by businesses for selection purposes came under fire in the late 1960s and 1970s for being biased against certain groups, the importance of tests has never been doubted. The issue at hand is to design tests that are both valid and reliable (check validity and reliability in Chapter 11). Testing procedures since the passage of the Civil Rights Act have become more job related, more comprehensive, and, in many ways, more sophisticated and complex.

Tests now provide selection information for management and information for employees to assist them in formulating their own career plans and training and development requirements. Possibly even more important, test-related information assists employees to obtain a better picture of their capabilities and fitness for particular types and levels of jobs. Developing a compatible match of employee skills, talents, and energy with job requirements is one of the most important assignments facing employers in the 1980s.

Some time after initial employment, the majority of employees begin to review their jobs and others available in their organization for future opportunities. From both a monetary point of view and the chance to learn and perform different job activities, promotion becomes an important consideration. From entry into an organization, performance appraisal plays an important role in the continuing growth and advancement of the employee. In the probationary period, the results of appraisal frequently determine who is to be retained and who is to be terminated. After completion of the probationary period, appraisals identify performance strengths and weaknesses. Management and employees identify where training is required for improving current job performance, for expanding current skills, and for developing new ones that are demanded in jobs that the employee may be seeking.

As already mentioned, a major determinant of promotability is performance in the current job, but this does not provide a sufficient or complete picture of an employee's capabilities for performing a higher level job or a job with similar degrees of responsibility in areas requiring different knowledge and skills. When an individual is analyzed for promotability, it is, for all practical purposes, impossible not to return to the area of personal characteristics—traits—that inevitably carry with them the issue of subjectivity. When traits are used, descriptions and definitions must be of sufficient detail and clarity to minimize ambiguity, which causes inconsistent interpretations that lead to subjective bias in ratings.

In addition to actual job performance and the behavioral qualities described in this chapter, other variables that limit potential for promotion are:

1   Breadth of knowledge;
2   Company experience; and
3   Overall comparison with others.

For these reasons, the integration of assessment center activities with the more traditional approaches to performance appraisal provide critically needed insights into human qualities that the traditional approaches alone do not reveal. Performance appraisal is no simple checklist of behavioral qualities, nor is it a grouping of performance dimensions. It is a system consisting of many components that, when properly joined together, provide the kind of valid and reliable information needed to make employee-related decisions.

# 14

# Appraisal, Employee Development, and Organizational Productivity

As important as pay adjustments that relate to performance are and as critical as promotions may be to many employees, the most vital output of a well designed, properly administered performance appraisal system is employee development. In the final two decades of the twentieth century, the employer of the well educated, highly motivated employee must recognize the employee's demands for growth and development opportunities. For many employees, the major opportunity for growth and development occurs at the work site.

Employee growth is a continuous process and is strictly an individual responsibility and opportunity. However, businesses facilitate growth opportunities through the environment that they establish at the workplace. The amount and quality of teaching, counseling, and coaching information and feedback that they provide to their employees further facilitate growth and development. The formalized responsibility–goal process requires supervisor and subordinate participation in the flow of job knowledge and job-related information. The employee has the opportunity to make decisions concerning the kind and degree of growth that he or she personally desires. The opportunity is there, but responsibility for acceptance and use rests with each person. Growth and development in this process are not a once-a-year occurrence or a particular event occurring at some specified time. Growth and development are continuous processes that end only when the individual makes that determination.

## Growth and Development

Growth and development have been magic words related to human resource utilization for the past thirty years or more. Over these three decades, mystical concepts such as sensitivity training, T-groups, encounter therapy, transactional analysis, organizational behavior (OB), and organizational development (OD) have received widespread acclaim as processes available for overcoming employee apathy and even employee hostility. The golden carrots dangled in front of managers who implement these enlightened endeavors are decreased absenteeism and turnover, improved quality and quantity of output, reductions in costs, and increases in profit. Although many of these organizational elixirs have proven to be of some value, the time has arrived to return to basics and to be willing to do the dirty, trench-digging work necessary to build and defend a trusting workplace environment.

It all starts with the job, but this is only the start because a job without a jobholder is as valuable as a set of false teeth for someone who has never had a tooth pulled. The productive, profitable organization requires the services of cooperative employees who actively want to assist their employers to achieve their missions, their objectives.

This is where and when employee growth and development emerge. Fear, frustration, and concern for survival do not facilitate growth and development. Communicating information concerning what the job is and how to perform it within an environment that must relate to ever-increasing rates of change shines a light into the tunnel of job uncertainty. Involvement in developing performance dimensions and performance standards assists employees to understand and recognize their obligations. It is this type of interchange that permits the supervisor and subordinate to identify job-related goals that encourage a spirit of self-reliance and. possibly even more importantly, a spirit of responsibility for self.

The groundwork for growth and development is now laid. Desire for success in the completion of current job assignments and future opportunities will identify individual employee deficiencies. These shortcomings may be identified by either the supervisor or subordinate as they work together in the goal-setting, goal achievement process. A lack of specific job-related knowledge and skills is a first cue for training requirements. The training may come on the job from a co-worker, from a specialist in the identified area, or from the supervisor. The training may be a formal program held by the organization or some other organization that provides such services or may include invaluable coaching and counseling sessions involving only the subordinate and supervisor. Other types of training may involve various specialists who relate to specific needs.

Development needs may go beyond immediate job-related demands. Recognizing the potential available within the specific individual, the supervisor and other personnel specialists may recommend any of a wide variety of learning opportunities that enhance employee growth and assist the employee to achieve what he or she is capable of attaining.

The concept underlying the performance dimension–standard–goal process is not to police employee behavior but rather to assist employees to utilize their own resources. It is important to recognize that performance appraisals are not only the consequences of employee behavior but also the stimuli—they cause and form behavior.

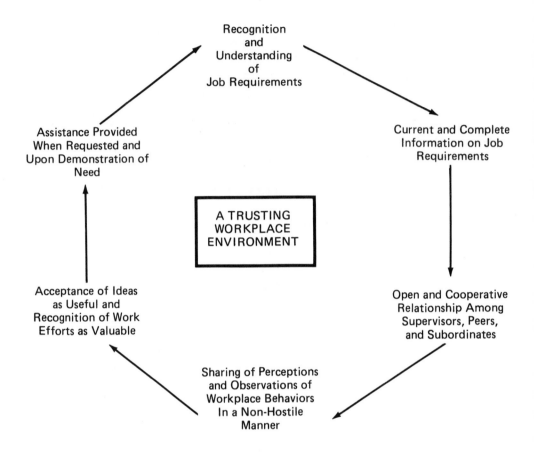

FIGURE 14-1     TRUST-DEVELOPING CYCLE

Focusing attention on employee growth and development is a major step in establishing a trusting workplace environment. Figure 14-1 identifies some of the key features in a trust-developing cycle.

## Barriers to Growth and Development

Few if any people like to be surprised, especially if the surprise can, in some way, damage or harm the individual. Survival or its workplace counterpart, job security, are of primary concern to most employees. Anything or any action that may have a damaging effect on job continuity in the immediate present or at some future time is going to be resisted with as much effort as required or possible.

A brief review of the influence of performance appraisal results indicates the importance that employees attach to the process.

*Claim on present assignment.* An unsatisfactory appraisal of performance may lead to loss of present job or even to complete termination of employment.

*Opportunity for desired job improvement.* Requests for more desirable work site, better equipment, more acceptable co-workers, etc., may rest on the performance rating.

*Transfer to new job.* A chance to develop new job skills, to obtain additional job knowledge, and to work in a different environment all may depend on the appraisal.

*Promotion to a higher level job.* For many employees, the most valuable reward that an organization can bestow is promotion to a higher level job. Increase in status, esteem of self and others, recognition, and additional compensation are only some of the valued rewards that accompany most promotions. Performance in current assignment is one of, if not the, most important determinant for advancement.

*Selection for Education and Training Program.* Opportunities to gain additional knowledge and acquire new skills may not only be useful within current organization but also as a stepping-stone to more lucrative opportunities in other organizations.

From an analysis of these five critical employee interest areas, it becomes rather easy to recognize the relationship between fear and performance appraisal. When employees feel that they have minimal influence over the appraisal process and that their final appraisal rating may depend on the whims and unfair or biased perceptions of the appraisers, fear quickly arises. This kind of situation promotes uncertainty, especially uncertainty as related to future workplace opportunities. As uncertainties begin to dominate the intellectual processes, they become exhibited through behaviors such as anxiety and tension. These stress-related behaviors, if of sufficient strength and duration, transfer into alienation, hostility, and unhealthy competition. As long as one individual is responsible for appraising the performance of another, some degree of stress will exist. The amount of stress varies according to individual qualities, environmental conditions, and the relationship between the appraiser and appraisee. When physical conditions such as increased pulse, pains in the back of the neck, butterflies in the stomach, and perspiration-soaked palms frequently accompany appraisal reviews, it may be time to analyze what is happening during the appraisal process.

There is no doubt that each individual requires some kind of competitive activities to activate and achieve innate potential. However, when the competition leads to barriers that appear to be insurmountable, hope fades away; despair, then fear dominate human behavior.

### Understanding

A major opportunity available to all managers for overcoming job-related fears is through the wise use of the very same performance appraisal process that, used unwisely, creates these fears. It is possible to attack and minimize the unhealthy effects of job-related fears through understanding. For the incumbent, understanding must include:

1   Recognition of job requirements—knowledge of job responsibilities and duties and their relative importance.

2   Mutual identification, description, and acceptance of job-related goals by supervisor and subordinate.

3   Availability of all information necessary to perform assignments in a satisfactory manner (necessary information must be considered from the perception of the incumbent).

4   Assurance that failure or mistake will not become a permanent blemish on the employee's record.

There is no sense in falling into the F. W. Taylor Scientific Management trap that there is a "one right way" to do anything. Among the many alternative processes available for appraising performance, none appears to provide more benefit than one that starts with a valid, accurate, and comprehensive description of job responsibilities and duties. The employee should have a vital role in developing these requirements or, after becoming fully acquainted with the job, in reviewing the responsibility and duty statements to ensure that they accurately describe the job as currently being performed.

As previously mentioned, the responsibilities and duties are what the organization identifies as the processes necessary to achieve standardized, job-required outputs that lead to the accomplishment of the mission of the unit, group, and, eventually, the total organization. These responsibilities and duties facilitate the identification of the situational and human variables that individualize each job and, in turn, assist jobholders in meeting the dynamic requirements of their jobs.

*The Impact of Change.* Even in the most highly structured, routine, repetitive assignment, variation or change occurs. The kinds and degrees of change do not occur in any well defined sequence. The ability to adapt and perform acceptably in an environment in which change is the rule requires the willingness to accept risk. Accompanying risk is the chance of failure. With failure comes fear of the unknown.

In the workplace, the more information that the employees have about the variables, factors, or forces that may cause change, the greater is the likelihood of successfully overcoming changing situations. When confronted with a novel situation, an employee who relates the possibility of errors or mistakes to an unsatisfactory performance review may do nothing. In the modern organization, which, in many cases, is large and impersonal and where individual desires, efforts, and reasoning go unnoticed or unrecognized, fear of making a mistake leads directly to doing nothing. This type of attitude stifles the courage to try something different, to implement an innovative approach. When employees demonstrate a "do nothing" behavior, they lose one of the great learning opportunities available—learning from past mistakes. When mistakes become part of the learning process and are not part of a punitive performance appraisal process, they reinforce the qualities that overcome job-related fear and minimize unhealthy stress.

The performance dimension–performance standard–performance goal cycle facilitates the sharing of information and perception between supervisor and subordinate. The possibility of a supervisor–subordinate adversary relationship diminishes when these two individuals work together to solve workplace problems. When both parties better understand the different set of issues facing the other party and also recognize mutual interdependencies, the opportunity for supportive interaction increases significantly.

*The Supervisor–Appraiser Role.* The supervisor in the modern organization seldom has the time, the necessary skills, or sufficient energy to be a director of subordinate action. Rather, the supervisor provides direction to the subordinate.

At first glance, these two phrases—"director" and "provides direction"—appear to be similar if not identical, but that is far from the case. The "director" type supervisor takes the position of telling the subordinate the how, when, and where of doing the assignment; in this case, the "why" is usually of importance only to the supervisor. On the other hand, the "provides direction" type supervisor assists subordinates to perform their assignments by providing the information, training, coaching, and counseling appropriate to the demands of the subordinate, the job, and the situation.

The performance dimension–performance standard–perform-ance goal cycle is a formalized process designed and implemented by the organization to facilitate the "provides direction" role. As stated throughout this book, the front-end costs of this process are extensive. But in the world of the 1980s, the cost considerations must include costs related to doing it right the first time and the costs related to review, repair, adjustment, and waste when "right the first time" occurs infrequently.

In the authoritarian, directive world, the burden is on the back of the director. The director must provide the how-to's, when's, where's, what's, and constant review necessary to ensure acceptable performance. Can the managers of the modern organization carry this weight? I, personally, do not think so.

On the other hand, in the "provides direction" role, the super-visor furnishes subordinates with sufficient quality and quantity of information to allow them to make their own decisions and to con-trol their own jobs. Training, coaching, and counseling are the in-puts made by this type of supervisor.

The well educated worker who has a relatively high level of aspirations and expectations cannot function in a productive man-ner in a job environment that requires conformity, blocks self-expression, and minimizes the need for employee intelligence and enthusiasm. When this occurs, the intelligence, enthusiasm, and energy are channeled into behavior that leads to "no growth" condi-tions and to more devastating behaviors that sabotage or block opportunities for achieving the goals and objectives of the organiza-tion. When employees recognize their responsibilities and super-visors provide the support necessary to achieve identified and ac-cepted goals, the burden moves to the back of the employee. The employee is now in a position to improve his or her own workplace conditions. Fear of the unknown begins to dissolve as employees accept the challenge of performing a job under conditions of uncer-tainty, recognizing that support is available when risk situations arise.

### Rewarding Growth and Development

Over the past 100 years, labor has been able to obtain an in-creasingly greater share of the total revenue of the business. The point has now been reached where there is little slack left in the revenue allocation process for increasing the amount available for compensating employees. In the past twenty years, private-sector businesses have increased labor's share of the revenue at the expense of dividends to shareholders, research and development, and capital investments. In the public sector, increased taxes on businesses and the public have been used to increase compensation payments to employees. A major result of these actions has been a rapid increase in costs with minimal increases in productivity. This cycle has been a major contributor to the inflation that is being felt around the world.

In the 1980s, as businesses attempt to increase their margins of profit and to improve their competitive advantage, they will continue to take the slack out of their organizational structures. Constant review of manpower requirements will result in relatively fewer promotion opportunities in the 1980s.

With a limited number of promotional opportunities and many intelligent, energetic, enthusiastic employees competing for them, businesses will be hard pressed to meet employee reward demands through promotions. Where does this leave the management that wishes to establish or maintain a workplace environment that rewards quality performance? A major opportunity for rewarding performance leading to improved organizational productivity may take this route:

1 Ensure that all employees know what is expected of them in performing their job assignments.

2 Adequately prepare employees to perform job assignments.

3 Provide employees with up-to-date and accurate job-related information.

4 Instill in each employee the feeling of importance of his or her role in processing productivity-improvement information.

5 Permit and facilitate employee involvement in setting work-related goals.

6 Support goal achievement behavior.

7 Review results of workplace efforts in an interactive and supportive manner.

8 Provide rewards relative to the quality of job performance.

Figure 14-2 describes the performance–reward relationship.

When taking this approach, the organization demonstrates through its actions that its employees are very important. The employees develop an awareness of the contributions that they can and are making. They enhance their self-images and, through their job efforts, obtain the intrinsic rewards that come from doing a good job.

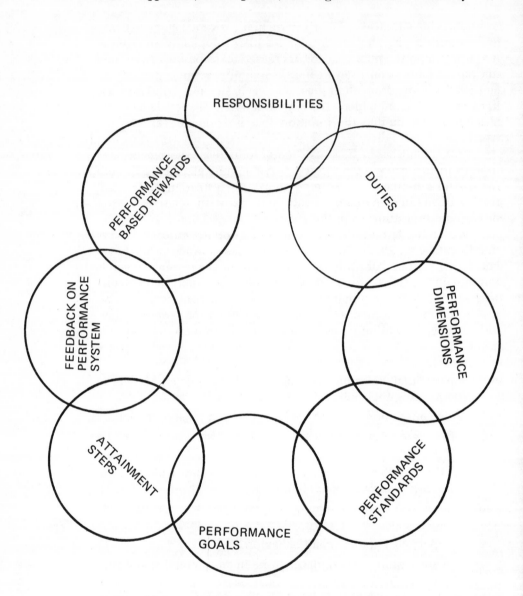

FIGURE 14-2     LINKING PERFORMANCE TO REWARDS

When an employee has the confidence to meet a job challenge, the opportunity for self-reliance and self-esteem increases dramatically. The responsibility–duty-based, goal achievement, performance appraisal system permits employees to improve their performance through expanded job knowledge and recognition that the supervisor is there to provide support. The job itself becomes a challenge; meeting situational variables provides variety to the work and also learning opportunities. This is how growth and development can flourish even in businesses where there are very few promotional opportunities.

In all businesses, management must sooner or later put its reward package on the table. Valid and accepted appraisals permit the earning of rewards through demonstrated workplace behavior.

Employee involvement in the development and establishment of performance dimensions, standards, and goals grants them the opportunity to share in decisions that shape their lives at work. These efforts become the final steps in the organizational planning process. Plan success occurs with individual acceptance and individual accomplishment of desired results. Plan accomplishment depends on (1) technical soundness of the plan, (2) flexibility of the plan to meet change, (3) plan implementers' influence over actions to be taken, (4) management's support of the plan and its implementers, and (5) implementers' knowledge and skill, willingness to be flexible, and desire to grow and develop.

A critical determinant of success for any business occurs when an employee decides to do or not to do something. The responsibility-based, goal-directed, performance appraisal system assists in getting employees to do something and ensuring that, in the process of their doing something, they:

1   Understand what they must do;
2   Recognize the impact of their actions; and
3   Appreciate collaborative efforts.

The entire work planning–results-oriented process is one that is productive. It is a positive initiation and expenditure of efforts to secure a result that benefits all involved parties. The posture of both the appraiser and appraisee in this process can be mutually supportive. Almost everyone wants to make friends, not enemies. Judging does not lead to cooperative, friendly relations. A supportive supervisor–subordinate relationship involves listening, teaching, and guiding. Attention is focused on job requirements and job efforts. Interpersonal skills interrelate with job knowledge and skills. Both the appraiser and appraisee are better able to cope with each other from a supportive position than from one requiring defensiveness. The entire appraisal process emphasizes problem identification and problem solving. It is in this type of a workplace atmosphere that trust develops. Within such an environment, there is a greater likelihood that each employee will accept the responsibility for improving his or her own effectiveness and will take as a personal challenge the improvement of organizational productivity.

If the organization of the 1980s is going to be able to increase the compensation rewards offered to its members, productivity improvement is critical. By relating performance ratings to demonstrated workplace behaviors and then tying compensation rewards to appraisal ratings, merit gains significant meaning to all members.

A secondary effect of the goal-setting approach is that employees who are satisfied with their present assignments and who perform acceptably in these assignments can opt to remain where they are. The process also provides as much or as little structure as the employee desires. The appraiser–appraisee interaction permits the appraiser to provide significant amounts of order and direction to the employee who feels comfortable in a structured environment. To the independently oriented appraisee, room for independent action with a minimal amount of supervisor interference is possible. The entire process from development of performance dimensions to the identification of goal attainment steps can be tailored to meet the needs and demands of the specific employee.

Any system designed and managed by man can be corrupted by man, but the opportunities available through the goal-setting process facilitate the rewarding of acceptable behavior and the reinforcement of desired behavior.

Improved technology to increase productivity will be an important factor for the organization of the 1980s. However, the *decisive* factor will be employee involvement and interaction with the technology.

A Checklist of Issues,
Methods, and Procedures
to be Considered in Designing,
Implementing, and Managing
a Performance
Appraisal Program

## 1. General Guidelines

1 Has senior management developed a *philosophy* regarding the worth of or necessity for performance appraisal?

2 Has a performance appraisal *policy* been established?

## 2. Senior Management Commitment

1 Does senior management understand costs involved in developing and operating a performance appraisal program?

2 Is senior management interested and willing to use performance-appraisal-derived information for executive level planning, operation, and control decisions?

## 3. Different Kinds of Performance Appraisal Plans

1 Does the organization require different kinds of performance appraisal plans for various

   (1) Levels of management
   (2) Professional, administrative, technical, and functional groups
   (3) Nonmanagement groups such as secretarial-clerical, crafts and trades, laborers and other operatives

## 4. Identified and Desired Uses

1 Compensation Administration (including pay adjustment, bonus determination, lump-sum allocations, budget decisions)

2 Training and Development (including identification of training needs, opportunity for coaching and counseling, developing employee career plans)

3 Personnel Movement Decisions (including promotions, lateral transfer, demotion, layoffs, termination)

4 Personnel Planning (relate employee growth and promotability to long-term organizational personnel plans)

5 Organizational Communication (provide flow of information in all directions regarding individual work group and organizational goals)

6   Personnel Research (measure effectiveness and validate hiring, selection, placement, promotion, and training procedures)

## 5. Conflict Arising From Different End Uses

1   Identify and describe potential areas of conflict arising because of various uses of performance appraisal.

## 6. Appraisal Instrument Design

1   Will criteria used for measuring performance be: (1) work activity related, (2) trait related, (3) results oriented?

2   Will scales used to measure performance criteria have: (1) numerical anchors and intervals, (2) adjective anchors and intervals, (3) behavioral-based anchors and intervals?

3   Will plan require appraiser to write a narrative or essay describing observed and identified behavior?

4   Is appraisee required to sign appraisal form acknowledging review has occurred?

5   Does instrument allow for appraisee rebuttal/feedback?

6   Does instrument require review by higher levels of management?

## 7. Special Features

1   Does performance appraisal plan include some type of forced-choice statements?

2   Does the appraisal plan require a ranking of employees? By work group? By kind of work? By organizational level?

3   Does the appraisal plan require a forced distribution of employees? By work group? By kind of work? By organizational level?

4   Is employee potential for promotion assessed with the same plan and at the same time as the appraisal of performance?

5   Are such objective criteria as absenteeism, tardiness, errors, and waste linked to performance appraisal?

6   Do appraisers use the Critical Incident Technique to document observed behaviors?

## 8.  Goal-Setting Features

1   Are goals set in a top-down manner?

2   Do employee goals integrate with and reinforce overall or-
    ganizational goals?

3   Does the employee participate in the goal-setting process?

4   Are activities involved in goal-achievement identified and de-
    scribed when measuring results achieved?

5   Is it possible to establish equivalency of goal achievement of
    an individual with that of others for reward purposes?

6   Does plan relate the equivalency of goal achievement of indi-
    viduals working in different jobs/occupations/disciplines?

## 9.  Individuals and Groups Involved in Rating

1   Immediate supervisor

2   Groups of supervisors

3   Project or team leader other than immediate supervisor

4   Supervisor(s) of immediate supervisor

5   Staff officials

6   Consultants

7   Peers/co-workers

8   Subordinates

9   Self

## 10.  Timing of Performance Appraisal

1   Does the program require a special date or time for the annual
    appraisal of performance (e.g., specific date in the calendar
    year for all employees, employee's anniversary date, special
    assigned date for specific groups or specified individuals)?

2   Does the program call for informal or interim performance
    reviews (e.g., bi-monthly, quarterly, semi-annually, at com-
    pletion of a specific project or work activity, upon demonstra-
    tion of a specific behavior)?

## 11.  Instructional Information

1   Are both appraisers and appraisees provided formal training
    on the purpose, uses, and operation of the performance ap-
    praisal system?

2   Does the program include a manual that describes the responsibilities and opportunities for the appraisers and appraisees?

## 12. Monitoring the Appraisal Program

1   Are specific individuals or groups delegated the authority to monitor the program to ensure compliance with established policies, rules, and procedures?

2   Is the appraisee provided with certain opportunities to monitor the correct operation of the appraisal system?

## 13. Auditing the Appraisal Program

1   Is the program audited to ensure proper operation and to identify errors, inaccuracies, or inconsistencies in the system?

2   Is the program computer-based wherever possible to ensure consistency of application and fair and impartial treatment?

3   Are numerical scores compared with narrative descriptions?

4   Are supervisors at levels higher than the appraiser and staff officials required to review appraiser ratings?

5   Does the appraisee participate in the auditing process?

## 14. Appeals

1   Is the appraisee granted the opportunity to appeal an appraisal rating?

2   Is an appeal heard before the appraisal rating becomes part of the permanent record of the employee?

## 15. Attitude Survey

1   Are employees surveyed regularly regarding their opinions and perceptions of the appraisal system?

2   Are both positive and negative influences of performance appraisal identified and measured?

3   Are the results of attitude surveys tied into the modification or redesign of the appraisal program?

## 16. Computer-Based Information

1   Is the computer used to store performance appraisal information (e.g., maintain individual rating over a period of time)?

2   Is the computer used to analyze ratings (e.g., compare appraisee with others performing similar work or with others in the same work group; compare supervisor's ratings and distribution of ratings with those given by other supervisors; compare work group ratings with group performance)?

3   Is appraiser provided with computer-based statistical analyses?

4   Is appraiser provided with computer-based statistical analyses?

# References and Resources

The following magazine and journal articles, books, films, audio-tapes, and training programs provide information to those interested in seeking additional knowledge about this crucial but extremely complex subject.

## Magazine and Journal Articles

Over the years, thousands of articles have been written on this subject. Those included in the following list provide additional insights into the topics covered in each of the chapters. Although the articles are listed by chapters, the content of nearly all articles is relevant to more than one chapter in this book.

### Chapter 1. An Introduction to Performance Appraisal

Conant, James C. "The Performance Appraisal: A Critique and an Alternative." *Business Horizons*, June 1973, pp. 73–78. A discussion of the negatives resulting from performance appraisal. The author recommends the use of management by objectives to overcome the inadequacies inherent in most performance appraisal methods.

Kearney, William J. "Performance Appraisal: Which Way to Go?" *MSU Business Topics*, Winter 1977, pp. 58–64. A development of answers to such relevant performance appraisal issues as purpose, what is appraised, how performance is appraised, who the appraisers are, the timing of the appraisal, and the use of feedback in the process.

Kelly, Philip R. "Reappraisal of Appraisals." *Harvard Business Review*, May–June 1958, pp. 59–68. An examination of the historical evaluation of formal management appraisals, including a questioning and even challenging of some of the assumptions and concepts underlying performance appraisal.

Kindall, Alva F., and Gatza, James. "Positive Program for Performance Appraisal." *Harvard Business Review*, Nov.–Dec. 1963, pp. 153–59, 162, 165, 166. Most managers recognize the shortcomings of traditional appraisal systems. Superiors judge subordinates in terms of their own personality traits. There is a significant difference in agreement over use of terms and scales used for rating. The result is that most managers receive high ratings and the system is useless in terms of differentiating among levels of performance.

Kipnis, D. "Some Determinants of Supervisory Esteem." *Personnel Psychology*, Vol. 13, 1960, pp. 377–91. The rating process in appraising performance is influenced by: (1) physical proximity of rater and ratee, (2) degree of job stress, (3) organizational climate, (4) superior–subordinate dependence.

"Managers Rate Performance Appraisal Programs." *Industry Week*, 30 May 1974, pp. 52, 56, 58. An in-depth discussion and comparison of the results of surveys on performance appraisal conducted by the Bureau of National Affairs in 1964 and 1974. It appears that more organizations are using performance appraisals, but discontent with the results is also growing.

Meyer, Herbert E. "The Science of Telling Executives How They're Doing." *Fortune*, January 1974, pp. 102–6, 110–12. An interesting review of how many top businesses appraise the performance of their managers. The message here is to stress the opportunities available through effective appraisal of performance and to minimize stress and develop candid and open exchange of performance information.

Patton, Arch. "Does Performance Appraisal Work?" *Business Horizons*, February 1973, pp. 83–91. The first step in improving performance is to establish an expected standard of performance. The setting of standards must be followed with information that adds objectivity to the appraisal process and the individual will to apply the information.

Patz, Alan H. "Performance Appraisal: Useful But Still Resisted." *Harvard Business Review*, May–June 1975, pp. 74–80. A discussion of the major barriers that continue to hinder effective performance appraisal. The author develops a four-point strategy that emphasizes manageability and directions. His four points are: keep it (1) simple, (2) separate, (3) contained, and (4) participative.

## Chapter 2. Accomplishing the Mission of the Organization

Miller, George A. "The Magical Number Seven Plus or Minus Two: Some Limits on Our Capacity for Processing Information." *The Psychological Review*, March 1956, pp. 81–97. A review and analysis of research into the relationship between information input and the ability of the brain to process this information in the short-term. An important piece of evidence uncovered by Miller is that the short-term memory has a finite and rather small capacity for making unidimensional judgments.

Miner, John B. "Bridging the Gulf in Organizational Performance." *Harvard Business Review*, July–Aug. 1968, pp. 102–10. An approach available for bridging the gulf between organizational performance and managerial motivation is to relate managerial behavior to company goals and clearly defined job requirements. The integration process requires an understanding of the value system of the company. Within the value system lies the key to accurately identifying performance standards, personal effectiveness, and compensation rewards.

O'Reilly, A. P. "Skill Requirements: Supervisor–Subordinate Conflict." *Personnel Psychology*, Spring 1973, pp. 75–80. A review of various research studies indicates that there are marked discrepancies between perceptions held by supervisors and subordinates as to what the subordinate understands the job to be and the levels of skill/knowledge needed to perform the job satisfactorily.

Villareal, Morey, J. "Improving Managerial Performance." *Personnel Journal*, February 1977, pp. 86–89, 96. The author describes a results-oriented performance appraisal system that focuses on well-defined performance standards that are developed through negotiations between supervisor and subordinate.

## Chapter 3. From Job Content to Individualized Performance Requirements

Haynes, Marion G. "Developing An Appraisal Program." *Personnel Journal*, January 1978, pp. 14–19; and February 1978, pp. 66–67. These articles stress the need for using objective criteria in measuring performance. Appraisals based on objective standards are more versatile and allow for more open discussion of performance.

Levinson, Harry. "Appraisal of *What* Performance?" *Harvard Business Review*, July–Aug. 1976, pp. 30–32, 34, 36, 40, 44, 46, 180. The importance of how results are achieved, as well as the actual results achieved, is the focus of this article. The author promotes the need to establish job descriptions that are behavior- as well as results-oriented.

## Chapter 5. Goal Setting

French, John R. P., Jr.; Kay, Emanuel; and Meyer, Herbert H. "Participation and the Appraisal System." *Human Relations*, February 1966, pp. 3–20. The effect of participation in the performance appraisal process is modified by a wide variety of individual variables; but the influence of participation appears to be widespread and long-lasting, although the impact itself may not be as strong as frequently discussed.

Koontz, Harold. "Making Managerial Appraisal Effective." *California Management Review*, Winter 1972, pp. 46–55. Developing a meaningful appraisal process requires setting the proper business objectives and measuring results against these objectives. The author discusses problems that arise when appraising against objectives.

Latham, Gary P., and Yukl, Gary A. "A Review of Research on the Application of Goal Setting in Organizations." *Academy of Management Review*, December 1975, pp. 824–45. A review of goal setting in organizations to determine whether goals that are heard, understood, appraised, and reacted to have an effect on performance. The results indicate that specific goals and the more difficult to achieve but accepted goals lead to improved performance. Individual traits, however, may moderate the effectiveness of goal setting.

Levinson, Harry. "Management by Whose Objectives?" *Harvard Business Review*, July–Aug. 1970, pp. 125–34. Making management by objectives more valuable to organizations is possible by analyzing group action and personal goals prior to or in conjunction with organizational goals.

Lewis, Robert W. "Measuring, Reporting, and Appraising Results of Operations With Reference to Goals, Plans, and Budgets in a Case Study of Management Planning and Control of General Electric." New York: *Controllership Foundation, Inc.*, 1955, pp. 29–41. A classic study of the key results areas used for directing and measuring the efforts of management personnel at General Electric. The eight key results areas are: (1) profitability, (2) market position, (3) productivity, (4) product leadership, (5) personal development, (6) employee attitudes, (7) public responsibility, (8) balance between short-range and long-range goals.

McConkie, Mark L. "A Clarification of the Goal Setting and Appraisal Processes in MBO." *Academy of Management Review*, Winter 1979, pp. 29–40. A review of the work of 39 authorities quoted in the field of MBO literature: what they consider the goal-setting process to include and how goals and objectives are defined, set, reviewed, and weighted.

Tosi, Henry L., and Carroll, Stephen. "Some Factors Affecting the Success of 'Management by Objective.'" *The Journal of Management Studies*, May 1970, pp. 209–23. A discussion of research that focuses on the consequences of MBO and various factors that influence the success of an MBO program.

## Chapter 6. Documenting Workplace Behavior

Flanagan, John C. "A New Approach to Evaluating Personnel." *Personnel*, July 1949, pp. 35–42. A classic article that advocates the use of critical job requirements for appraising employee performance. By using these requirements, it is possible to observe and measure performance and behaviors that relate directly to the work required of the employee.

Kavanagh, Michael J. "The Content Issue in Performance Appraisal: A Review." *Personnel Psychology*, Winter 1971, pp. 653–68. Job-oriented traits are still useful in rating job performance. Personality traits, however, should be relevant to job performance and should be described in sufficient detail so that raters are identifying the same qualities. To improve identification of relevant dimensions of job performance, more than one rater should provide rating information.

McGregor, Douglas. "An Uneasy Look at Performance Appraisal." *Harvard Business Review*, May–June 1957, pp. 89–94. A classic in the literature of performance appraisal in which the author discusses one of the most distasteful and disliked activities facing managers—the appraisal of subordinate performance. Placing the major responsibility on subordinates for establishing short-term targets and appraising progress is a potential approach for overcoming the undesirable features of performance appraisal.

## Chapter 7. Performance Interviewing and Counseling

Burke, Ronald J. "Why Performance Appraisal Systems Fail." *Personnel Administration*, May–June 1972, pp. 32–40. The author identifies and describes a number of problem areas related to accomplishing successful appraisal of performance. A major determinant appears to relate to the ability of the appraiser to provide feedback during an appraisal interview.

Farson, Richard E. "Praise Reappraised." *Harvard Business Review*, Sept.–Oct. 1963, pp. 61–66. An interesting and valuable discussion regarding the pitfalls that may develop when involved in praising an employee. The author presents various alternatives available for establishing a relationship in which praise is accepted as positive and useful in creating a motivating workplace environment.

Fletcher, Clive, and Williams, Richard. "The Influence of Performance Feedback in Appraisal Interviews." *Journal of Occupational Psychology*, Spring 1976, pp. 75–83. A study of discussing individual strengths and weaknesses during appraisal interviews indicates that the most productive interviews contain a balanced review of individual strengths and weaknesses. This type of interview achieved the greatest positive effect overall.

Kay, Emanuel; Meyer, Herbert H.; and French, John R. P., Jr. "Effects of Threat in a Performance Appraisal Interview." *Journal of Applied Psychology*, October 1965, pp. 311–17. Through an intensive study conducted at General Electric, the authors found that when subordinates perceived their supervisor's identification of areas needing improvement as a threat, the result was defensive behavior. The more threatening the recommendations to employee self-esteem, the less favorable the attitude of the employee to other appraisals and to the company.

Kellogg, Marion S. "The Ethics of Employee Appraisal." *Personnel*, July–Aug. 1965, pp. 33–39. Whether deliberate or not, all too often managers violate ethical principles when making appraisals. This article develops a checklist for appraisers to follow to keep the appraisals honest.

LeBoeuf, M. Michael, and Villere, Maurice F. "TAMBO—Applying TA to MBO." *Atlanta Economic Review*, March–April, 1975, pp. 29–35. An improvement in communication in goal-setting sessions is possible when the concepts of transactional analysis are placed into the MBO goal-setting process.

Mayfield, Harold. "In Defense of Performance Appraisal." *Harvard Business Review*, March–April 1960, pp. 81–87. A useful discussion of differences in perceptions between supervisors and subordinates, and why and how the performance appraisal interview is a valuable tool for overcoming perception problems.

Wexley, Kenneth N.; Singh, J. P.; and Yukl, Gary A. "Subordinate Personality as a Moderator of the Effects of Participation in Three Types of Appraisal Interviews." *Journal of Applied Psychology*, August 1973, pp. 54–59. An investigation into problem-solving, tell–listen, and tell–sell types of appraisal interviews indicates that satisfaction and motivation increase for individuals with different personality variables related to the need for authoritarianism and the need for independence when involved in a problem-solving (participation) type appraisal interview.

White, B. Frank, and Barnes, Louis B. "Power Networks in the Appraisal Process." *Harvard Business Review*, May–June 1971, pp. 101–9. Do superiors have the right to control subordinates, and, more importantly, will subordinates accept the control? Performance appraisal leads to a de-emphasis of control, and that control should be exercised on a mutual basis between superior and subordinate.

## Chapter 8. Performance Appraisal
## Techniques and Methods

Blanz, Friedrich, and Ghiselli, Edwin E. "The Mixed Standard Scale: A New Rating System." *Personnel Psychology*, Vol. 25, 1972, pp. 185–99. The authors present a method for minimizing rating errors such as halo error and leniency and provide a useful index for measuring the reliability of rating. This study uses 18 traits and three statements to measure each trait. The 18 traits are further reduced to four general trait factors.

Campbell, John P.; Dunnette, Marvin D.; Avery, Richard D.; and Hellervik, Lowell V. "The Development and Evaluation of Behaviorally Based Rating Scales." *Journal of Applied Psychology*, February 1973, pp. 15–22. A discussion of a procedure used for identifying and weighting workplace behaviors and translating those behaviors into Behavioral Anchored Rating Scales.

Cohen, Barry M. "A New Look at Performance Appraisal: The Specimen Check-List." *Human Resource Management*, Spring 1972, pp. 18–22. A brief review of the strengths and weaknesses of four principal methods of performance appraisal: ranking, rating, essay, and checklist. The author focuses on the development and use of behavior-oriented checklists that identify and measure employee behavior, yet also relate to job behaviors ranging from highly effective to highly ineffective.

Cozan, Lee W. "Forced Choice: Better Than Other Rating Methods?" *Personnel*, May–June 1959, pp. 80–83. Research indicates that the forced-choice techniques do not provide consistently more valid ratings than do graphic or peer rating techniques. They do, however, appear to insure greater objectivity in rating.

Fogli, Lawrence L.; Hulin, Charles L.; and Blood, Milton R. "Development of First-Level Behavioral Job Criteria." *Journal of Applied Psychology*, February 1971, pp. 3–8. A discussion of the methods used for identifying job criteria and developing performance dimensions with behaviorally anchored rating scales. The researchers defined the dimensions and the staff members of a grocery chain then allocated behavioral examples to the dimensions.

Holley, William H.; Feild, Hubert S.; and Barnett, Nora J. "Analyzing Performance Appraisal Systems: An Empirical Study." *Personnel Journal*, September 1976, pp. 457–63. This study identifies the types of performance criteria—traits, behaviors, results—and their frequency of use in manufacturing, non-manufacturing, and government organizations. The authors identify three types of rating techniques used by respondents: (1) numerical scale rating, (2) essay evaluations, and (3) a combination of the two.

Keeley, Michael. "A Contingency Framework for Performance Evaluation." *Academy of Management Review*, July 1978, pp. 428–38. The author identifies three fairly distinct classes of appraisal techniques: (1) behavior-based procedures, (2) objective-based procedures, and (3) judgment-based procedures. He further states that behavior-based procedures are most suited to jobs that are highly mechanistic in struc-

ture; objective-based procedures relate to jobs more "organic" in structure; and judgment-based procedures relate to jobs highly organic in
structure. Organic refers to less routine jobs or jobs having a high
degree of change or uncertainty.

Lochner, Allan, H., and Teel, Kenneth S. "Performance Appraisal: A Survey
of Current Practices." *Personnel Journal*, May 1977, pp. 245–54. In a
survey conducted in California, the author found that three major
types of techniques were used in appraisals: rating scales, essays, and
MBO. Four seldom-used techniques were critical incident, behavioral
statement checklists, forced-choice questionnaire, and ranking.

McAfee, Bruce, and Green, Blake. "Selecting a Performance Appraisal
Method." *The Personnel Administrator*, June 1977, pp. 61–64. The
authors present a five-step approach for selecting a performance appraisal method. This article also presents a procedure for analyzing
the strengths and weaknesses of an appraisal method relative to various criteria.

Salton, Gary J. "VARIMAT: Variable Format Performance Appraisal." *The
Personnel Administrator*, June 1977, pp. 53–58. The development of a
flexible performance appraisal instrument through the use of the computer. This approach requires the development of a catalog of appraisal criteria applicable to jobs in an organization. The appraiser
checks off those items to be used in the appraisal process and develops
a tailor-made appraisal plan for each employee.

Schwab, Donald P.; Heneman, Herbert G. III; and DeCotiis, Thomas A. "Behaviorally Anchored Rating Scales: A Review of the Literature." *Personnel Psychology*, Winter 1975, pp. 549–62. A brief discussion on
how to develop BARS, followed by a discussion of research using
BARS and the results of the research. The researchers investigated
such areas as the impact of BARS on (1) learning effects, (2) dimension
independence, and (3) reliability. The research has, to date, not been
encouraging.

## Chapter 9.  Appraisers and Timing of Appraisals

Bassett, Glen A., and Meyer, Herbert H. "Performance Appraisal Based on
Self-Review." *Personnel Psychology*, Winter 1968, pp. 421–30. A discussion of research conducted at General Electric, where comparisons
were made on the effectiveness of appraisals in which: (1) the supervisor completed an appraisal form before the interview; (2) subordinates only completed the appraisal form; and (3) during the review
session, the supervisor and subordinate came to agreement on each
subordinate rating. In this study, the self-prepared form resulted in (1)
superior upward flow of information, (2) self-raters required to do
systematic thinking about jobs and their performance, (3) clarification
of differences of opinions and perceptions.

Borman, Walter C. "The Rating of Individuals in Organizations: An Alter-
nate Approach." *Organizational Behavior and Human Performance*,
August 1974, pp. 105–24. A problem arising when using a multi-rater
analysis of employee performance is that raters holding jobs at dif-

ferent levels observe different behaviors and have difficulty reaching agreement on various performance dimensions. The author develops a hybrid matrix for analyzing performance ratings.

Brouner, Paul J. "The Power to See Ourselves." *Harvard Business Review*, Nov.–Dec. 1964, pp. 156–65. If employees are to fulfill their potential, a vital part of any development program is permitting employees to develop a useful and workable self-concept. This requires self-examination, self-expectation, self-direction, and broadened perceptions.

Dayal, Ishwar. "Some Issues in Performance Appraisal." *Personnel Administration*, Jan.–Feb. 1969, pp. 27–30. A review of barriers to effective performance appraisal and some suggestions for improving the performance appraisal process.

Fritz, Roger J. "Self-Appraisal for Results." *The Personnel Administrator*, August 1977, pp. 26–29. Involving the employee in performing a self-appraisal is a positive step in developing an effective appraisal system. Reasons for and rewards to be gained from self-appraisal are discussed.

Massey, Don J. "Narrow the Gap Between Intended and Existing Results of Appraisal Systems." *Personnel Journal*, October 1975, pp. 522–24. A recommendation for the use of standards to measure demonstrated behavior (performance) and the use of a team approach for the actual rating. The standards proposed in this article are the rating group's standards.

Meyer, Herbert H. "The Annual Performance Review Discussion: Making It Constructive." *Personnel Journal*, October 1977, pp. 508–11. Deviating from his earlier stand, Meyer states that salary issues may be covered in the appraisal interview, but skill in providing feedback is critical for a successful review discussion.

# Chapter 10. Designing a Performance Appraisal System

Hayden, Robert J. "Performance Appraisal: A Better Way." *Personnel Journal*, July 1973, pp. 606–13. Appraisal system design requires the use of various appraisal techniques if it is to satisfy the various demands placed on it by management. This article reviews the various parts of the performance appraisal system and recommends approaches relative to each part.

Marcus, Edward E. "What Do You Mean, 'Evaluation'?" *Personnel Journal*, May 1971, pp. 354–58, 411. Performance appraisal includes weighting measuring, testing, averaging, persuasion and negotiation, mechanical feedback, and autopsy. These procedures may be employed upon completion, at timed intervals, at critical junctures, by exception, by random sampling, and continuously.

Miner, John B. "Management Appraisal: A Capsule Review and Current References." *Business Horizons*, October 1968, pp. 83–96. An excellent review of the performance appraisal process. The author describes the various components of the appraisal process and identifies research to support his concepts and views regarding acceptable approaches available to management.

Thompson, Paul H., and Dalton, Gene W. "Performance Appraisal: Managers Beware." *Harvard Business Review*, Jan.–Feb. 1970, pp. 149–57. Using a goal-oriented approach for appraising performance assists in overcoming widespread discouragement, cynicism, and alienation found to accompany appraisal of performance and feedback in technology-based companies.

Varney, Glenn H. "Performance Appraisal—Inside and Out." *Personnel Administrator*, Nov.–Dec. 1972, pp. 15–17. A survey conducted in 1972 found that formal appraisal of performance of exempt-salaried employees is widespread. The use of MBO type appraisal plans appears to be common. Businesses use performance appraisal for pay decisions and for management development.

## Chapter 11. Government Involvement, Validation Processes, and Training Opportunities

Holley, William H., and Feild, Hubert S. "Performance Appraisal and the Law." *Labor Law Journal*, July 1975, pp. 423–30. A review of appraisal systems and problems that exist within the systems leading to unfair and illegal discriminatory practices. This article focuses on job content as the starting point for developing a valid appraisal effort.

Lasagna, John B. "Make Your MBO Pragmatic." *Harvard Business Review*, Nov.–Dec. 1971, pp. 64–69. A review of the type of training program one organization developed to assist in implementing an MBO appraisal program.

Lawshe, C. H. "A Quantitative Approach to Content Validity." *Personnel Psychology*, Winter 1975, pp. 563–75. A thorough discussion of content validity that will assist those involved in validating performance appraisal in understanding this crucial topic. The article includes a discussion on how to identify, describe, and weight job information for establishing content validity.

## Chapter 12. Performance Appraisal and Compensation Opportunities

Deci, Edward L. "The Hidden Costs of Rewards." *Organizational Dynamics*, Fall 1976, pp. 61–72. When receipt of the reward—pay—is directly related to performance, there is great likelihood that the reward will be viewed as a control device and will limit the possibility of gaining intrinsic satisfaction from the work performed.

Meyer, Herbert H. "The Pay for Performance Dilemma." *Organizational Dynamics*, Winter 1975, pp. 39–49. Focusing on a potential area of conflict between intrinsic and extrinsic rewards and employee motivation, the author stresses the need to relate pay to performance.

Mobley, William H. "The Link Between MBO and Merit Compensation." *Personnel Journal*, June 1974, pp. 423–27. A discussion of the arguments for and against linking MBO to merit compensation, followed by a discussion of the need to tie MBO to compensation. This link between MBO and compensation then serves to enhance role clarity and feedback aspects of the MBO process.

Winstanley, Nathan B. "Performance Appraisal: Another Pollution Problem?" *The Conference Board Record*, September 1972, pp. 59–63. The author recommends that if the objective of performance appraisal is pay information, then the performance criteria should be results-oriented. If, however, the intent is personal development, then the focus should be on skills and abilities.

————. "The Use of Performance Appraisal in Compensation Administration." *The Conference Board Record*, March 1975, pp. 42–46. If a business wishes to get out of the merit increase trap, there are these alternatives: (1) base increases strictly on company service, time in grade, internal and external economics; (2) rate employees relative to three categories: marginal, competent, exceptional; (3) use merit pool to finance an award program for 5% of covered employees who receive 5% of annual salary for exceptional work.

## Chapter 13.  Assessing Potential

McIntyre, Francis M. "Use of Coached Rating Appraisal Data in Development," in Banker, K. A., ed., *Performance Appraisal Necessities. Verities and Strategies* proceedings. Palm Beach, Fla., 1974 Executive Study Conference, pp. 21–32. A discussion of a performance appraisal system developed by Chevrolet Sales Division of General Motors Co., detailing procedures used by appraisers for rating subordinates on nine primary factors: (1) responsiveness to job demands, (2) interpersonal relations–communications, (3) relations to supervisor, (4) practical judgment, (5) marketing strategy, (6) work problems, (7) time utilization, (8) development of subordinates, and (9) job knowledge and skill.

Randle, C. Wilson. "How to Identify Promotable Executives." *Harvard Business Review*, May–June 1956, pp. 122–34. An early study that identifies and classifies behavior qualities promotable individuals possess. From an initial group of 30 qualities, eight qualities tend to distinguish promotable individuals from those who are non-promotable.

Roadman, Harry E. "An Industrial Use of Peer Ratings." *Journal of Applied Psychology*, August 1964, pp. 211–14. A discussion of the results of peer ratings of 13 behavioral qualities and subsequent promotions of the individuals involved in the peer assessment. Four of the 13 qualities appear to be significant indicators of future potential.

## Chapter 14.  Appraisal, Employee Development, and Organizational Productivity

Meyer, Herbert H.; Kay, Emanuel; and French, John R. P., Jr. "Split Roles in Performance Appraisal." *Harvard Business Review*, Jan.–Feb. 1965, pp. 123–29. A classic article that describes performance appraisal research and processes at General Electric. A discussion of G.E.'s Work Planning and Review (WP&R), which uses job responsibilities as the basis for setting goals and goal achievement as the basis for appraising performance. The appraisal interview was split into two sessions: one session focused on appraisal of performance and salary review; the second session focused on performance improvement plans.

## Books

Barrett, Richard S. *Performance Rating*. Chicago, IL: Science Research Associates, Inc., 1966. An outstanding technical book on the mechanics of developing appraisal procedures and reasons for their use. Includes a discussion of various rating procedures and forms that are useful in the appraisal process.

Beatty, Richard W., and Schneier, Craig Eric. *Personnel Administration: An Experiential Skill-Building Approach*. Reading, MA: Addison Wesley Publishing Co., 1977. The section from pages 103–152 provides exercises that build familiarity with Behavioral Anchored Rating Scales (BARS) and develop skills for deriving the scales.

Cummings, L. L., and Schwab, Donald P. *Performance In Organizations: Determinants and Appraisal*. Glenview, IL: Scott, Foresman and Company, 1973. An integrated approach toward performance appraisal that focuses on organizational objectives and proceeds in developing a model that links the major components of the appraisal system.

Drucker, Peter F. *The Practice of Management*. New York: Harper and Row, Publishers, 1956. In this classic, Drucker discusses the use of MBO and calls for the "substitution of management by self-control for management by domination." Drucker further states that managers must be able to measure their own performance on a continuing basis using clear, simple, rational, and relevant measures of performance in all key areas.

Fournies, Ferdinand F. *Coaching For Improved Work Performance*. New York: Van Nostrand, Reinhold Co., 1978. Theories of motivation are integrated into specific techniques useful in achieving optimum work performance. The author discusses five steps of coaching, which coaching technique is appropriate for a specific situation, how to use rewards and punishment, and how to recognize problem attitudes.

*How to Increase Sales and Profit Through Salesman Performance Evaluation*. Chicago, IL: Dartnell Corp. Help your salesforce in meeting its sales and goals by analyzing seven basic measurement tools that assist in evaluating and pinpointing new and existing markets. There are also examples of reports useful in tracking the progress of sales personnel and ways to evaluate sales call activities.

*How to Review and Evaluate Employee Performance*. Chicago, IL: Dartnell Corp. This book describes a method for setting up a program to determine how well employees are performing. It provides guidelines to determine the need for performance analysis and review, and points out how to analyze and rate employee performance.

Hughes, Charles L. *Goal Setting*. New York: AMACOM, 1965. A practical guide that shows how to recognize employee needs for self-fulfillment and job satisfaction. Identifies tested methods for stimulating goal-seeking behavior in workers at all levels in the organization.

Humble, John W. *How to Manage By Objectives*. New York: AMACOM, 1978. A discussion of how MBO can be used as a tool for overcoming tactical errors commonly made by managers. Provides insights into when to use MBO and how to use it effectively.

Keil, E. C. *Performance Appraisal and the Manager*. New York: Lebhar-Friedman Books, 1977. Focusing on the performance appraisal interview, the author analyzes the opportunities available to managers for improving productivity and, at the same time, assisting employees grow and become more satisfied workers.

Kellogg, Marion S. *What to do about Performance Appraisal*, Rev. ed. New York: AMACOM, 1975. An outline on how to appraise performance and potential for such management uses as coaching, salary administration, employee growth, and career counseling. The book provides goal charts, summaries, and step-by-step plans to assist those involved in developing a performance appraisal system.

Lazer, Robert I., and Wikstrom, Walter S. *Appraising Managerial Performance: Current Practices and Future Directions, Report # 727*. New York: The Conference Board, Inc., 1977. A report on an extensive mid-1970s study of almost 300 businesses that found that approximately 75 percent of all respondents had formal appraisal programs. Although more than half of the businesses stated their programs were less than three years old, many problems were identified relative to their design and use.

Lefton, Robert E.; Buzzotta, V. R.; Sherberg, Manuel; Karraker, Dean L. *Effective Motivation Through Performance Appraisal: Dimensional Appraisal Strategies*. New York: John Wiley & Sons, 1977. Through the use of two models, the authors show how to conduct performance appraisal with increased pay-offs. The two models, the Dimensional Model of Superior Appraisal Behavior and the Dimensional Model of Subordinate Appraisal Behavior, provide a basis for explaining how an effective performance appraisal system operates.

Lopez, Felix M. *Evaluating Employee Performance*. Chicago, IL: Public Personnel Association, 1968. An analysis of techniques available for appraising performance and how they are useful with regard to the intended purpose of the appraisal. There is a particular focus on appraisal in the public sector.

———. *Personnel Interviewing: Theory and Practice*, 2nd ed. New York: McGraw-Hill, 1975. This book provides background information and specific techniques that are valuable in improving interviewing skills. Interviewing activities in job analysis, performance appraisal, and employee career counseling are covered. Interview forms and a comprehensive bibliography are included.

Mager, Robert F., and Pipe, Peter. *Analyzing Performance Problems or "You Really Ought a Wanna."* Belmont CA: Fearon, 1970. Is there a performance discrepancy? If there is, the authors develop a flow diagram that assists in identifying performance problems and what to do with them. A quick-reference checklist provides a guide for determining what to do when an unacceptable performance situation arises.

Maier, N. R. F. *The Appraisal Interview: Objectives, Methods, and Skills.* New York: John Wiley, 1958. This classic categorizes appraisal methods into: (1) tell and sell, (2) tell and listen, and (3) problem-solving. The author discusses each method and identifies where each is useful in improving superior–subordinate relations.

Maier, Norman R. F. *The Appraisal Interview: Three Basic Approaches.* LaJolla, CA: University Associates, Inc., 1976. A discussion of the three dimensions of appraisal interviewing—objectives, methods, and skills—with a discussion of the principles of problem solving as related to the interview. The three approaches used in appraisal—sell, tell and listen, and problem solving—are explored and discussed in detail.

Mali, Paul. *Improving Total Productivity: MBO Strategies for Business, Government and Not-for-Profit Organizations.* New York: John Wiley & Sons, Inc., 1978. A step-by-step practical operating guideline on how the MBO strategy can be developed, installed, and managed. The book identifies 12 of the most critical areas of reduced performance and offers approaches to minimize efforts.

Margulies, Newton, and Wallace, John. *Organization Change: Techniques and Applications.* Glenview, IL: Scott, Foresman and Company, 1973. An excellent resource for those involved in designing and implementing a performance appraisal system. The authors present a systematic approach to bringing about organizational change. They provide knowledge and understanding to assist those willing to expend the effort to develop innovative approaches for improving human interaction within the organizational structure.

McConkey, Dale D. *How to Manage By Results*, 3rd ed. New York: AMACOM, 1977. Provides valuable instruction on how to make MBO work, focusing on procedures to increase productivity and improve communication and work flow, and stressing individual achievement and rewards for results achieved.

————. *MBO for Nonprofit Organizations.* New York: AMACOM, 1975. Pragmatic and useful insights into MBO in non-profit organizations, with case studies describing how particular organizations have implemented MBO programs.

Migliore, R. Henry. *MBO: Blue Collar to Top Executive.* Rockville, MD: Bureau of National Affairs, 1977. The author recommends a review of the organizational environment before setting objectives. He further recommends the setting of objectives at every level. "How-to" advice is provided on setting and writing objectives at lower levels in the organization and in measuring MBO effectiveness.

Morrisey, George L. *Appraisal and Development Through Objectives and Results.* Reading, MA: Addison-Wesley Publishing Co., 1972. The philosophy and techniques of MBO are suitable and useful to employee appraisal and development. The author provides a variety of ways to apply goal setting to employee appraisal and development.

Odiorne, George S. *MBO II: A System of Managerial Leadership for the 80's.* Belmont, CA: Fearon–Pitman Publishers, Inc., 1979. Odiorne states that the hardest part of MBO is making it work, but only two of the six chapters actually address this issue. MBO is seen as an overall way of managing an organization—public or private—a department, or an individual job. Many useful insights on implementing MBO are provided, such as 27 rules by managers who have made MBO work, the politics of implementing MBO, and a number of chapters on goal-setting techniques.

Porter, Lyman W.; Lawler, Edward E. III; and Hackman, J. Richard. *Behavior in Organizations*. New York: McGraw-Hill, 1975. The authors conclude that a good appraisal system must have the following characteristics: (1) it must measure both behavior and results; (2) it must be objective and tied to behavior; (3) moderately difficult goals and standards must be set; (4) subordinates must be able to influence the measures; (5) time cycle of appraisal feedback must be appropriate to the task; (6) subordinates must participate in setting goals and establishing measures; and (7) appraisals must be effectively linked with the reward system.

Raia, Anthony P. *Managing by Objectives*. Glenview, IL: Scott, Foresman and Company, 1974. One of the pioneers of MBO, provides excellent descriptions of the fundamental tools required to design and implement an effective MBO system.

Smith, Howard P., and Brouner, Paul J. *Performance Appraisal and Human Development: A Practical Guide to Effective Managing*. Reading, MA: Addison-Wesley Publishing Co., 1977. Recognizing that the human resources of an organization are truly its most valuable assets, the authors provide an example-oriented approach for understanding how an appraisal system functions and the role management plays in developing an effective program.

Whisler, Thomas L., and Harper, Shirley F., eds. *Performance Appraisal, Research and Practice*. New York: Holt, Rhinehart & Winston, 1962. A basic review of the elements that comprise the performance appraisal process. An excellent primer for anyone wishing to learn about performance appraisal.

Winstanley, Nathan B., ed. *Current Readings in Performance Appraisal*. Pittsburgh, PA: American Compensation Association, 1974. A broad and comprehensive review of what has been taking place during the past 15 years in the appraisal of employee performance. It focuses on emerging knowledge of the need for feedback in the appraisal process. In addition, it notes the trend away from rating scales, particularly when performance appraisal centers on personnel development.

## Cassettes

*Appraisal and Career Counseling Interview*, Donald Faber. AMACOM Division, American Management Associations, 135 West 50th Street, New York, NY 10020.

*Appraising Performance: An Interview-Skills Course*, Norman R. F. Maier. University Associates, Inc., 7596 Eads Ave., LaJolla, CA 92037.

*How to Evaluate Performance and Assess Potential.* AMACOM Division, American Management Associations, 135 West 50th Street, New York, NY 10020.

*Management Assessment Centers*, Joseph L. Moses. Management Decision Systems, Inc., P. O. Box 35, Darien, CT 06820.

*Managing by Objectives Program.* AMACOM Division, American Management Associations, 135 West 50th Street, New York, NY 10020.

*Objective-Focused Management*, George S. Odiorne. AMACOM Division, American Management Associations, 135 West 50th Street, New York, NY 10020.

*Performance Appraisal*, Herbert H. Meyer. Management Decision Systems, Inc., P. O. Box 35, Darien, CT 06820.

*Performance Dynamics*, Felix M. Lopez. Universal Training Systems Co., 7101 N. Cicero, Lincolnwood, IL 60646.

## Films

*Pay for Performance*, BNA Communications, Bureau of National Affairs, 5615 Fishers Lane, Rockville, MD 20552.

*Performance Appraisal: The Human Dynamics.* CRM/McGraw-Hill Films, 110 Fifteenth St., Del Mar, CA 92104.

*Performance Counseling and Appraisal*, Management Decision Systems, Inc., P.O. Box 35, Darien, CT 06820.

*Where Are You? Where Are You Going?* Roundtable Films, 113 North San Vicente Blvd., Beverly Hills, CA 90211.

*You're Coming Along Fine.* Roundtable Films, 113 North San Vicente Blvd., Beverly Hills, CA 90211.

## Training Programs

Many different kinds of organizations provide training programs on performance appraisal. The following list identifies some organizations that currently offer these services. In addition, universities and community colleges throughout the nation provide training programs that relate to many of the components of performance appraisal. It is quite likely that the nearest college or university would develop a tailor-made training program for any organization that identifies such a need and requests such a service.

American Compensation Association (ACA), P. O. Box 1176, Scottsdale, AZ 85250

American Management Associations (AMA), 135 West 50th Street, New York, NY 10020

American Society for Personnel Administration (ASPA), 19 Church St., Berea, OH 44017

Applied Management Seminars International, 1700 Ygnacio Valley Rd., #220, Walnut Creek, CA 94596

Center for Creative Leadership, 5000 Laurinda Dr., P.O. Box P-1, Greensboro, NC 27402

Development Dimensions, Inc., 250 Mt. Lebanon Blvd., Pittsburgh, PA 15234

Industrial Relations Counselors, Inc., P. O. Box 1550, New York, NY 10019

PENTON—University Seminar, 420 Lexington Ave., Suite 2846, New York, NY 10017

Special recognition must be given to the AT&T professionals who have done so much to further an understanding of the issues involved with performance appraisal and assessment of potential in general and the area of training and development in particular. "FORMATIVE YEARS IN BUSINESS: A Long-Term Study of Managerial Lives" is a classic product of three AT&T professionals, Douglas W. Bray, Richard J. Campbell, and Donald L. Grant, that provides a vast amount of information to those involved in improving organizational productivity through a better understanding of the critical criterion, human resource utilization.

Index